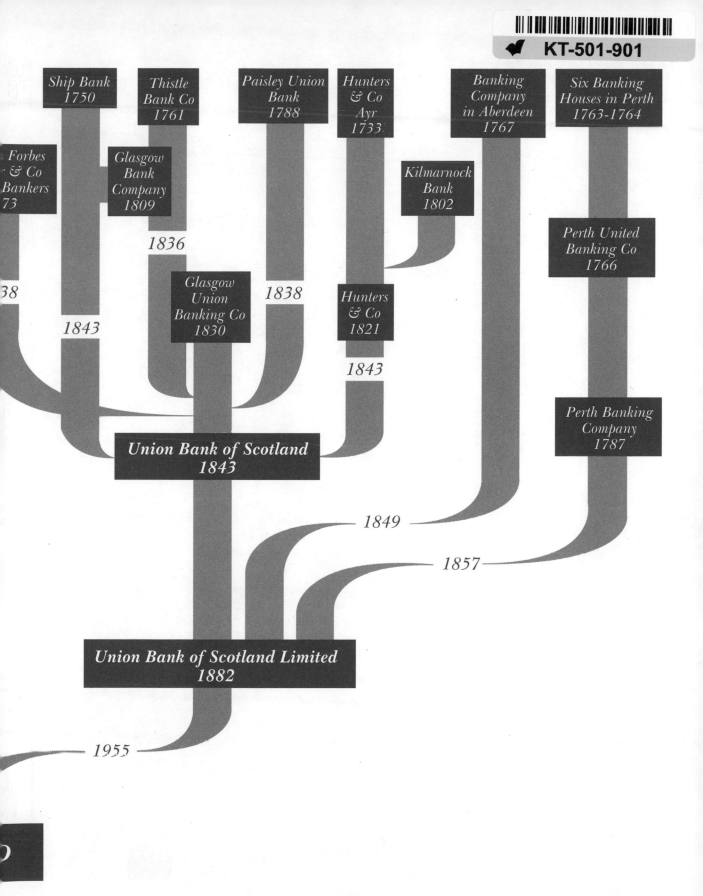

Ship Bank
1750

Thistle
Bank Co
1761

Paisley Union
Bank
1788

Hunters
& Co
Ayr
1733

Banking
Company
in Aberdeen
1767

Six Banking
Houses in Perth
1763-1764

Forbes
& Co
Bankers
73

Glasgow
Bank
Company
1809

Kilmarnock
Bank
1802

1836

Perth United
Banking Co
1766

Glasgow
Union
Banking Co
1830

1838

Hunters
& Co
1821

38

1843

1843

Union Bank of Scotland
1843

Perth Banking
Company
1787

1849

1857

Union Bank of Scotland Limited
1882

1955

BANK OF SCOTLAND
1695–1995

A Very Singular Institution

ALAN CAMERON

MAINSTREAM
PUBLISHING

EDINBURGH AND LONDON

First published in Great Britain in 1995 by
MAINSTREAM PUBLISHING COMPANY (EDINBURGH) LTD
7 Albany Street
Edinburgh EH1 3UG

ISBN 1 85158 691 1

A catalogue record for this book is available from the British Library

Designed by John Martin

Typeset in New Baskerville by Litho Link Ltd, Welshpool, Powys, Wales

Printed and bound in Great Britain by Butler & Tanner Ltd, Frome, Somerset

CONTENTS

*Act of the Parliament of Scotland of 17 July 1695, setting up
Bank of Scotland*

FOREWORD

I N a turbulent and unpredictable world most commercial concerns have a period of vigour, but then the energy wanes and eventually they die or are absorbed by other, newer organisations. A small number of companies survive more than one economic cycle. This is the story of how Bank of Scotland has traded under the same name for three hundred years. The Bank has been visited periodically by 'plague and pestilence'; it has experienced war and peace; and it has survived bouts of excessive rivalry and intrigue. At times the tale is romantic and eventful. At other times the progress of the Bank is frustratingly slow. It is a remarkable story of tenacity and of lessons learned the hard way, set against the social and economic history of the time. I believe it to be the story of a very special company.

SIR BRUCE PATTULLO
Governor and Group Chief Executive
Bank of Scotland

March 1995

Edinburgh from Calton Hill by Thomas Grant

PREFACE

ARCHIVISTS of major banks are in a very privileged position in relation to both colleagues and the public. They are insiders, privy to some of the discussions and decisions which shape their employers' policies, and at the same time observers, assessing the history, character and collective culture of the organisations of which they are part. As a matter of routine, judgment is passed on such matters and on the effects of time and change upon the business. It is small wonder, therefore, that many colleagues feel that the Archivist ought to arrive with the health warning that Robert Burns provided for the antiquarian Captain Francis George Grose, undertaking his tour of Scotland in 1789:

> If there's a hole in a' your coats,
> I rede ye tent it:
> A chield's amang you taking notes,
> And faith he'll prent it.

All businesses are convinced that their own story is unique. Yet precisely what this uniqueness amounts to is difficult to convey in an academic history, concerned as it is to establish long-term patterns of activity and change, and the impact of personality, or changes of personnel, upon policy; in short, the formal history of an institution. Lying alongside this, sometimes as a part of the larger story but more often only touching upon it at particular points, is the informal history, which is probably the part which matters most to those who work within any organisation. This can in turns be pithy, idiosyncratic, funny, boring, frustrating and, very occasionally, tragic. If it is recorded at all, this history merits at most a few lines in the formal record. But it is this collective consciousness (it cannot be called wisdom) which passes down the generations, while the organisation itself sails on, apparently oblivious to the tremors within.

So far as can be judged, Bank of Scotland has always possessed a 'guid conceit o' itself', which has shaped its view of the world in which it operates. This has not been an unqualified blessing. There are troughs as

8   well as peaks in the story and, over three hundred years, not a few miscalculations.

It is inevitable that in the preparation of a work like this many personal and private debts have been incurred. My thanks are therefore due to Dr Richard Saville of St Andrews University, with whom many of the issues were discussed and whose major study of the Bank will appear later in the year. Both of us would be much the poorer without the first-rate work done by our research assistant, Seonaid McDonald, and the calm competence of Sandra Morrison, who typed (and revised) the text many times. My thanks are also due to Win Elliott, whose editing skills and eagle eye have added substantially to the finished result. Dr Charles Munn, Archie Gibson and Michael Strachan have read and commented on the text. Their comments have been very welcome, although I have not always followed their advice. My colleagues Ron Herriot and Helen Redmond-Cooper have shouldered the burden of a distracted boss who must often have seemed 'away with the fairies'. The team at Mainstream deserve thanks for their patience and forbearance on this book. There is, however, a much wider debt which I have incurred over the last nine years: that is to all the members and pensioners of the Bank who were prepared, in informal conversations and in the oral history project, to teach me about the Bank and bankers. Their contribution is incalculable and I can only hope that the present work provides some compensation. None of my work as Archivist would have been possible without the consistent support and encouragement of the Bank's successive Governors, Sir Thomas Risk and Sir Bruce Pattullo, the Treasurer and Chief General Manager, Peter Burt, and Hugh Young, the Bank Secretary. My biggest debt of all is to Alison my wife, and my family. They have lived through the ups and downs of this project with me and sustained me at the low points. For that and much more, many thanks. In thanking friends and relatives (not mutually exclusive categories) for help and advice, it is not my intention to saddle them with the blame for shortcomings or errors in this book. Those are, and remain, mine.

A. C.

Bank of Scotland, Edinburgh, March 1995

—1—

INTRODUCTION

I N 1826 Sir Walter Scott, writing under the pseudonym of Malachi Malagrowther, argued that the banking system in Scotland possessed unique qualities:

> It is not less unquestionable, that the consequence of this Banking system, as conducted in Scotland, has been attended with the greatest advantage to the country. The facility which it has afforded to the industrious and enterprising agriculturist or manufacturer, as well as to the trustees of the public in executing national works, has converted Scotland, from a poor, miserable, and barren country, into one, where, if Nature has done less, Art and Industry have done more, than in perhaps any country in Europe, England herself not excepted.

Even if allowance is made for the propaganda explicit in this statement, the *Second Statistical Account of Scotland* bears eloquent testimony to the changes in the rural landscape and to the increasing tempo of industrialisation throughout Scotland in the period between 1750 and 1820. Scott's purpose was to defend that achievement against over-regulation by Parliament in London, whose intention was to provide a national financial system for the United Kingdom, supervised by the Bank of England. Specifically the legislation included the abolition of the one pound bank-note, whose widespread use throughout Scotland for over a century had been a key element in the move from a barter to a cash economy. There had been no alternative source of ready money in a small and poor country which was chronically short of gold and silver coin

Sir Walter Scott by Sir Henry Raeburn (National Gallery of Scotland)

First Letter on the Scottish Currency by Malachi Malagrowther (Sir Walter Scott)

A LETTER.

TO THE

Editor of the Edinburgh Weekly Journal,

FROM

MALACHI MALAGROWTHER, Esq.

ON THE

PROPOSED CHANGE OF CURRENCY,

AND

OTHER LATE ALTERATIONS,

AS THEY AFFECT, OR ARE INTENDED TO AFFECT,

THE

KINGDOM OF SCOTLAND.

Ergo, Caledonia, nomen inane, Vale!

FOURTH EDITION.

EDINBURGH:
Printed by James Ballantyne and Company,
FOR WILLIAM BLACKWOOD, EDINBURGH: AND
T. CADELL, STRAND, LONDON.

1826.

throughout the eighteenth century. Even by 1825 the move to a cash economy had not been completed. In the year 1833 a roup of the lands and chattels of Archibald McNab of McNab (the McNab), of Glendochart in Perthshire, revealed that of an estimated rental income of £1,300, no less than £500 was paid in kind: in cheeses, bolls of oatmeal, beasts and chickens. The estate was regarded by most contemporaries as old-fashioned and ill-managed (and beyond the Highland line), but the change in the context in which this was set had been very dramatic, and was still within the living memory of Scott's contemporaries.

To Sir Walter Scott, as to the economist Adam Smith a generation earlier, the rise of Scottish banking and its continuing success seemed to depend upon rejecting Government regulation and allowing unrestricted competition between banks. In *The Wealth of Nations* Adam Smith calculated that the whole circulation of money in Scotland amounted to £2 million, of which gold and silver coin provided only 25 per cent. The remainder was in paper money issued by the Scottish banks. Since the Union in 1707 the amount of coin had effectively halved. Despite this, Smith could see all around him evidence of increasing prosperity and economic activity. His conclusion was that unregulated banking was an unqualified benefit to a country. In truth, Adam Smith viewed Scottish banking from the outside and there was a gap between perception and actuality.

The Governor and Company of the Bank of Scotland, founded as a public bank by an Act of the Parliament of Scotland on 17 July 1695, is the original cornerstone upon which this banking system was erected. The story of Bank of Scotland as it exists in 1995 is the story not just of one bank through three hundred years, but also of 21 other banks which have been absorbed over those years. At the time of writing, two – the Union Bank of Scotland (merged in 1955), founded in 1843 and itself an amalgamation of no fewer than 13 partnership banks, and The British Linen Bank (merged in 1971), founded by an Act of the UK Parliament in October 1746 – still make a contribution to the corporate culture, adding weight to the old saying that the whole is greater than the sum of its parts. The story of these two banks will be woven into the story of Bank of Scotland as appropriate.

This history will tell the story of the fundamental part played by Bank of Scotland in creating a banking system north of the Border whose distinctive qualities persist to the present day.

Map of Scotland in 1693

—2—
THE FOUNDATION OF BANK OF SCOTLAND

ALTHOUGH it is possible to provide an exact foundation date for Bank of Scotland, in reality the founding Act was the result of discussions spread over several years. These involved Scottish merchants in Edinburgh and London and their English friends and required the active support of the Scottish political establishment of the day. It is one of the more curious ironies of history that while the Bank of England, founded in 1694, was promoted by a Scotsman, William Paterson, it is an Englishman, John Holland, who is generally credited with the foundation of Bank of Scotland. Holland, of whom there is no known portrait, was a paid employee of the East India Company and a prosperous merchant in his own right. He and a Dutchman, Francis Beyer, the Auditor-General of the East India Company, were acquainted with many of the Scots merchants in London, whose interests they supported. Three common threads bound them. First, most of these merchants had been trained in Dutch accounting methods in Antwerp and Amsterdam and may well have been acquainted with each other for over twenty years. Second, a number of them already had experience of working in 1693 with John Holland as partners in a scheme for the manufacture of baize cloth. Third, all had a common interest in the success of the Protestant settlement under William II (III) and Queen Mary and in the peace and improvement in trade which would result. John Holland is reputed to have told the story that 'an earnest and ingeneous friend of mine, a *Scotch* gentleman, importuned me one day to think of a Bank for Scotland . . . so I did'. His main qualification was that he was an experienced and able man

14   of business who was trusted by all those involved.

The bank which they created was unique. It was, and is, the only bank ever to be established by an Act of the Parliament of Scotland. It is the first example in Europe of a joint-stock bank being founded by private persons, to make a trade of banking, wholly dependent upon the capital raised from its stockholders – Adventurers as they are described in the Act, or Proprietors as they have been called since around 1780.

The contrast between the founding Acts for the Bank of England and Bank of Scotland is quite striking. The foundation of the former is contained in a very imprecise clause in a Bill of Ways and Means of the 1694 Parliament at Westminster which indicates that the Bank of England was set up to handle Government revenues. The capital of £1,200,000 sterling raised by the subscribers was to be loaned to the Government to finance the wars against Louis XIV. The Bank of Scotland Act, on the other hand, is carefully drawn up, with a series of detailed clauses for the regulation of the Bank (see Appendix 1). It has to be said that the overall concept has stood the test of time, because the Bank still trades under this founding document. The nominal capital of the Bank was to be £1,200,000 Scots (£100,000 sterling), of which one-third was to be raised in London and the rest in Edinburgh. A Foundation Committee of twelve was authorised, five in Edinburgh and seven in London. The Act specified the books which the Company should maintain for so long as it had a corporate existence (the reason for the completeness of the Bank's archive), but it also included three specific and unique privileges. First, the Company was granted a banking monopoly in Scotland for a period of 21 years. Second, the Adventurers were granted limited liability; that is to say that, in the event of Company failure, they were liable to lose only the value of their subscription, a situation not available to most business organisations until the 1856 and 1862 Companies Acts. Third – and in view of the subsequent history of Scotland, a peculiarity – up to 1920 anyone becoming a Proprietor of the Bank could claim Scottish nationality. The likeliest reason for this clause is that it protected *English* shareholders from prosecution for attempting to break the Bank of England's monopoly, which would have been petty treason.

The reasons for wanting to establish a bank with a strong London presence are not clear, but a number of threads can be teased out. By the 1690s the settlement of bills of exchange, the principal method of financing international trade, was already concentrated in London. Scots traders, as aliens, were at a distinct disadvantage in this market. They were offered less favourable rates than the English and often had to use rival

*Front and reverse of
Scots coins in
circulation in the
reign of William
and Mary*

CHARLES II
A Dollar

CHARLES II
Half Merk

WILLIAM II
Forty Shillings

CHARLES II
Sixteenth Dollar

CHARLES II
A Bawbee or Scots 6d.

WILLIAM II
Forty Shillings

JAMES II
Ten Shillings

Entrance to the Old Scots Mint

*French drawing of the Procession to the
Scottish Parliament in James II's reign*

English traders as intermediaries in negotiations. A second and more serious reason was that ever since the collapse of the Scottish Mint in 1681 the Scots coinage had been one of the more unreliable European currencies. Between 1660 and 1690, fluctuations against the pound sterling varied between £8 and £16 Scots before being finally fixed at £12 Scots. It was this uncertainty which made even Scots merchants prefer to make their settlements in sterling. The situation within Scotland was complicated by the fact that, while copper and bullion coin in circulation was almost exclusively Scottish in origin, among silver and gold denominations the coins of other European mints circulated as freely as those of the Scottish Mint. Merchants involved in trade wanted security and certainty. Paper currency, in the shape of bills of exchange expressed in pounds sterling, seemed to offer precisely what the Scots coinage could not. A third element was the need for credit facilities within Scotland. Scottish merchants were on the whole 'general' merchants, dealing with agricultural and fishery produce, textiles, trade and cash in equal measure. In the eyes of soured English contemporaries they were little better than pedlars. To be fair, this was not exclusively an English prejudice. In much of eastern Europe in the early eighteenth century *Scoti* equalled 'packman' or 'travelling salesman'.

As suggested earlier, the Scottish economy of the 1690s was one in which goods played as prominent a part as cash. The merchant's minimum requirement was for credit to cover cash flow for the period between purchase of produce and its subsequent sale. This could take months. On his own, the individual merchant was vulnerable to the vagaries of weather, politics and the social status of those to whom he was lending. Collectively, and as a member of a bank in which his liability was limited, he could afford to take a more long-term view of credit and so, with care, extend his operations.

In the generation before 1695 the Scots merchant had operated within Scotland in a very difficult economic and political environment. The Highland war which had been a feature of the first years of William and Mary's reign subsided during 1691. The final act in the tragedy, the massacre of the Macdonalds of Glencoe on 6 February 1692, drew this phase of Scotland's history to a close. Most merchants were involved with participants on all sides of the argument, and part of their necessary skills included knowing (or rather guessing) some of the outcomes. Large areas of Scotland, particularly in the Highlands, had suffered severely from the depredations of war. The Earl of Argyll, for example, needed peace and long-term credit to rebuild his estates – and therefore his income – in order

18 to sustain his political position. The problem for all landowners was complicated by the serious deterioration of climate associated with the 'little ice age'. The whole of Europe north of the Alps was affected, producing from 1695 onwards serious subsistence crises in France, England and northern Germany. In Scotland, the effects on people seem to have been more mixed, and depended upon whether they relied for income on arable agriculture or pasture. Even so, this was the beginning of the period called, in Jacobite propaganda, the 'seven ill years'. Crucially in 1695 and 1696 the harvests failed, and by the autumn of 1696 the price of grain had more than doubled. Indirect evidence of the impact of this near-famine is to be found in the increase in recorded death rates in burghs such as Edinburgh and Aberdeen. But a greater reliance on subsistence farming could not generate the cash surpluses to fund the purchase of consumer goods without a complex network of markets and a ready source of credit.

Therefore, when the sixth session of the Scots Parliament at last turned to economic affairs in 1695, those prepared to support the creation of the Bank did so with a variety of hopes and a range of ambitions: landowners were looking for long-term credit at reasonable rates; merchants were looking for long-term security and the collective strength which could be afforded to them by pooling a portion of their resources and limiting their individual liability; the Scots merchants in London, who appear to have been prime movers in the project, wished to offset some of the disadvantages they faced in competing with their English rivals.

Although the Act for founding a 'publick Bank' in Scotland is the only piece of legislation which has survived from the session of 1695, contemporaries did not see it as the most important business of that Parliament. Measures dealing with moral and religious regulation in Scotland, an 'Act against blasphemy' and an 'Act against profaneness', which were capital offences, were undoubtedly more important, but in the economic sphere the key piece of legislation passed at the end of May was an Act which created the Company of Scotland trading to Africa and the Indies. This Company, promoted by William Paterson, founder of the Bank of England, and supported with enthusiasm in Scotland, seemed to offer the possibility of breaking free from the trading and economic constraints of the previous century. From the first the Company of Scotland, or the Darien Company as it became known, viewed Bank of Scotland as a rival, particularly since, in the shape of John Holland, it seemed to be backed, albeit unofficially, by the English East India Company. This underlying rivalry and distrust is the key to many of the difficulties in which the Bank found itself before 1707.

— John Holland 1658-1721 —

John Holland, so important in the founding of Bank of Scotland, has always proved an elusive figure. His surviving correspondence indicates friendship with the London Scots who promoted the Bank, and his concern for it, even after his immediate connection as first Governor had ended. He came from an Essex sea-faring family whose original home was in Colchester.

John Holland was born in the Bridewell Precinct in the City of London in 1658. More exact information will never be available, because both the marriage and baptismal registers were destroyed in the Great Fire of London in 1666. His father, Philip Holland, was a friend of Samuel Pepys of the Admiralty, and during the Baltic Expedition of 1659 was captain of the *Assurance* on which Admiral of the Fleet Edward Montague (later first Earl of Sandwich) flew his flag.

With the Restoration of Charles II in 1660, Captain Philip Holland lost his command. He tried the merchant trade, but was so unsuccessful that on 24 April 1663 (according to Pepys's *Diary*) he attempted to cut his own throat with a razor. The failure turned him to religion. In 1665, being a non-conforming Protestant, he left England, joined the Dutch, and during the second Dutch War piloted their fleet into the Medway, where it burned most of the English fleet at anchor. It is clear that Holland's sons were still in England, because on 3 May 1668 Pepys records that he went to the King's Head in Islington 'and there by chance two pretty fat boys each of them a cake. They proved to be Captain Holland's children, whom therefore I did pity.'

The family moved to Holland where during the 1670s John Holland completed his education and met Scots merchants. He returned to England around 1681–82 and secured the position of clerk assistant to the Dutchman Francis Beyer, who in 1675 had been appointed Auditor-General of the East India Company. John Holland specialised in accounting for cotton imports at a salary of £40 a year, rising to £60 by 1692. He was reasonably prosperous, and wealthier than his salary would suggest. The best explanation is that he had taken a share in a number of successful East India Company voyages.

In 1687 he married Jane Fowke, the daughter by a second marriage of Walter Fowke of Brewood in Staffordshire. The couple leased Brewood Hall from the Fowke family, possibly for Jane's lifetime, and their three children, Richard (1688), Jane (1689) and Fowke (1700), were born and brought up there. A London house was kept as a business base as John was both a Merchant of the Staple and a member of the London Mercers Company. After his return from Scotland in 1697 he appears to have lived in semi-retirement. He died on 30 November 1721 and was interred in the Fowke family vault in Brewood Parish Church. Jane Holland, his wife, died on 24 December 1740, having been pre-deceased by all three children.

Att Edinburgh anno Domini 1695.

Wee underwritten in pursuance of an Act passed the last Session of Parliament allowing a Joynt Stock, amounting to the summe of Twelve hundred thousand pounds scots money to be raised for carrying on and manadgeing a publick Bank Do subscrive for the severall summes hereafter in this Book set against our respective names and upon the conditions expressed in the foregoing preliminaries by us signed at the same tyme.

November 8 — n° 1 Wee John Marques of Tweeddale &c. Lord high Chancellor of Scotland, Do subscrive for Four Thousand pounds scots money ... 4000

Tweeddale

2 Wee John Lord Yester, Do subscrive for Three Thousand pounds scots money ... 3000

3 Wee C... subscriv...

4 George ... burgh ... scots mo...

London the 8 of November 1695.

Wee whose Names are hereunder written Residenters in the Kingdome of England In pursuance of an Act passed the last Session of Parliament in Scotland allowing a Joint Stock of Twelve Hundred Thousand Pounds Money to be raised for erecting and carrying on a publick Bank do subscribe the severall summs set against our respective Names, And We do hereby agree, and declare that these Our Subscriptions being put into the Book for Subscription of the said Joint Stock shall to all Intents and Purposes oblige Us as much as if each of Us had imediatly signed at Edinburgh.

£
J James Foulis do Subscribe for Twenty Thousand Pounds Scots Money ... 20000
J John Holland do Subscribe for Twenty Thousand pounds Scots Money ... 20000
J David Nairn do Subscribe for Twenty Thousand pounds Scots Money ... 20000
J Walter Stuart do Subscribe for Twenty Thousand Pounds Scots Money ... 20000
J Hugh Fraser do Subscribe for Twenty Thousand Pounds Scots Money ... 20000
J Thomas Coutts do Subscribe for Twenty Thousand Pounds Scots ... 20000
J James Foulis for Account of Thomas Deans do Subscribe Twenty Thousand Pounds Scots Money ... 12000
J James Johnstoun Secretary of State for Scotland do Subscribe for Twelve Thousand pounds Scots Mony ... 8000
J William Stonehewer do Subscribe Eight Thousand Pounds Scots Money ... 16000
J William Hamilton do Subscribe for Sixteene Thousand Pounds Scots Money ... 8000
J James Gray do Subscribe for Eight Thousand pounds Scots Mony ... 8000
J Walter Stewart for Account of James Campbell do Subscribe Eight thousand pounds Scots Mony ... 8000
J William Graham do Subscribe Eight Thousand pounds Scots Money ... 8000
J Nathaniel Carpenter do Subscribe Eight Thousand ... 8000

Opening pages of the Subscription Books in Edinburgh and London, November 1695, and (inset) John, Marquess of Tweeddale, Lord High Chancellor of Scotland (the first Subscriber), by Sir Peter Lely (National Gallery of Scotland)

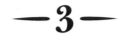

—3—

THE EARLY YEARS, 1695–1707

THE first act of the Foundation Committee of the Bank was to place a subscription book in Patrick Steill's Cross Keys Tavern in Covenant Close, midway between Parliament Close and the Tron Church in Edinburgh's High Street. It was open for two months from 1 November 1695 and was supervised by Alexander Campbell, WS, a cousin of the Earl of Argyll, whom Parliament had appointed collector of subscriptions. A similar volume was kept in London. An initial call of 10 per cent of the nominal capital was made before the Bank opened for business in April 1696. Of the total of £1,200,000 Scots (£100,000 sterling), one-third was left in London and its use supervised by a committee of London subscribers, chaired by James Foulis. In the first instance there were 172 Adventurers, of whom 136 lived in Scotland and the remaining 36 in London. A detailed examination of who they were reveals that in Scotland they included 24 nobles, 39 landed proprietors, 41 merchants, 14 lawyers and judges, with seven women subscribing in their own right. The London subscribers included the Scottish Secretary of State, James Johnston, a number of Government office-holders and four officials of the East India Company; the rest were merchants, mostly with strong Edinburgh connections. One of these, Thomas Coutts, was involved in banking in his own right, and the partnership of which he was a member became and remained Bank of Scotland's London Agents until the Bank opened a branch in Lothbury in the City of London in 1867.

On New Year's Day 1696 an office was leased in Mylne Square, near the present-day North Bridge in Edinburgh, and the first official, David

22   Spence, was appointed Secretary of the Bank. His duties involved care of the kist or chest in which coins and bills were stored and the care and custody of all the Bank's papers. The subscribers then got down to the business of electing a Governor and Deputy Governor and appointing a Treasurer, Accountant and tellers. It now seems clear that John Holland's election as Governor was an attempt to deflect the hostility of the English Parliament to all matters Scots. The activities of the Darien Company, to which many of the Bank's Adventurers also subscribed, were the main source of this hostility, and a number of London-Scots merchants narrowly escaped prosecution for treason. Edinburgh's reputation for parsimony is well earned: Holland was instructed to come to Scotland at his own expense, and his salary was settled at 10 per cent of the Company's profits after a dividend of 12 per cent had been paid to the Adventurers.

The first Accountant, George Watson, was appointed to set up the bookkeeping system, and the new Directors drew up regulations which defined and limited the activities of the new Bank. The key clause was the one which forbade the Directors and managers collectively from using the joint-stock or profits of the Bank for any purpose other than the trade of lending and borrowing money on interest, and the negotiation of bills of exchange. This ensured that the Bank would not develop into a general trading company and allow sidelines to dominate its business. Effectively this ensured that the Bank would provide accommodation for borrowers, deal with money transmission to and from London and elsewhere, and discount bills of exchange. It also ensured that the Bank's capital would not become tied up in long-term loans to landowners, a disappointment to many of the original supporters and a continuing source of criticism. Central to these concerns was the decision to issue a paper currency, backed by the Bank's capital, to expand credit and facilitate payments. There were precedents elsewhere for this, in negotiable goldsmiths' notes in England and again in Amsterdam and among northern Italian banks. Scottish bank-notes had to be derived from first principles, which included the establishment of a paper mill on Lord Yester's estate at Gifford in East Lothian and later at Colinton near Edinburgh. Two types of bank-note were issued, both valued in sterling: one was negotiable only at the point of issue and included the name of the payee (the forerunner of the cheque); the other was payable in cash on sight to a bearer who need not be named. The latter could pass from hand to hand and is therefore the direct ancestor of the modern bank-note. The concept of 'legal tender' was confined to coin issued under royal authority. Every note was hand-numbered and recorded, as well as having a 'stub' against which it was matched. After various experiments, the note issue represented roughly

Mylne Square, Edinburgh

*The Darien Kist, the first safe, inherited with the
Mylne Square premises*

40 per cent of the Bank's nominal capital by about 1700, and denominations of £100 down to £5 sterling were used. Local offices were established in Glasgow, Aberdeen, Dundee and Montrose, and a proportion of notes placed in each for local circulation, returnable only to the issuing office.

Loans by the Bank were made on heritable bonds in the name of the individual requiring the loan, usually guaranteed by two 'cautioners'. Loans were also granted on personal security but only up to a maximum of £500 Scots. The maximum legal interest of 6 per cent per annum was charged on these loans. The earlier comment that Bank of Scotland was not a 'Government' bank requires some modification. Many of those granted loans in the first two years of the Bank's existence were the tacksmen, or commissioners of supply for Government revenues. Lt-Col John Erskine borrowed money to pay the troops in Stirling Castle against security of Government payment. The connection, therefore, was at one remove from the Government but it was not entirely absent.

The Bank opened for business in the teeth of competition and faced the first of a series of bank wars which marked Bank of Scotland's history for the first hundred years.

The activities of the Darien Company in London infringed the monopolies granted to both the Bank of England and the English East India Company; so, fearing prosecution, Darien's main promoters, William Paterson (ironically, founder of the Bank of England) and Roderick Mackenzie, fled back to Scotland in February 1696 and immediately opened subscription ledgers. By the beginning of August some £400,000 sterling had been pledged, and the Company held over £34,000 in coin, rather more than six times the amount held by Bank of Scotland. By this time the split between Bank and Darien Company directors was complete, and it is clear that Paterson intended to establish the Company as a bank in all but name, thereby destroying Bank of Scotland's legal monopoly. Loans were made, notes were printed and sums of money sent to London to enter the discount market for exchequer bills. Paterson's supporters treated Bank of Scotland as little better than a front for the East India Company.

Left: *George Watson, the first Accountant, and two pages of the first running cash book of the Bank*

Right: *The first ledger of the Bank*

Grant of Arms to the Bank, 1 March 1701.
The motto 'Tanto Uberior' means 'Ever more Prosperous'

The Bank's second home, above John's
Coffee House, Parliament Square, Edinburgh

Claim and counterclaim are to be found in pamphlets preserved in the National Library of Scotland, in which each side sets out its position. To compound matters further, it is clear that by this time the directors of the Bank of England regarded Paterson as a scoundrel who had betrayed them. During the summer of 1696 the Darien Company's intention to break Bank of Scotland became open. Bank-notes of the Darien Company were placed in all the main burghs, and Bank of Scotland's notes were bought up and accumulated, so that they could be returned all together with a demand for cash. By August Bank of Scotland was in crisis. Bank lending was stopped, and a further call of 20 per cent of the nominal capital was necessary. This was described as a 'loan', and in the event was sufficient to tide the Bank over, accompanied as it was by rigorous cuts in expenses and a strict watch on lending. The major casualty was the branch network, which was closed down. Two events shifted the balance back in the Bank's favour. The political establishment realised that the Government and its friends in Scotland would suffer if Bank of Scotland went under. Secondly, the Darien Company's incompetence in financial matters began to emerge, culminating with revelations in early November that nearly half the subscription had disappeared and could not be accounted for. Most of this had been embezzled, and 9 per cent of the total subscription was never recovered. It was only at this point that the Darien Company began to look seriously at colonisation schemes in Central America.

A Pistole of William II's reign, one-twelfth of all the gold in Scotland won in the Isthmus of Panama

In the event, the Directors' report to the Adventurers indicated that Bank of Scotland had survived, but only just. John Holland left Edinburgh in March 1697; and in the subsequent elections for Governor, the Earl of Leven, Governor of Edinburgh Castle, was chosen, with George Clerk of Penicuik the Younger as his Deputy, while the Londoners re-appointed Francis Beyer and John Holland. Despite the instinctive caution of Leven and his Directors, the Bank had no choice but to increase the circulation of paper, because the crisis in agriculture, accompanied by the outflows of coin associated with the Darien Company's activities, meant that from 1697 there was a severe cash shortage in Scotland which was to last up to and beyond the Act of Union. As might be expected in a period of agricultural crisis, the Bank's loans to landowners performed poorly, if at all.

By 1699 the Bank had moved to premises above John's Coffee House in Parliament Square, Edinburgh, had repaid the 'loan' of £20,000 Scots

28   from the nominal capital, and even managed to declare a dividend of 12 per cent for the year. On 3 February 1700 a great fire destroyed the Bank and most of the property on the east side of Parliament Square. The Earl of Leven and his troops managed to rescue the books, securities and cash, whose loss would have spelt disaster for the Bank. These difficulties were compounded by its first recorded example of forgery of bank-notes. Although the perpetrator was caught and the trade in forgeries stopped, there was not sufficient evidence to convict him. No dividend was paid in 1700, a new bank-note was designed, and stricter controls instituted on their manufacture and distribution. The Bank moved into premises in Gourlay's Close in the Lawnmarket, where it was to remain for nearly a century, and the bill trade proved sufficiently profitable for dividends to be declared in each of the succeeding four years: 20 per cent in 1701, 1702 and 1704, and 18 per cent in 1703.

Bank of Scotland, as conceived and run by its Directors, was increasingly based in Scotland as the English subscribers fell away. Thomas Coutts and James Campbell had both left the list of London supporters by 1701 – although Coutts remained the Bank's London agent. The practical consequence of this weakening of the London link was that the Bank became less attuned to the political situation. A further threat arose in 1702, when James Armour proposed a scheme for a national land bank. He suggested that the Government issue paper money against the capitalisation of annual land values in Scotland. Its attractions were obvious to those who had provided funds for the Darien Scheme and hoped to recoup their losses. A plan to merge this new bank with Bank of Scotland came to nothing, but it made the Directors realise that they needed to do more to support local trade in Scotland. The Bank's answer was twofold: to increase its volume of business in loans and bills; and to issue a bank-note for £12 Scots or £1 sterling. The unfortunate result was that the Bank over-extended its trading. All might have been well had not economic and political events south of the Border seriously affected Scotland. The export of coin to pay for the Duke of Marlborough's military campaigns on the Continent caused a scarcity of money throughout Britain. In the autumn of 1703 a hurricane destroyed a huge volume of Dutch and English shipping in the Channel and wrought havoc along much of the south coast of England. Finally, confidence in the Government fell with a series of military reverses in the war, and all the main London stocks fell in value. The result was that on 18 December 1704 the Bank was forced to stop cash payments and all lending and discounts. This stop lasted for five months and required firm Scottish Government intervention.

The Scots Privy Council, chaired by the Marquess of Tweeddale,

David E. of Leven
dr 1728

J. B. Medina

*David, third Earl of Leven, Governor of Bank of Scotland 1697-1728, and
Governor of Edinburgh Castle, by Sir John de Medina (National Gallery of Scotland)*

30 required that the Bank issue a balance sheet. This statement showed that, in theory at least, all creditors could be paid. The practical problem which was concealed from the public was that this presupposed that all loans could be recovered quickly, which was very far from the case. Most of Scotland's remaining gold and silver coinage disappeared from circulation at this time, and there was effectively a total stop on credit. To compound the situation further, Queen Anne's health gave cause for concern, and the future succession demanded serious discussion between the English and Scots Parliaments. This was Bank of Scotland's nadir.

In this climate a variety of new banking schemes were proposed, but all involved Bank of Scotland being absorbed in a new Government bank. The most plausible and superficially attractive was that proposed in 1705 by John Law of Lauriston. Its essential features were to combine the trading functions of Bank of Scotland with the benefits of a land bank. This project was strongly supported by the Duke of Argyll (as he had become in 1701) and backed by the *Squadrone,* the name usually given to those who were increasingly moving into political power in Scotland and were committed to a Union of Parliaments. Had the project been successful, it would have given Argyll and his supporters total control over the supply of credit in Scotland and therefore the Scottish economy.

For these reasons, all who were not of Argyll's persuasion were keen to see the Bank reopen, and the *Squadrone* over-played their hand. But it is from this date that the Argyll interest was opposed to Bank of Scotland. On the other hand, the Bank's Directors supported the Act of Union because they believed that the agreements contained in the negotiations would lead to an increase in trade and therefore to more settled conditions, which would in turn lead to an increase in the Bank's business. In short, the Union was seen as contributing directly to the Bank's good health.

In its first eleven years of business the Bank had weathered major political and economic storms. It had, moreover, learned a great deal about the business of banking, more often than not by the pragmatic lesson of 'getting it wrong'. The crucial change in its situation by 1707 was that it was no longer run by Scotland's ruling élite and tacitly backed by the Government.

—4—

THE ACT OF UNION AND AFTER, 1707–50

HE Act of 1707 uniting the parliaments of England and Scotland – in the words of the Treaty, 'An Incorporating Union' – was the outcome of tortuous discussions on both sides of the Border lasting four years. The conclusion, that it represented the only real future for the Scottish economy, was not seriously challenged until the 1970s and the advent of North Sea oil. The benefits and costs of merging the economy of a small, poor country with that of a large, wealthy one has been much debated by historians. The incorporation of the former East Germany into the Federal Republic of Germany in the 1990s has given us a much clearer idea of the difficulties and costs involved in amalgamating two economic systems at different stages of development. Previously it had not been appreciated that, in the short term at least, there could be severe economic strains on the larger partner.

For most Lowland Scots the crucial part of the Act (apart from the Presbyterian settlement of Scotland's national Church) was contained in the financial arrangements of clause XV. England was to pay Scotland £398,026 sterling, with an additional sum, called the 'arising equivalent', which represented a proportion of the increased tax revenue resulting from the Union. The 'arising equivalent' did not arise for almost a generation after 1707 and in itself indicates some of the immediate consequences of the Union upon Scotland. The sums of money were to be used in five ways. Scotland's public debts, which stood at £200,000 sterling, were to be paid. The costs and losses incurred in the recoinage of Scots coin were to be reimbursed, a matter of crucial importance to Bank of

32 Scotland. The bulk of the payment, some £232,884 sterling, was to be used to compensate those who had lost money in the failed Darien Scheme to establish a Scottish colony on the Isthmus of Panama in Central America, and a development fund was to be created to encourage fisheries, textiles and other industries. Finally, the expenses of the Scots commissioners, some £30,000, were to be met. In the event only the last item was met in full, giving rise to the gibe made by Andrew Fletcher of Saltoun, a consistent opponent of the Union, that the Scots commissioners were 'a parcel of rogues bought with English gold'.

For Scottish merchants the crucial outcome of the Union was the removal of disabilities, for example, the English Navigation Acts, which they had faced when competing with their English rivals. For Bank of Scotland, appointment as agent to oversee the recoinage offered immediate profits and the prospect of longer-term benefits from the changes.

The outflow of coin from England to Scotland which these payments

Edinburgh from the north in Queen Anne's reign by John Slezer

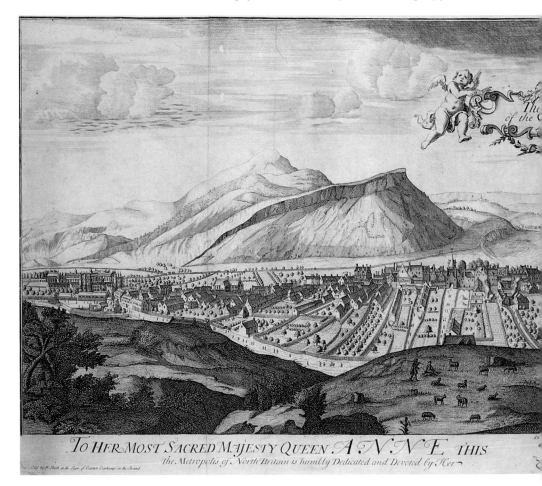

represented seriously worried the directors of the Bank of England. It ran contrary to the accepted economic wisdom of the day. Mercantilism taught that any export of specie (coin or bullion) from a country equalled loss of wealth. There was also one very practical consideration. The removal of coin from England to Scotland simultaneously with the cash requirements of Marlborough's armies on the Continent meant that more Exchequer bills and bank paper would have to be placed with Government contractors. Any military reverse could cause a run on the bank, and the paper itself was unpopular because it had to be held longer before it could be redeemed for cash. The directors of the Bank of England took a decision to attempt to save coin by sending to Edinburgh only £100,086 sterling in coin, making up the balance with Exchequer bills. Effectively a new paper currency was to be launched in Scotland which was designed, quite deliberately, to challenge Bank of Scotland's monopoly and extend the Bank of England's operations in Scotland.

PROSPECT OF HER ANCIENT CITY OF EDENBURGH.
Majesties most Dutifull and most Obedient Subject and Servant

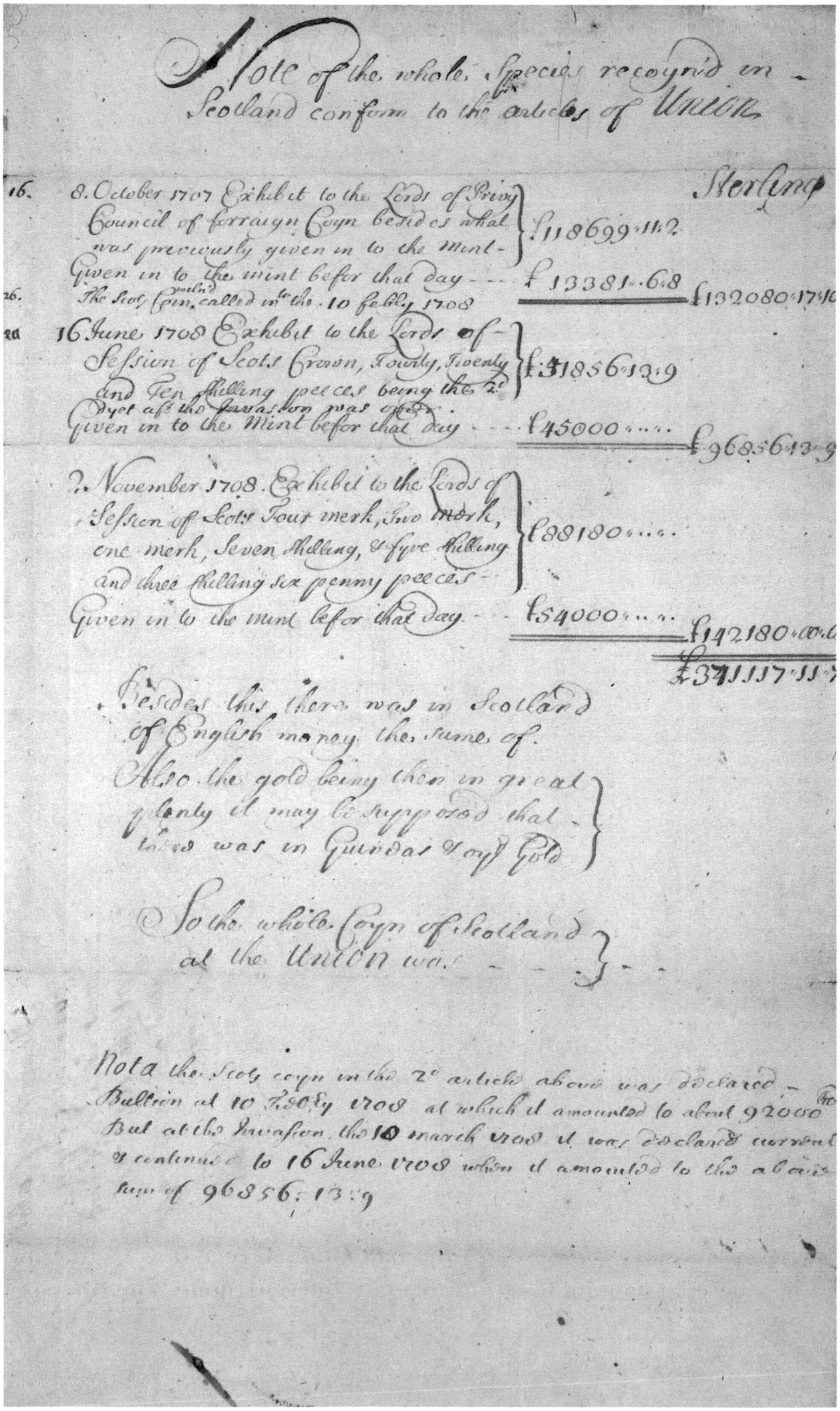

34

Note of the whole Species recoynd in Scotland conform to the articles of Union

Sterling

16.   8. October 1707 Exhibit to the Lords of Privy
Council of forraign Coyn besides what
was previously given in to the Mint-   £118699.11.2
      Given in to the mint befor that day ----   £ 13381.6.8
26.   The Scots Coin called in the 10 Febry 1708   £132080.17.10

      16 June 1708 Exhibit to the Lords of
      Session of Scots Crown, Fourty, Twenty
      and Ten shilling peeces being the 2d   £ 51856.13.9
      dyet aft the Invasion was over -
      given in to the Mint befor that day ---   £45000 .....   £96856.13.9

      2. November 1708. Exhibit to the Lords of
      Session of Scots Four merk, Two merk,
      one merk, Seven Shilling, & fyve shilling   £88180 .....
      and three shilling six penny peeces -
      Given in to the mint befor that day ---   £54000 .....   £142180.00.0
                                                                        £371117.11.7

      Besides this there was in Scotland
      of English money the sume of.
      Also the gold being then in great
      plenty it may be supposed that
      there was in Guineas & oyr Gold

      So the whole Coyn of Scotland
      at the Union was. --- ---

      Nota the Scots coyn in the 2d articles above was declared
      Bullion at 10 Febry 1708 at which it amounted to about 92000
      But at the Invasion tho 10 march 1708 it was declared current
      & continued to 16 June 1708 when it amounted to the above
      sum of 96856: 13: 9

Part of the tactic for forcing Scotland to accept English paper was to delay sending coin north for as long as possible so that coin shortage, resulting from the recoinage, would make exchequer bills seem a reasonable alternative. The added attraction was that Scots, desperate for money, would allow the bills to be discounted at less than face value, ensuring either a profit for the discount business in London or a lower cost to the Exchequer than the sums agreed in the Act of Union. Predictably, this was kept secret from all but the inner cabal of Scots ministers and it was the beginning of August before the money arrived in Edinburgh. The news leaked out at precisely the same time as a rumour was circulating that the Scottish Privy Council had been abolished. Scots refused to accept English paper, and amid riots the Scots commissioners demanded a further £50,000 in cash to settle the most pressing obligations. By Christmas 1707 most of the Darien debt had been paid, and the costs of exchange in and out of London fell sharply. Even so, this left many Scots holding debentures payable against the customs and excise or against the 'equivalent', a matter which was to be of crucial concern to the Bank ten years later.

In the meantime, the officials of Bank of Scotland were dealing with the reminting of the Scottish coinage. The process began in Edinburgh at six o'clock on the morning of 17 April 1707. The Lord President of the Court of Session, Sir Hew Dalrymple, and Bailie James Nairn both presented themselves to David Drummond, the Bank's Treasurer, to begin the process. All the English coin was checked, counted and certified, then all foreign coin in circulation in Scotland and finally all Scots coin. The last two categories were then taken to the Mint in the Cowgate for melting, refining and recoining. The whole process took nearly three years and the final products of the Scottish Mint between 1707 and 1709 can be recognised by the letter 'E' (signifying Edinburgh) under the Queen's portrait on the crown, half-crown, shilling and sixpence. The loss in value which this represented was to be reimbursed by the commissioners of the equivalent, as were the costs incurred by the Bank. By the time the coinage books were closed in 1709, some £411,000 sterling had been dealt with. The fee to the Bank was set at 0.5 per cent of the sterling value and this went straight into the dividend paid to the Proprietors. One unsolved puzzle in this story (but perhaps the Bank was exaggerating) is that the Bank believed it had not been fully paid for the work done. The Directors petitioned the Lords of Session for some unpaid costs, which were granted.

Note in the hand of David Spence, the Bank Secretary, about the Scottish coin reminted into United Kingdom denomination

36   In 1711 the larger issue was taken up by the Earl of Leven with both the Privy Council and the Lord High Treasurer, but without result.

The payment of the equivalent resulted in cash deposits in the Bank, which improved the cash reserve, and it is from this time, in 1708, that rules were devised for the acceptance, payment of interest, and repayment of cash deposits. In March 1708 a French fleet appeared in the Forth on behalf of James III (the Old Pretender) which, although causing a brief run on the Bank's cash, led directly to the system of depositing items of value on security with the Bank. It was a mere hiccup, because the fleet was dispersed by bad weather before it was able to make any meaningful intervention.

The period from 1707 to 1714 was one of considerable prosperity for the Bank, and a dividend of not less than 20 per cent was declared each year. The certainty of that dividend would be curious to an accountant today. It was achieved by the creation of a hidden reserve. Some of this reserve was the Bank's own stock which was released only to those whom the Directors chose to become Proprietors. There were at least two aspects to this. On the one hand, had Bank stock been freely available, it would almost certainly have been acquired by the political interest of the day, which was increasingly Whig and dominated by the Duke of Argyll. On the other hand, the practice gave credence to the accusation that the Bank was a self-perpetuating and complacent oligarchy, more concerned with its own narrow profit than with Scotland's wider needs.

The Jacobite rebellion of 1715 was a major interruption in the Bank's business. News of the Jacobite army's early successes caused a panic in Edinburgh, and the citizens were determined to change their bank-notes for cash. By 19 September the Bank's cash reserves were exhausted and payments were suspended. Immediately the Bank began to call in loans, and those holding bank-notes were reassured that they would be redeemed with interest as soon as possible. Normal business resumed on 19 May 1716 when lending, first on bills, and then on personal security, and finally in 1717 on heritable property, began again. The loss of business for eight months and the interest to be paid on bank-notes meant that no dividend was declared in 1715. The reputation of Bank of Scotland as the Jacobite bank does not stand up to a close examination of the evidence. As with many institutions and organisations in Scotland, it probably had many Jacobite sympathisers, but even now only the Earl of Panmure, a Director and Proprietor, and Lord Basil Hamilton, also a Director, can be identified as having been 'out' in the rebellion. Colour is added to the story by the fact that the Bank's Treasurer, David Drummond, acted as treasurer to a

Left: *Proprietors' receipts for the dividend on their
stockholding in 1721*
Right: *Old Bank Close, the Lawnmarket, Edinburgh, showing Robert
Gourlay's house, the Bank's office from 1700 to 1806. This property
was demolished in 1835*

fund for the defence of prisoners tried after the Rising. Nevertheless, the
Bank's Jacobite reputation stuck in London and ensured that in 1716,
when its monopoly of banking in Scotland came up for renewal, this was
decisively rejected by the Privy Council.

One consequence of the Union of 1707 was to raise the general level
of taxation in Scotland and also to introduce many more excise officers to
enforce this. The results were the growth of smuggling as a national
occupation and something close to an excise war in which the sympathies
of the local inhabitants were always with the smuggler. Numerous
occasions are recorded in which excisemen were on the receiving end of
bloody riots. The best known example is the Shawfield Riot in Glasgow,
when the imposition of 2d Scots on Scottish malt was greeted with
widespread public outrage; but riots were common throughout the
Lowland towns and ports in the 1720s and 1730s. In 1720 there was also a

The Porteous Mob in 1736 (City of Edinburgh Museums and Galleries)

series of food riots which affected most of the towns on the North Sea littoral. In Dysart in Fife over 2,000 people overran both the bailies and the military. The cause was a shortage of meal, which should have been plentiful since the harvest of 1719 had been good. Once again this situation could be traced back to an additional clause in the Act of Union which offered a bounty to exporters, and as a consequence caused a rapid growth in the meal and grain traffic. In this context the ferocity of the Edinburgh populace's handling of Captain Porteous in 1736 is more understandable. The citizens were incensed when Porteous was reprieved for his part in the shooting of protestors who were objecting to the execution of a smuggler. This was not simply an isolated example of an urban lynch mob, but part of a more widespread popular resistance to the new British state. Such acts confirmed the London view of Scots, in Daniel Defoe's words, as a 'hardened, refractory and unruly people'.

Part of the resistance to the exciseman could be seen as a 'class' matter. The repayment of the Government debentures issued in 1707, and even interest on them, depended upon revenue from the Scottish customs, which fell far short of the demands made on it. In the circumstances the resale value fell sharply to about 20 per cent of their face value. From 1713 debenture holders demanded redress from Parliament in London and began to meet on a regular basis in Edinburgh and London; they included the Governor of the Bank, the Earl of Leven. In 1714 Parliament considered all the claims, which amounted to £230,309, and replaced the old debentures with new ones at 5 per cent interest, again payable out of the revenues specified in the Treaty. The need for cash in Scotland was acute and by 1719 around £170,000 was held by London or foreign financial interests. George Middleton, the London banker, Campbell of Monzie and other Argyll kinsmen led the fight for redemption, refunding of the debt or an improvement in compensation. The model they had in mind was the South Sea Company, which appeared to be very successful. (It is one of history's ironies that Bank of Scotland's present-day London Chief Office occupies the Threadneedle Street site of the South Sea Company.) In June 1719 a new compensation and provision for interest payments were made. Administrative control came directly under the Treasury and the whole operation was outwith the jurisdiction of the Scottish courts. In addition, provision was made for the holders of the debentures to form themselves into a corporation. In essence what was achieved was the possibility of a London-based bank with a secure revenue of £10,600 a year based on Scottish taxation. The core of Scotsmen

The Bishop of Down and Connor's attempt to sell his South Sea Company Stock in 1725

Below: *An early bank-note on which £1 sterling is expressed as £12 Scots. This practice continued until 1750*

40   involved, broadly speaking the Argyll interest, were also investors in the Mississippi and Bank of France schemes of their friend John Law.

It was at this juncture that the Directors of Bank of Scotland made a serious error of judgment. Up to this point the Bank had co-operated with the 'equivalent' men and had opposed the Bank of England's attempts to restrict their activities. In the winter of 1719-20, Edinburgh-based equivalent interests offered a merger to the Directors of Bank of Scotland. The details of the scheme owed a great deal to John Law's ideas and little to the careful banking techniques which the Bank had learned. Ten per cent of equivalent stock would be added to the existing paid-up capital of the Bank while the remaining 90 per cent would be exchanged for Bank of Scotland notes. In exchange, the interest of £10,600 a year on the equivalent stock would be added to the Bank's assets to back the note issue. In essence a large-scale convertible paper currency was to be launched, backed only by unredeemable paper, some interest and vague undertakings. Bank of Scotland's unease was compounded by the fact that London speculation in the Mississippi Company and France drained gold and silver out of Scotland. The Directors rejected the offer.

The Edinburgh Society of the Equivalent (simply those people living in Edinburgh who had been granted 'equivalent' money as part of the Act of Union) then formed a project to provide fire insurance, but this was simply a cover to provoke a run on the Bank. In April 1720, notes worth £8,400 were presented with a demand for cash. This was met by calling up another £10,000 of shareholders' capital and restricting discounts on bills of exchange. Again a merger was proposed by the Edinburgh Society and rejected by the Bank. The collapse of the South Sea Company provoked legislation in the Parliament of 1722 which ruled that only six partners were to be allowed in a joint-stock company unless the capital was incorporated by Act of Parliament; but no mention was made of the equivalent, so only a royal charter would be required to create a bank. A tentative proposal to set up an equivalent bank in London was strongly opposed by the Bank of England. However, the Walpole-Newcastle-Islay group, strongly supported by George Middleton, who dealt with much of the finance for the army in Scotland, secured the passage of the charter which founded the Royal Bank of Scotland in 1727. From this time two quite specific rumours about the 'Old' Bank (as Bank of Scotland was known for one hundred years) circulated in Edinburgh, each of which had an impact on the Bank's business before 1740: firstly, it was unreliable from the Government's point of view – that is to say, it was Jacobite and had been unwilling to lend the Government money during the Fifteen; secondly, the

Edinburgh from the west by John Slezer

The Bank's balance sheet, issued on 18 June 1728
in response to forced closure

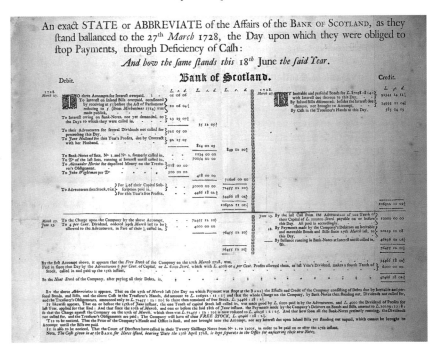

Alexander, second Earl of Marchmont, Governor 1728-40
(Scottish National Portrait Gallery)

Bank was over-cautious and partial in its lending policies. These were restatements of accusations which had been made since 1705 but, in the way of repeated calumnies, the suspicion remained.

Neither the economic theory of the day nor the political situation in Scotland favoured the existence of banking competition. Even before the Royal Bank was formally set up, its agents were accumulating Bank of Scotland notes to be presented in due course for payment. The 'Old' Bank husbanded its resources by calling in its loans and restricting new loans, knowing very well that a struggle for survival would result. Matters came to a head in March 1728, when £900 worth of notes presented by the Royal's agent in Glasgow could not be honoured immediately. Although the cash was found, the offer of payment was rejected because it was claimed that interest was also due. Bank of Scotland suspended payment and closed its doors. The immediate response by the Directors was to look for a further £10,000 of subscription from the shareholders (bringing the Bank's capital up to £40,000) and to publish a pamphlet describing the Bank's history and achievements since its foundation.

In April of that year, George Drummond, Lord Provost of Edinburgh, believing that the 'Old' Bank would be sufficiently chastened, proposed that the two banks should amalgamate. To assist in the persuasion Andrew Cochrane of Glasgow, who had started the proceedings, raised a suit for debt against the Directors of Bank of Scotland until the interest had been paid. The Royal Bank cashier also looked for the arrestment of funds and 'inhibition' of the Bank office, now in Gourlay's Close in the Lawnmarket. As the negotiations dragged on and the Court of Session rejected the legal process, Drummond delivered what he believed would be the *coup de grâce*. He was a commissioner of the Customs and Excise and persuaded the London commissioners that Bank of Scotland notes should not be received as payment for tax or customs revenue. Many local customs officials had already received payment of taxes and customs dues in Bank of Scotland notes. They were reluctant to take the loss if these were not redeemed. In fact, when in late May, early June the notes were presented for payment, the Bank was able to find gold and silver in exchange. The crisis was effectively over.

By July the 'Old' Bank had reopened its doors, paid its creditors and resumed lending. It had survived the onslaught, but the active hostility of Lords Islay and Milton and Provost Drummond was a constant feature of the background to the business of the next twenty years. As if to emphasise its independence of the Argyll connection, the Bank elected as Governor in August 1728 Alexander, second Earl of Marchmont – a man dismissed

44 from all his crown appointments by Sir Robert Walpole, despite a successful diplomatic career from 1714 as minister plenipotentiary in Prussia and between 1722 and 1725 as joint ambassador with Lord Whitworth to the Congress of Cambrai. A number of changes were introduced into the Bank's procedures as a result of its experiences. First, in March 1729 the Directors issued the following statement:

> Now all the money borrowed at interest for support of the company's credit *is paid*, or ordered to be paid off . . . therefore they agree to commence lending at five per cent with the provision: that the several committees shall at each monthly court make a report of what money has been lent out by them the preceding month.

This was accompanied by a series of alterations to bookkeeping practices so that a balance or 'state' could be produced more quickly. Secondly, after the new £5 note issue of 19 November 1730, an option clause was added to

A £1 bank-note of the 1729 design bearing the 'option' clause

The Bank's salary sheet for the half-year ending 27 March 1740 (£250 and eight employed in total!)

the notes. This promised to 'pay the bearer on demand or at the option of the directors five pounds two shillings and sixpence sterling at the end of six months after the day of the demand'. From 1732 a similar phrase was added to the £1 note. In other words, if the 'Old' Bank could not meet the immediate demands for cash of its note issue, it undertook to pay interest on the sum at the rate of 5 per cent a year.

Following the Royal or 'New' Bank's lead, in 1729 the cash credit was introduced, the direct banking ancestor of the overdraft. The first recorded facility was to John Whyte, merchant of Edinburgh, who was granted credit to the extent of £1,000 sterling, with John Craig, WS, as his cautioner. The rules regarding deposits were overhauled and regularised. If interest was to be paid on such accounts, the account was to be for a term of six months at 3 per cent or twelve months at 4 per cent. No deposit of less than £100 was accepted and the bond was to be signed by the Treasurer. Finally, the importance of branches in the main trading burghs was realised and in 1731 a fresh start was made at creating a branch network when agents were appointed in Aberdeen, Dundee and Glasgow. All the branches were unsuccessful, however, and closed within two years.

Despite this, the Bank made steady progress during the 1730s and was able to pay a dividend of at least 5 per cent to the Proprietors. The open hostility between the 'Old' and 'New' banks also began to fade, as each realised that, against the background of a Scottish economy which was beginning to expand, there was room for both to make a living. As in 1720 and 1727 there were serious food riots in Scotland, the result of poor harvests and rising grain prices. In Edinburgh, mobs attacked granaries at the Dean Village, Gilmerton and Leith. The Bank made an interest-free loan of £5,000 to the Provost and bailies of Edinburgh to be spent on poor relief, the first of a number of similar loans it made throughout the eighteenth century.

Phrases such as 'steady progress to prosperity' were shattered by news of the arrival of Prince Charles Edward Stuart at Moidart on 6 August 1745. The Highland army's progress towards Edinburgh was preceded by rumour and counter-rumour and accompanied by many secret hopes and fears. The Directors' reaction to the Forty-five must surely give the lie to the belief that the 'Old' Bank remained Jacobite in anything more than nostalgic sympathy. Quite simply, rebellion was bad for business, and bankers acted, so far as was possible, in ways to protect it. The minute books of the Bank make it clear that great efforts were made to gather in bank-notes ahead of the Highlanders. Roughly 50 per cent of the issue was withdrawn and destroyed between August and November 1745, so that credit was

46 effectively withdrawn from Highlanders. The Royal Bank was not so lucky, and the diary of John Campbell, Cashier of the Royal, provides a vivid account of the consequences of Prince Charles's secretary, Murray of Broughton, having £10,000 of Royal Bank notes in his possession. John Campbell was on the horns of a dilemma. On the one hand, he was required by law to provide coin on demand for bank-notes when presented. On the other hand, too ready compliance with Murray's demands might have brought the charge of colluding in rebellion. On 13 September Bank of Scotland's cash, ledgers, title deeds, bonds and books were moved into the house of Major Robertson – Adjutant of the Garrison at Edinburgh Castle – in three iron chests. One room became a 'safe', which was locked and the keys handed to the Treasurer. In gratitude (or perhaps as an insurance policy) the Bank lent General Preston, the governor of Edinburgh Castle, £10,000 to ensure payment of the garrison's wages.

On 16 September, Prince Charles's Cameron Regiment, under their Clan Chief, Lochiel, rushed the Netherbow, and Edinburgh fell to the Highland Army without bloodshed. The Bank remained closed for eight weeks while Prince Charles's army occupied the city and all business came to a standstill. The Castle remained in Government hands. On 31 October, after the Highlanders had left, three of the Bank's Directors went to the Castle and brought out sufficient cash and notes for business to reopen in a modest way. In January 1746 a duplicate set of ledgers and minutes was commissioned in case of accidents. By March, matters were slowly returning to normal and cash accounts were reopened where good security could be offered. Finally, on 5 April 1746, all the books and cash were brought back to Old Bank Close and the full business of the Bank was restored. The help of Major Robertson was acknowledged by a gift of thirty guineas 'for preserving the cash in his rooms during the late unhappy confusions', a phrase which captures exactly the Bank's attitude to the Forty-five. The main impact of six months' closure on the Bank's archive is to be found, not in the laconic entries in minute books and ledgers, but in the file of letters either complaining about the Bank's closure or attempting to secure payment for sums of money allegedly 'lost' during the rebellion.

OPPOSITE PAGE:
Top left: *Portrait of The Old Pretender attr. to Antonio David*
Top right: *Charles Edward Stuart, The Young Pretender, in 1752 by Cosmo Alexander (detail)*
(The Drambuie Collection)
Board minute book for August 1745–December 1745
Background: *Entry of the Highlanders into Edinburgh, 16 September 1745, by Thomas Duncan*
(detail) (City of Edinburgh Museums and Galleries)

Lt Ferguson's
——— Bank-notes ———

On 16 August 1745, Lt James Ferguson was leading two companies of St Clairs, or the Royal Regiment of Foot, when they were ambushed 'by a much superior force of rebels' – that is, Lochiel's Camerons. This first skirmish of the Forty-five took place at Highbridge in Lochaber, and Lt Ferguson was carrying the pay for his men – some £59 sterling in Bank of Scotland notes (the 1995 equivalent would be about £3,000). Ducking behind a convenient rock while the bullets whistled over their heads, Lt Ferguson and his sergeant proceeded to destroy the notes, Lt Ferguson putting the numbers into his coat lining while Sgt Johnston mutilated the rest. Both men were captured and paroled, and on 6 September appeared before the Bank directors to reclaim the money due. After a certain amount of discussion, because the amount claimed did not match the numbers in the bank-note issue ledger, the sum was repaid in full and the two men were instructed to join the garrison at Edinburgh Castle.

Private, Grenadier Company
1751
The 1st of Foot (Royal Scots)

Private, Grenadier Company
1742
The 1st of Foot (Royal Scots)
(Royal Scots Museum)

Lt Ferguson's petition

—5—
NEW BANKS AND NEW HORIZONS, 1746–75

I N the quarter-century after the defeat of the Jacobites at Culloden, the banking system of Scotland developed very rapidly to service the needs of an economy which was finally beginning to feel the real benefits of the Act of Union. In one matter Scotland was unique: most of its business was settled in paper currency, issued by one of the country's many banks, while gold and silver coin almost disappeared from circulation. This was commented on by Adam Smith in *The Wealth of Nations*. It seemed to Smith that unregulated competition between banks was the key which opened the door for a small, poor country on the periphery of Europe to 'punch above its weight' (a phrase used in a different context by Foreign Secretary Douglas Hurd) in international affairs, and to improve dramatically on its economic inheritance.

1 The British Linen Company

On 5 October 1746 a third company whose shareholders also had limited liability was added to the 'Old' and 'New' banks by royal charter. The British Linen Company (so called because the concepts of *Scottishness* and *Englishness* were to give way to the Britishness created by the Union) opened its doors in Halkerston's Wynd, Edinburgh, 'to carry on the linen manufactury in all its branches'. It brought together and formalised a variety of interests, including the Edinburgh Linen Co-partnery, which had been concerned with improving the quality of linen manufacture in Scotland in the previous generation. The key political figures were the third

50   Duke of Argyll, Lord Milton (a nephew of Andrew Fletcher of Saltoun, who had fought a duel in opposition to the Union of 1707), the Earl of Panmure and the London banker George Middleton. Work on converting the Edinburgh Linen Co-partnery into a chartered company had begun before the Forty-five, and its managers, William Tod and Ebenezer McCulloch, were convinced that progress of the petition had been delayed by the rebellion. The charter gave the Company limited liability and power to raise a capital of £100,000; however, the trustees decided in the first instance to raise only half that sum. The essential need was to begin business quickly and persuade weavers and linen manufacturers to sell direct to the Company, but also for the Company to employ spinners and weavers without any intermediary. A cash account was granted by the Royal Bank on the security of the shareholding. The overall aim was to raise the quality of linen manufactured in Scotland and to produce a series of standard-quality linens which would be certified and marketed by the Company, thereby making Scotland independent of Dutch and German cloth manufacturers. A subsidiary, and perhaps moral, purpose of the promoters of the Company was to encourage the development of both a widespread cash economy and the habits of regular industry and thrift among working people.

By 1748 the capital had been increased to £70,000 and McCulloch, finding the supply of local flax inadequate, had begun to buy abroad through Scots merchants resident in Riga, St Petersburg, Rotterdam and Amsterdam. One agent, John Coutts of Danzig, was the son of Edinburgh's Lord Provost and belonged to a family which had been trading to the Baltic out of Montrose since the 1670s. The first letter books of the Company give a fascinating insight into the mechanics of linen trade and manufacture, which were controlled from a warehouse in Halkerston's Wynd, off the Canongate in Edinburgh. Warehouses for both flax and cloth were opened in other towns: London in 1747, Glasgow in 1749 and Leith in 1750. To these were added a bleaching green and a cloth-finishing works. The crucial step for the Company's future as a bank was taken in 1747, when promissory notes were issued, inscribed 'for value received in goods'. This is the earliest recorded example in Scotland of merchants issuing notes of hand, and one that was followed shortly by a number of Glasgow merchants. In fact, the offer of trade credit was a necessary part of the Linen Company's normal business. It was also one very simple way of helping to manage a geographically dispersed business which by its very nature relied on small-scale producers with individual spinners and weavers throughout Scotland. This is not the place to detail the ups and downs of the linen trade before 1760, but by 1763 the problems facing the

*Coat-of-arms of the British Linen
Company*

Moray House, Canongate, Edinburgh, home of the British Linen Company, 1753-90

52 Company had become so formidable that winding up the business seemed to many of its directors the most sensible option. One major issue was the fluctuating price of the raw material, flax, which turned importation, at first a profitable part of the business, into a steady loss. There was also the problem of a consistent shortage of ready cash in the countryside. Unlike Bank of Scotland notes, Linen Company paper was payable on demand for cash. New notes were printed in 1763 containing the 'option' clause offering to pay on demand or at six months plus interest. The immediate result was a run on the Company's resources, at one stage to the value of £3,000 a week, which drained its cash account with the Royal Bank. These runs continued to 1767 and could have been much worse had not the Lord Provost of Edinburgh, George Drummond (known to Bank of Scotland from his activities of 1728), instructed revenue agents in the various towns to accept the notes as payment and recirculate them. The cornerstone of a successful note issue was (and is) public confidence in its security and value. In this case it was not helped by growing public differences among the Linen Company's directors. The affairs of the Linen Company were well known to the 'Old' Bank by way of Patrick Miller of Dalswinton, remembered now as the man who first applied steam power in seagoing vessels and as Robert Burns's landlord in Dumfries, but in 1765 as a man with a foot in both camps; and one of the main sources of the runs on the Linen Company was Bank of Scotland, which over a number of years ingathered Linen Company bank-notes and presented them for payment.

Early British Linen Company one guinea note dated 5 April 1768

The transformation of the Linen Company to a bank occurred over a number of years and almost by stealth. Serious attempts at debt recovery were begun in 1764, and the business of granting cash credits (overdrafts) to linen manufacturers was extended to other types of business. From 1765 and the passing of the Bank Act, the banking side of the business began to predominate and the Linen Company advertised that its cash office would be open daily like those of other banks. It must be emphasised that the Company's directors, despite their earlier misgivings, had no intention of abandoning the linen business. The problem was that the few successful manufacturers no longer needed the Company, and the majority faced severe competition from cheaper foreign linens once import duties were lowered and the subsidy on raising flax in Britain was removed. There was one respect in which the Linen Company was different from its older rivals: it possessed the kernel of a branch network, with agents in Forres, Inverness, Peterhead, Aberdeen, Dundee, Dumfries, Eyemouth and Dunbar who were eager to introduce new business.

The Royal Bank recognised the Linen Company as a bank in 1765 and was prepared to support it, but it was not until 1771 that Bank of Scotland was ready to accept its bank-notes and to form a more neighbourly relationship.

2 Banking in Glasgow

The origins of banking in Glasgow and the Glasgow tobacco trade are two facets of the same story – a remarkable historical tale in its own right. The Glasgow merchants trading to North America, unlike their London competitors who tended to act as commission agents, followed the older Scots tradition of buying direct in America, shipping the products to Glasgow and then selling them on. The main product and source of their prosperity was tobacco from Virginia and the mid-southern states. From 1720 onwards, these men were accustomed to providing working capital to cover the needs of trade, but were also prepared to invest in goods, grant credit to planters in the colonies and to invest in port facilities and ships. In short, Glasgow and the tobacco trade were dominated by a group of perhaps twenty families who lent and borrowed from each other to cover the ups and downs of their trade and who could largely depend upon their mutual resources. They included well-known families such as the Dunlops and the Montgomeries, whose social coherence was strengthened by intermarriage. Until recently most historians have argued that there was a close relationship between the formation of banks in Glasgow in the 1750s and the needs of the Virginia merchants for

Glasgow from the east by John Slezer

increased capital to expand their trade rapidly. Although this thesis has now been modified in some important respects, the connection between the two remains clear.

Two of the three banks founded in Glasgow before 1770 – the Ship Bank, founded in 1749, and the Thistle Bank, founded in 1761 – are part of Bank of Scotland's story; the third, the Arms Bank, founded in 1750, is not. All were established as partnerships and in each case the main partners were tobacco lords. The founders of the Ship Bank were Colin Dunlop, Allan Dreghorn, Robert Dunlop and Andrew Buchanan, with two West India merchants, William McDowell and Alexander Houston. The first partners of the Thistle Bank – John Glassford, James Ritchie, John McCall and James Coats Campbell – were all Virginia merchants; only Sir James Maxwell represented domestic interests.

Initially the Ship Bank was seen as a possible partner for Bank of Scotland in the West following the failure to establish a branch in Glasgow. It was launched with full approval and a cash credit of £10,000 from Bank of Scotland in July 1749. The official name of the company was Dunlop, Houston & Co., but it was popularly known as the Ship Bank from the device of a ship in full sail which appeared on all its bank-notes after 1750. The introduction of the bank-notes upset the 'Old' Bank, but an accommodation was reached and they were permitted to circulate. In like manner the Arms Bank, founded in 1750, was supported by the Royal Bank. But by 1752 the two Edinburgh banks were taking fright at the competition which was developing from the Glasgow banks. The breaking-point was the setting up of agencies in Edinburgh by the Glasgow banks to redeem their notes and at the same time to use the Edinburgh banks' notes as part of their reserves. In other words, Bank of Scotland and Royal Bank notes would be withdrawn from circulation by the Glasgow banks and held as part of their reserve, with consequent damage to Edinburgh profits. The outcome was a pact between the Bank and the Royal in July 1752. Each agreed that it would never organise a 'run' on the other; moreover, they would provide mutual support if any third party attempted to do so. Other parts of the understanding covered arrangements for regular meetings (the forerunner of the Committee of Scottish Clearing Bankers), regular note exchanges (a feature of the Scottish banking scene to this day), combined pursuit of forgers, and joint action to make life difficult for anyone attempting to export specie from Scotland.

With their backs secure, the two Edinburgh banks launched an all-out assault on the Arms and Ship banks. Legal action was unsuccessful. The main line of attack was to withdraw credit from anyone who dealt with the Glasgow banks, withdraw the banks' cash credits in the two Edinburgh banks and refuse to honour their bank-notes. The Aberdeen Banking Company, formed in 1747, collapsed in 1753, a casualty in the note war, but the British Linen Company, although resented by Bank of Scotland, was left alone. The simplest explanation for this is that a number of cross-directorships existed; that it had powerful political patrons; and that it was perceived to be operating in a particular niche, which did not represent the same sort of threat as did the Glasgow banks. In fairness, the intention was not to drive the Glasgow banks out of business but to reach a reasonable division which would give room for all. On 18 October 1756 Lord Milton, a director of the Royal Bank, tried to negotiate terms. The Glasgow banks proposed that they would confine themselves to the counties of Ayr, Lanark, Renfrew, Stirling and

*A flintlock blunderbus carried by Bank
messengers between Edinburgh, Glasgow and Dumfries*

Argyll and would not increase their combined capital beyond £120,000 sterling. The counter-proposal was that the Edinburgh banks would open a joint office in Glasgow and would help the Glasgow banks to wind up their operations; alternatively the Glasgow banks could limit their combined capital to £50,000 sterling and trade only in Glasgow, Paisley and Port Glasgow. No progress was made and the two Edinburgh banks appointed Archibald Trotter, with sufficient notes and credit, to harass the Glasgow banks. The tactic, as before, was to collect bank-notes of the opposition and present them with a demand for specie. The Glasgow banks adopted two tactics: the 'option clause' was inserted into the bank-notes; and instead of redeeming the notes in cash, they paid for them by bills drawn on London. The net effect of this in Scotland was the virtual disappearance of gold and silver coin and an almost total reliance on paper currency. It was not popular with the public, particularly when notes were issued for values as low as sixpence, and a number of 'skit' or spoof notes appeared, ostensibly valued at a penny.

Some of the tactics adopted by the Arms and Ship banks were designed to make the collection of cash as tedious as possible. The teller of the Arms Bank was particularly adept at delaying tactics. He would deliberately miscount the money, drop some on the floor so that counting had to begin again, test the coin to see that it was true, and sometimes arrange to be called away on urgent business, which meant restarting the count from scratch. Archibald Trotter, the Edinburgh banks' agent, complained that on one occasion it took 34 working days to count out £2,893, and on another that the daily average never exceeded £36. It was Trotter's patience which broke first and he raised a law suit for vexatious delays. Although he was the nominal victor, Bank of Scotland and the Royal Bank decided in March 1761 not to continue the battle and withdrew their advances to him.

The same year saw the founding of the third Glasgow bank, whose principal partner was John Glassford (1715–83), also a founding partner of the Arms Bank. He was the wealthiest of all the tobacco merchants, and one who is immortalised as the hero of Tobias Smollett's *The Expedition of Humphrey Clinker*. He had a great variety of business interests, as had the bank's other five partners. The connecting link between them once again was the Virginia trade, and the evidence suggests that they were more adventurous, that is to say more aggressive, in their attitude to banking than either the Ship Bank or the Arms Bank, in the latter of which three of the other partners were also involved. The official name of the new bank was Sir Walter Maxwell, James Ritchie & Company, but it was more usually known as the Thistle Bank, after the device which

*Colin Dunlop, Virginia merchant
and founding partner in the Ship Bank*

*The Ship Bank Chest – a wrought-iron and
painted 'kist' from around 1710*

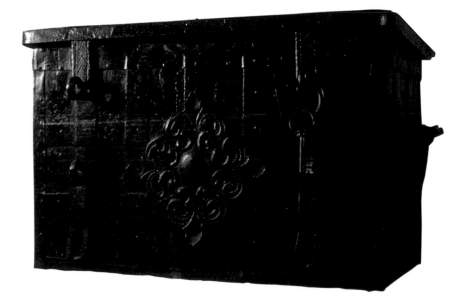

58 appeared on its bank-notes. It began to expand its note issue throughout Scotland, concentrating on the north-east, with a secondary base in Aberdeen. As early as 1763, and just when Bank of Scotland thought the note war was coming to an end, private bankers in Edinburgh became worried about the attempts to push Thistle Bank notes. The Thistle Bank adopted a different tactic for dealing with the Edinburgh banks. As a result, the bank-note war degenerated into pure farce. Archibald Trotter wrote to the joint committee on 9 December 1763, describing an unexpectedly convivial meeting with Sir James Maxwell and his colleagues at the Thistle Bank:

> After drinking a few glasses of wine Sir James Maxwell broke the ice and told me he was sorry on his first acquaintance with me, to be obliged, him, and his company to take a protest against me, to which I answered I know no difference that was betwixt us, upon that Barclay [a Glasgow lawyer] pull'd out a long paper cut and read over. This conduct of theirs was unexpected by me. . . . After that was over Sir James and the rest of the gentlemen insisted on my staying to sup with them . . . and we spent a very merry night together till past one a clock, and not one word of banking passed more . . . Last night's gambol has thrown me back greatly in health today. I wish I was with you to get these troublesome affairs out of head for a few days . . .

Edinburgh was not amused and delivered a sharp instruction to 'avoid like

Two 'Bank' notes issued by merchants – the proliferation of these threatened the stability of paper currency and they became non-negotiable after the 1765 Bank Act

entanglements in future'. One major problem was that Thistle Bank notes became a prime target for forgery and by 1768 a large number of known forgeries were in circulation. It was at least partly in response to this that the cashier of the newly formed Banking Company in Aberdeen refused to accept Thistle Bank notes and thereby provoked a note war in the north of Scotland. The capture, trial and conviction (and hanging) of William Herrics of Ayr for forgery improved matters but did not eliminate the problem. The

Above: *Aberdeen from the south in 1750 by Mossman. The Banking Company in Aberdeen opened its doors on 1 January 1767. It became one of the constituent banks of the Union Bank of Scotland in 1849 (Aberdeen City Art Gallery and Museum)*

Right: *A Glasgow 'skit' note for one penny, including an option clause of a song in exchange for interest due*

60   note war had brought the whole matter of the issue of paper bank-notes into disrepute, and an alternative method of regulation was required.

Despite the note war it has to be said that the Glasgow banks, the Ship Bank in particular, prospered. Great profits were to be made supplying and supporting the British war effort in North America, and the end of the war with France (known as the Seven Years War) in 1763 opened vast new areas of Nova Scotia, Quebec and the Allegheny region to settlement and trade. By 1761 the Neat Stock, which we would now understand as net profit, for division among the partners stood at £12,900. In fact the partners consistently reinvested their profits in the business, which in part explains the rapid and secure growth of their working capital. When drawing up new articles of partnership in 1765 the Ship Bank proprietors could record that:

> we . . . find the amounts of debts owing by us to be (including our own signed notes) £127,550: 16s.: 8½ sterling and interest &c. on accounts not settled £705: 18: 4¾. The amount of debts owing to us we find to be £129,702: 14: 0¼d., and interest owing to us on accounts &c. not settled £1,554: 1: 1d. sterling, from which there appears to be a balance owing to us of £3,000 sterling, which is our Neat Stock this 30th of August 1753.

In 1765 Bank of Scotland led a lobby of Parliament at Westminster, and a statute was passed – 'an Act to prevent the inconveniences arising from the present method of issuing notes and bills, by the banks, banking companies, and bankers in that part of Great Britain called Scotland'. This contained three main provisions: bank-notes containing the option clause were outlawed as from 15 May 1766; summary diligence (instant legal redress) was permitted against anyone issuing bank-notes and not redeeming them on demand; and finally the issue of bank-notes for sums of money less than twenty shillings (£1) sterling was forbidden.

The Bank Act of 1765 was in part an acknowledgment by Bank of Scotland that the climate in which it was operating had changed. In summary, by 1770 there were two banks with limited liability and a third, the British Linen Company, *en route* to joining them; and there were three partnership banks in Glasgow, seven private banks in Edinburgh and probably two in Glasgow. In addition, small partnerships had coalesced into larger organisations in Aberdeen, Perth and Dundee, with Douglas, Heron and Co. of Ayr absorbing previous banking operations in Ayr and Dumfries in 1770–71. Part of Bank of Scotland's response was a radical reorganisation of its internal management and structure, effectively the first for over fifty years. The key figure was Patrick Miller of Dalswinton, who became a Director in 1767 and pushed for the changes required. These were opposed by a number of Directors, who were voted out of office in 1771, and some reforms were instituted; the most important was that voting rights would rest with the share rather than with the shareholder. In other words, one Proprietor with 200 shares could not be outvoted by two with 20 shares each. It was also agreed that each year the three longest-serving Directors would retire and would not be eligible for re-election for at least a year thereafter. The paid-up capital of the Bank was increased to £80,000. Perhaps most important of all, in 1771 formal arrangements were set up to provide for a regular and general exchange of bank-notes. Hand in hand with this there developed a system of settling inter-bank accounts on a weekly basis.

Bank of Scotland's policy was determined by the Directors, with all salaried staff occupying a subsidiary role. Responsibility for implementing the Directors' policy before 1772 rested with the three senior officers of the Bank – the Treasurer, the Secretary and the Accountant, each heading a 'department' dealing with a particular aspect of the Bank's business. The Treasurer was responsible for dealing with bills of exchange, inland bills and cash accounts, the vehicle through which the Bank's notes were circulated. The Secretary handled all legal matters, dealt with correspondence and kept the minutes, while the Accountant ran and organised the Bank's bookkeeping systems. The general impression given by the Bank's own records is that its staff structure was stable over long periods of time. Most men entered as clerks and might after ten years or so move on to a higher position or to become a teller, a key position of trust. All staff came from 'respectable' families who were able to offer the Bank security against defalcation. There does not, at this time, appear to have been any formal system of apprenticeship. All members of staff were literate and it is perhaps noteworthy that the porters and messengers were all capable of signing their own names in the salary books. The range of salaries was quite small throughout the eighteenth century, the Treasurer and Secretary and Accountant each receiving £100 to £150 a year, with the Treasurer having a bonus calculated as a percentage of deposits, the use of the Bank house and allowances for 'coal and candle'. Tellers were paid between £30 and £50 depending on seniority, while the Bank servant was paid £15 a year. In every case, salaries were paid six-monthly in arrears. Requests for rises in salary were dealt with on an individual basis, but it was more than common for length of service or merit to be dealt with by a bonus or present rather than by a permanent salary increase.

A LIST of the NAMES of the ADVENTURERS

IN THE

BANK OF SCOTLAND.

FEBRUARY 6th, 1771.

Nota, *That those marked* ***, *are, by their Adventure, qualified to be chosen* GOVERNOR, DEPUTY-GOVERNOR, *or* DIRECTORS; *those marked* **, DEPUTY-GOVERNOR, *or* DIRECTORS; *and those marked* *, DIRECTORS.

A
* Sir Anthony Thomas Abdy of Lincolns-in, in the county of Middlesex, Baronet.
* Sir Robert Anstruther of Balcaskie, Brt.
* William Alexander Merchant in Edinburgh.
* Archibald Arbuthnott Merchant in Edinburgh.
  Helen Arbuthnott, daughter of Robert Arbuthnott, Merchant in Edinburgh.

B
*** The Hon. George Baillie of Jarviswood.
  Grizel Baillie, eldest daughter of the Hon. George Baillie of Jarviswood.
  Elizabeth Baldwin, of the parish of Enfield, in the county of Middlesex, widow.
* James Balfour, son of the deceased George Balfour, Writer to the Signet.
** Thomas Belsches, Presenter of Signatures in the Exchequer.
  John Blackader, son of the deceased John Blackader, late of St. Leonards.
* John Blair of Balthyock, Esq;
  Mrs. Margaret Blair, spouse to Lieutenant-Colonel William Fullarton-Blair.
  Thomas Boyes Writer in Edinburgh.
* Archibald Brown of Greenbank, Esq;

C
*** Sir Hew Crawfurd of Jordanhill, Bt.
** James Carmichael Writer to the Signet.
*** George Chalmers Merchant in Edin.
* James Chalmer Writer to the Signet.
* William Clarke of Bush-hill, in the county of Middlesex, Esq;
*** George Clephan of Carslogie, Esq;
* Robert Clerk of Mavisbank, Esq;
*** Oliver Coult of Auldhame, Esq;
* Hugh Craig of Corsartoun, Esq;
* Thomas Craig of Riccarton, Esq;
  Capt. William Craig, his Executors.
* Charles Craigie of Glendoick, Esq;
** Laurence Craigie Writer to the Signet.
  Andrew Crosbie, Esq; Advocate.
*** Thomas Cuming Merchant in Edin.
* William Cuming Merchant in Edin.

D
  Her Grace Margaret Dutchess of Douglas.
*** Sir Laurence Dundas, Bart.
* William Dallas Wright in Edinburgh.
* William Dempster Goldsmith in Edinburgh.
  Anne Dewar, widow of George Napier of Kilmahew, Esq;
*** Archibald Douglas of Cavers, Esq;
  Henry Douglas Merchant in London.
* David Dundas of Newhalls, Esq;
* Henry Dundas, Esq; his Majesty's Solicitor-General.

E
* James Erskine of Barjarg, Esq; one of the Senators of the College of Justice.
*** Martin Eccles, M. D.
* James Edmonstone Writer in Edin.

F
** The Right Hon. James Earl Fife.
* Sir Adam Fergusson of Kilkerran, Baronet.
* Sir William Forbes, Bart. Merchant in Edinburgh.
*** Adam Fairholme of Greenhill, Esq;
* George Falconar Merchant in Cadiz.
* James Falconar of Monkton, Esq;
  Mary Falconar, daughter of the deceased George Falconar, Merchant in Edinburgh.
*** George Farquhar-Kinloch, Merchant in London.
  Trustees of the deceased Captain James Farquhar.
* Alexander Fergusson, Esq; Advocate.
* Anthony Ferguson Merchant in Edin.
  Jean Finlayson, widow of John Porterfield of Fullwood, Esq; Advocate.
* David Forbes Writer in Edinburgh.
* James Forrest of Comieston, Esq;
* John Forrest Merchant in Edinburgh.
* John Forrest junior Merchant in Edinburgh.

G
*** The Right Hon. John Earl of Glasgow.
* David Gavin of Langton, Esq;
** Alexander Gibson of Cliftonhall, Esq; Goldsmiths of Edinburgh.
* James Gordon, youngest son of Alexander Gordon of Cairnfield, Esq;
* Mr. William Gordon, late Fellow of Bennet College, Cambridge.
* James Grant Merchant in Edinburgh.
  Executors and Trustees of the deceased William Grant of Prestongrange, Esq;
*** James Guthrie Merchant in Edin.

H
*** The Right Hon. John Earl of Hopetoun.
* William Hall of Whitehall, Esq;
* John Hamilton Merchant in Edin.
  Mrs. Mary Hamilton-Nisbet, spouse of William Nisbet of Dirleton, Esq;
  John Hay of Belton, Esq;
* Willam Hay of Lawfield, Esq;
* Robert Hepburn of Baads, Esq;
* Roger Hog of Newliston, Esq;
*** Roger Hog jun. Merchant in London.
* Thomas Hog, Esq ; Advocate.
* James Home of Gamelshiels, Esq;
* Dr. John Hope Physician in Edinburgh.
*** James Hotchkis Brewer in Edinburgh.
* Alexander Houston Merchant in Edinburgh.
*** Alexander Hunter Merchant in Edinburgh.

* James Hunter Merchant in Edinburgh.

I
*** Sir John Inglis of Cramond, Bart.
* George Inglis of Redhall, Esq;
* John Inglis Merchant in Edinburgh.
* George Innes, one of the Cashiers of the Royal Bank of Scotland.

J
*** Robert Jamieson Writer to the Signet.

K
*** Alexander Keith, one of the Underclerks of Session.
  Mrs. Elizabeth Ker, Widow of James Ker, late Goldsmith in Edinburgh.

L
* The Right Hon. James Earl of Lauderdale.
* The Right Hon. David Earl of Leven.
* George Leslie Merchant in Edinburgh.
  Montague, Francis, and George Lind, children of the deceased Captain Francis Lind.
*** William Loch Writer in Edinburgh.

M
*** His Grace William Duke of Montrose.
*** The Right Honourable Hugh Earl of Marchmont.
** Sir John Mylne, Bart. Lieut. Governor of the Island of Guernsey.
  Lt. Col. George Moncrieffe of Reidie, his Representatives.
*** Lieut. General Alexander Marjoribanks, in the service of the States-General.
* James Macdowall Merchant in Edinburgh.
  James Mackenzie, Esq; M. D. his Executors.
* John Mackenzie Writer to the Signet.
* Robert Mackintosh, Esq; Advocate.
* John Maclaurin, Esq; Advocate.
* Edward Marjoribanks of Lees, Esq;
*** Patrick Miller Merchant in Edinburgh.
* John Monro, Esq; Advocate.
** Mr. James Murison, Principal of the New-college of St. Andrews.
* Archibald Murray, Esq; Advocate.
  Mrs. Barbara Musgrave, widow of John Idle, Esq; late Lord Chief Baron of his Majesty's Court of Exchequer.

N
* James Newbigging Writer in Edinburgh.

O
*** William Ogilvie of Hartswoodmyres, Esq;

P
*** The Right Hon. William Earl Panmure.
* Sir Robert Pringle of Stitchel, Bart.
  Margaret and Agnes Pitcairn, daughters of the deceased Dr. Archibald Pitcairn.
* Andrew Plummer of Middlestead, Esq;

*** George Pringle of Torwoodlie, Esq; Advocate.
** James Pringle, one of the Principal Clerks of Session.
* John Pringle Writer to the Signet.

R
* George Ramsay of Whitehill, Esq;
* James Ramsay Saddler in London.
* William Ramsay Merchant in Edinburgh.
* Thomas Rigg of Morton, Esq;
* Alexander Robertson Writer to the Signet.
  Katharine Robertson, daughter of the deceased William Robertson, one of the Depute-clerks to the Bills.
** James Rocheid of Inverleith, Esq;

S
* Sir John Sinclair of Stevenstoun, Bart.
*** Andrew St. Clair Merchant in Edinburgh.
* Charles St. Clair, Esq; Advocate.
* Col. James St. Clair of Sinclair.
* John Scot Esq; late of Gottenburgh, now of Crigie.
* Robert Scott of Benholme, Esq;
* Robert Scott-Moncrieff Merchant in Edinburgh.
* Daniel Seton Merchant in Edinburgh.
* James Seton Merchant in Edinburgh.
  James Short Optician in London, his Representatives.
  Mrs. Susanna Sinclair, daughter of the deceased Sir Robert Sinclair, Bart. her Executors.
* Andrew Skene of Dyce, Esq;
  Mrs. Katharine Skene, daughter of the deceased James Skene of Grange, Esq ;
* James Smollet, Esq; Advocate, one of the Commissaries of Edinburgh.
* James Spence, Treasurer of the Bank of Scotland.
* John Spottiswood of that Ilk, Esq;
* James Stuart, Esq; late Lord Provost of Edinburgh.

T
* Alexander Tait, one of the Principal Clerks of Session.
* John Tod Merchant in Edinburgh.

W
  David Warrander Writer in Edinburgh, his Representatives.
** George Warrander of Burntsfield, Esq;
  Grizel and Eupham Warrander, daughters of the deceased Sir George Warrander of Lochend, Bt.
* James Wemyss younger of Winthank, Esq;
*** Robert Whyt, Esq; Collector of his Majesty's Customs in Kirkaldy.
* Alexander Wight, Esq; Advocate.
* Robert Williamson Merchant in Edinburgh.

Y
* James Yeaman of Murie, Esq;

N. B. Oldest Directors { Ordinary, THOMAS BELSCHES, ANDREW ST. CLAIR, ALEXANDER TAIT. { Extraordinary, ADAM FAIRHOLME, Earl of HOPETOUN, GEORGE WARRANDER.

John Forrest has been Dep.ᵗ Gov.ʳ since 1750

List of Bank of Scotland Adventurers (stockholders)
as at 6 February 1771

The next major challenge to Bank of Scotland, and indeed traumatic to the whole banking system in Scotland, was the collapse in 1772 of Douglas, Heron and Co., more usually known as the Ayr Bank. This bank had been formed in November 1769 with a nominal capital of £150,000 and a paid-up capital of £96,000. The Duke of Queensberry, also Governor of the British Linen Company, was elected chairman, and the directors included the Duke of Buccleuch – Adam Smith's pupil – and the Earl of Dumfries. All three were supporters of 'improvement', keen to develop both their own estates and the wider Scottish economy. The majority of the 140 founding partners belonged to the landowning and business classes of the south-west of Scotland. It was a private co-partnery, and therefore without limited liability, but was felt to be very secure because its activities were backed by the land values of the property of its partners. In many respects, though not all, it reflected the land bank ideas of John Law. From the day it opened its doors in Ayr, Dumfries and Edinburgh the bank traded on an almost national scale. Cash credits for development of property were granted easily, which permitted a great expansion of its bank-note issue. One consequence was that the Edinburgh banks contracted theirs, forcing a loss on the Royal Bank in 1771. By the beginning of 1772 it was stated that Ayr Bank notes represented two-thirds of the note circulation in Scotland. This note issue was backed by short-term credits from London bankers at substantial premiums. Many of the cash credits were spent on speculation, and the bank found itself over-extended and over-trading. A system developed of borrowing on bills in London to meet bills due. By banking standards it was a recipe for disaster, particularly since few of the directors of the bank had any real banking experience, and the reality was deliberately hidden from the shareholders by the managers. Essentially, the bank committed the cardinal banking sin of lending long-term and covering this with short-term borrowing on the commercial money market. In June 1772 the liabilities of the company amounted to about £1,120,000 and the assets stood at £409,079 in bills of exchange and £827,963 in loans. Roughly half of these loans were to the Ayr Bank's own partners. At this point the London-based bank of Neale, James, Fordyce and Downe collapsed owing some £243,000. Others followed, and in the crisis Scottish paper was heavily discounted, particularly since the Bank of England would not touch it. In fairness, the collapse of confidence in 1772 was part of a Europe-wide problem, and demands upon the Bank of England for loans and cash appeared from all sides. A large number of the Edinburgh private banks failed and there was a panic. Ayr Bank notes were returned to the bank with demands for cash.

64   The two dukes led a deputation to the Bank of England to ask for a loan on the security of their lands. A sum of £300,000 was offered but the terms were so severe that the Ayr Bank felt it had no choice but to refuse. An approach to Bank of Scotland and the Royal Bank for loans of £50,000 was also rejected. They had borne the brunt of the Ayr Bank's activities and such a loan would have severely strained their own resources. The crisis spread to Glasgow, and Bank of Scotland granted loans of £10,000 to each of the Arms, Thistle and Ship banks and ordered up a supply of coin from London. This was vitally necessary to prevent a collapse of confidence in banks throughout Scotland. In other words, it was enlightened self-interest.

Clearing up the mess fell on the two chartered banks, which decided to accept Ayr Bank notes on the landed security of its proprietors. Basically, the two dukes and other partners had to raise loans on their estates to pay off their debts, a burden which some families were still repaying some sixty years later. In 1788 the owner of a £500 share not only forfeited that, but was liable in addition for some £2,200 of the bank's debts. Of the eventual 226 partners in the Ayr Bank in 1772 it is estimated that 114 became bankrupt. As a result, estates were split up and one estimate suggests that £750,000 of landed property changed hands. Much of this was concentrated geographically. One consequence was a great change in the pattern of land ownership in Ayrshire, Kirkcudbrightshire and Dumfries.

Scotch Money: an English lampoon on the collapse of the Ayr Bank

It goes without saying that paper currency on the Scottish pattern was viewed with immense suspicion and distrust in London (a view which over two hundred years of success since then has not entirely eliminated).

The Ayr Bank experience taught the banks two important lessons. First, that despite their comparatively limited resources the two Edinburgh chartered banks acting together could in practice operate as a quasi-reserve bank for the whole Scottish system, and therefore could discipline the more aggressive new banks. Second, each realised that it was undercapitalised for Scotland's requirements. In 1774 an Act of Parliament permitted Bank of Scotland to double its authorised capital to £200,000. This was called up and available by the beginning of 1775. For one observer of the Ayr Bank disaster the years between 1772 and 1775 were spent reflecting and writing about what he had observed. Adam Smith's *The Wealth of Nations* appeared in 1776.

Auld Robin Carrick of the Ship Bank

—6—

TWO CITIES;
TWO BANKERS

FOR much of the last quarter of the eighteenth century two bankers, one from Glasgow and one from Edinburgh, came to epitomise the banking practices and attitudes of their own cities. They shared three essential characteristics: honesty, scrupulous attention to detail in all business dealings, and success. And both were remembered in anecdote and literature long after their deaths. For once Glasgow had a slight seniority, if only in the matter of birth date.

Robert or (as he was more usually known) Robin Carrick was manager of the Ship Bank in Glasgow from 1775 to 1821 and his portrait now hangs in Glasgow Chief Office of Bank of Scotland. He was born in Houston, Renfrewshire, in 1737, the fourth son of Robert Carrick, a minister, and Margaret Paisley. The father had been tutor to Andrew Buchanan of Drumpellier, one of the founders of the Ship Bank, and it was in 1752, a year after its foundation, that Robin was appointed clerk at a salary of £25 a year. He was just 14. Six years later, in 1758, he became accountant at £70 a year, and subsequently cashier. By 1760 he was also in business on his own account under the name of Brown, Carrick and Company, which was allowed a cash credit of £990 from the Ship Bank. He became a partner in the second co-partnery of the Ship Bank in 1775, the year in which the Clyde was dredged. This allowed ships which previously had to unload at Greenock or Port Glasgow passage up to the Broomielaw in the city centre for the first time. It was also the year in which the American War of Independence started. The tobacco trade and the tobacco lords suffered a severe decline, but by way of consolation Glasgow's trade to the West Indies improved, bringing cotton,

68 rum and molasses into the city and creating a new business area just west of the old High Street, between Ingram and Jamaica Streets – the district now known as the Merchant City. One of Robin Carrick's first steps was to move the bank office to the corner of Glassford Street, a building which some thirty years previously had housed the Young Pretender. The windows were

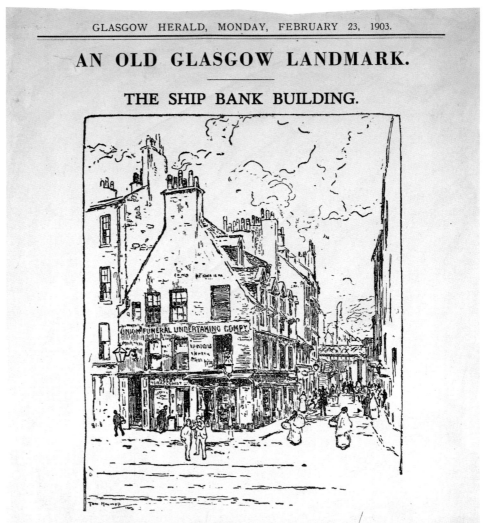

GLASGOW HERALD, MONDAY, FEBRUARY 23, 1903.

AN OLD GLASGOW LANDMARK.

THE SHIP BANK BUILDING.

The quaint old tenement at the corner of Bridgegate and Saltmarket, known as the "Old Ship Bank Building"—having housed the Ship Bank for 25 years from 1750—is about to be removed to allow for the widening of Bridgegate; and it is interesting to learn that the Improvements Committee has offered it to the Parks Committee for re-erection in one of the Parks. Early in the thirties, this dwelling was known as Coulter's House; and it was said that here Cromwell convened a Parliament. An inscribed stone, which formerly marked the height of the great river flood of 12th March, 1782, on Silvercraig's Land, a building which stood on the east side of Saltmarket, may be seen on the wall of the Old Ship Bank, where it was inserted for preservation. The house has been described in the Corporation as "a monument of ugliness"—but it is just a few hundred such "ugly" buildings which go to make up the picturesque streets Glasgow people admire in other cities. The desire of the Improvements Committee to preserve, as far as possible, the old landmarks should have the support of the citizens; and if a use can be found for this example of the early domestic architecture of Glasgow, it should certainly be rebuilt in, or near, the Green.

strengthened by iron bars so that its external appearance was 'not unlike a county jail'. There are many descriptions of the interior but there was little (in that generation of Glaswegians) for mere show:

> On entering the rather dark lobby from Argyle Street a passage led to the right, at an acute angle into the business rooms of which there were two on opposite sides . . . the one room looked into Argyle Street and had a small low counter, behind which stood a teller . . . like a grocer's shopman. The room opposite contained the élite of the establishment . . . everything was, as it were, defended from the public; and people transacting business had to stand almost on tiptoe to look over the high wooden screen, with a narrow shelf on the top, which separated them from the bank employes [sic], and bawl out what was wanted . . .

Business was transacted methodically, and slowly, and any customer wanting a bill honoured had to wait while it was taken to 'Auld Robin' for approval. The rejection phrase 'it's no convenient' became so well known in Scottish banking circles that in the Kilmarnock Banking Company it was actually printed on bill rejection slips. One other trick of Robin's was to mark the corner of a rejected bill with his thumb-nail so that if it ever reappeared he would know it instantly. One rejected customer refused to take the bill back and said, 'Na, na, it maun be discounted noo. Ye ken naebody will tak it wi' the deil's mark on it.' The stark and forbidding nature of Auld Robin and his bank produced a sense of awe and apprehension in those fated to do business with him. In later life his very appearance was old-fashioned and strange:

> He was usually attired in a brown-coloured coat, queerly made, with deep flaps on the outside pockets, the broad skirts reaching nearly down to his heels, and adorned with large brass buttons; drab knee-breeches; a striped woollen waistcoat of hotch-potch tinge . . . white neckcloth, with longish ends; white worsted stockings and buckles in his shoes; while a small brown wig covered the pate of this singular looking but able old financier.

The success of his methods is abundantly clear from the Ship Bank records. Balance sheet totals of 1777, which showed £120,352 in the books, had risen to £346,638 in 1792 and stood at £1,028,456 10s. in 1821, the year of Robin Carrick's death. The partnership's profits fluctuated from £6,000 to £12,600 in 1818, the year in which the capital stock of the partnership stood at £67,695, which translates into a yield of 18 per cent at a time when the Proprietors of Bank of Scotland were securing an ordinary dividend of 9 per cent. The core of the business was

70 bank-note issue and bill-discounting. In both, the policy was, in banking terms, conservative. It was precisely for this reason that the Ship Bank was able to weather the economic crisis of 1793 caused by the outbreak of war with France. Similarly in 1797, when the Bank of England was forced to close its doors, the Ship was able to maintain its customers' credit. A printed list of borrowers in 1789 mentions eighty firms or people, reflecting the full range of Glasgow's business and commercial interests at that time.

Robin Carrick's business interests were widespread and included linen drapery and manufacturing such as muslin production. It has been estimated that his personal fortune amounted to half a million pounds, much of which was invested in landed property, the core being an estate at Mount Vernon, where he had a country house. He was a bachelor and usually lived above the bank, but during the summer he tended to live in the country and travelled daily to town:

> Two plough horses composed his whole stud, and most leisurely was their sombre pace much like a funeral pageant. The millionaire banker sat in his carriage surrounded with baskets of all kinds of vegetables in their seasons, and when he extricated himself from the verdant mass, his equerry John Culbertson drove the carriage slowly by way of Argyle Street to the Green Market, then in Candleriggs. He there deposited the contents with the greengrocer, and had faithfully to account for the sales to his master.

His personal frugality extended to his domestic arrangements, which were presided over by his niece, Jenny Paisley. It must not be thought that Robin lived meanly, however. The bank house was handsomely furnished and there were occasional parties. Some of the food for these dinners was taken on 'sale or return', and Miss Paisley had no hesitation in returning uneaten cheeses or fruit to the suppliers. Some of the anecdotes about Robin are recorded in Peter Mackenzie's *Reminiscences of Glasgow and the West of Scotland* (1865), and many may be apocryphal. They tend to centre on his public stinginess, for which there is ample objective evidence, and on attempts to 'put one over on him', for which there is none. There is the story of a prosperous young man about town who presented a bill for payment which was for a large sum of money. It was 'no convenient'. One of his other customers protested, 'Oh you need not hesitate about him, Mr Carrick, for he has started, and keeps his carriage.' 'Oh aye,' said Robin, 'but the question wi' me is, can he keep his legs?'

When Robin Carrick died in 1821 the capital stock of the Ship Bank stood at £91,859. When Auld Robin's portion of £47,695 was withdrawn, the Ship

Bank itself lost its driving force, amalgamating in 1836 with the more recently formed Glasgow Bank Company to create the Glasgow and Ship Bank. In fact, it has been shown that by the 1820s the days of partnership banks like the Ship Bank were numbered. The future of banking lay with large joint-stock banks, which had a much larger capital base.

Robin's Edinburgh contemporary was Sir William Forbes of Pitsligo (1739-1806), who inherited his baronetcy and very little else when his father died in 1743. A baronetcy of Nova Scotia conferred few real advantages since it had been devised as one of James VI and I's money-making ploys, and the actual land had been part of French Canada since 1641. Initially Sir William was brought up in Aberdeen in the Episcopalian tradition – one which was closely associated with Jacobitism. His great-uncle Alexander, fourth Lord Forbes of Pitsligo, raised a regiment for Charles Edward Stuart in the Forty-five and paid the price in hiding, exile and forfeiture. In 1753 the widowed Lady Forbes moved to Edinburgh and through a friend of his father the young William secured a place as a clerk in the counting house of Coutts Brothers & Company in Parliament Square. As the years passed, he became an active member of all the city's

Ship Bank £1 note, 1828 design

72   societies for literature, thought and improvement and a generous friend to all those who from 1760 onwards made Edinburgh 'a hotbed of genius' and a centre of the European Enlightenment. In 1773, aged just 34, he was introduced to Dr Johnson by James Boswell at the beginning of their great tour of the Highlands and Islands of Scotland. Boswell's comments on Forbes are remarkable:

> . . . a man of whom too much good cannot be said: who with distinguished abilities and application in his profession of a banker, is at once a good companion, and a good christian; which I think is saying enough. Yet it is but justice to record, that once, when he was in dangerous illness, he was watched with the anxious apprehension of a general calamity; day and night his house was beset with affectionate inquiries; and upon his recovery, *te deum*, was the universal chorus from the *hearts* of his countrymen . . .

Given James Boswell's reputation, it would be easy to dismiss the portrait as mere flattery. However, since the first edition of *Journal of a Tour to the*

Sir William Forbes of Pitsligo Bt by Sir Henry Raeburn

Unissued twenty shilling note from Forbes, Hunter & Co

Hebrides was published in 1785, and the traits of character are repeated by others throughout Sir William Forbes's life, it would seem to be correct in all its essentials. The main source of information about his bank is an autobiographical essay which Sir William wrote for the instruction of his eldest son, also William, and which gives many insights into the business of a private bank.

The firm which Sir William joined in 1754 was known as Coutts Brothers & Company, the main partners being the four sons of Provost John Coutts of Edinburgh, who had died in 1749. The eldest and youngest brothers took over the London business and under the tutorship of Thomas Stephen developed a profitable banking business, the ancestor of the London bank which still bears the name Coutts. The middle brothers, James and John, were minors, and the Edinburgh house was supervised by Archibald Trotter, whose later career is mentioned in the previous chapter. A large part of the business depended on corn trading and import and export business. In some years it made great profits, in others, losses.

In 1761 the death of John Coutts left the Edinburgh part of the business without a resident member of the Coutts family. So although a new partnership agreement was drawn up among the remaining Edinburgh partners, which included Sir William as a partner, the firm retained the name of Coutts & Co. The new partners resolved to confine their business to taking deposits, granting loans, discounting bills and dealing on the exchanges of London, Rotterdam and Paris. In 1773 the name of the bank

74 was changed to Sir Wm Forbes, James Hunter & Company. Then, diversifying from its purely financial role, it secured the exclusive contract for supplying Virginia tobacco to France. Distribution in France was a government monopoly and the supply was routed through Glasgow. This trade lasted formally until 1778, when war broke out between Britain and France, but it had been in steep decline after 1775, when the beginning of the American War of Independence closed down the Virginia trade.

The key to the bank's success was its care and prudence, of which the autobiography gives many instances. Throughout the 1770s and up to the end of the American War of Independence (1783), the bank invested steadily in Government stock, primarily Navy and exchequer bills. Many of the purchases were made when stock prices were low and resold when prices rose at the end of the war. This greatly increased the personal fortune of Sir William and permitted the bank to exchange a cash credit with the Royal Bank into deposits of £20,000 and to hold a further £20,000 of Royal Bank notes as a reserve. Sir William was always careful not to offend either Bank of Scotland or the Royal Bank, and he gave ample warning of changes of policy. In 1782 the partnership began to issue bank-notes and faced none of the problems of acceptance which others experienced. It is a measure of the stature of Sir William Forbes that during the bank crises of 1793 and 1797 he was automatically included by the two banks in their discussions.

It is, however, for his foresight, energy and charity that he truly lived up to his family motto, 'Neither timidly nor rashly'. He was a founder member of both the Society of Antiquaries of Scotland (1780) and the Royal Society of Edinburgh (1783). He was among those who entertained the young Ayrshire poet Robert Burns on his first visit to Edinburgh. New Pitsligo in Aberdeenshire is a planned village and a monument to his desire for agricultural improvement, while the Episcopal Church of St Paul and St George, in Edinburgh's York Place, owes its existence to the benefactions which arose out of his loyalty to his origins. Edinburgh's Blind Asylum, Morningside Lunatic Asylum, the High School and the Merchant Company were all supported by him. Perhaps most interestingly of all, his eldest son William and Walter Scott were school and university friends, a friendship which cooled only temporarily in 1797 when both pursued Williamina Belches, heiress to the Fettercairn estates, and Walter Scott lost.

It was Walter Scott who provided the most eloquent epitaph when Sir William died in 1806. The lines are to be found in the introduction to the fourth canto of *Marmion*.

Scarce had lamented Forbes paid
The tribute to his Minstrel's shade,
The tale of friendship scarce was told,
Ere the narrator's heart was cold –
Far may we search before we find
A heart so manly and so kind!
But not around his honoured urn
Shall friends alone and kindred mourn;
The thousand eyes his care had dried,
Pour at his name a bitter tide;
And frequent falls the grateful dew,
For benefits the world ne'er knew.
If mortal charity dare claim
The Almighty's attributed name,
Inscribe above his mouldering clay,
'The widow's shield, the orphan's stay'.
Nor, though it wake thy sorrow, deem
My verse intrudes on this sad theme;
For sacred was the pen that wrote,
'Thy father's friend forget thou not'.
And grateful title may I plead
For many a kindly word and deed,
To bring my tribute to his grave:-
''Tis little – but 'tis all I have'.

The phrase 'A shield and stay' was in due course adopted as the motto on the coat of arms of the Union Bank of Scotland, the inheritor of the traditions and businesses of both Robin Carrick and Sir William Forbes, two men who epitomised the creative tension of style and substance which still characterises the Edinburgh-Glasgow debate in Scotland – but reversing the usual stereotypes.

Henry Dundas, first Viscount Melville, Governor 1790-1811, by Sir Henry Raeburn

—7—

FROM AYR BANK
TO WATERLOO,
1775–1815

T HE thirty years from 1775 to 1805 saw Bank of Scotland at the
then zenith of its power and influence over the banking system
in Scotland. The system, and we must call it that, developed
rapidly during the 1770s and '80s. In part this was the direct response of
Scotland's political élite to the Ayr Bank disaster and the resultant need to
provide an underlying stability for banking in Scotland. In part it
was the result of providing capital for both industrial and agricultural
development. This was in turn influenced by the American War of
Independence (1775–83) and then by the French Wars of the 1790s. It is
a measure of the success of the strategy that in 1793 the London banker
Thomas Coutts could refer to Bank of Scotland as the Scots National Bank
without irony or parentheses.

The major element of the story is political, a core part of the way in which
Henry Dundas (later first Viscount Melville) managed to weld a variety of
interests in Scotland into a solid political platform for the North-Pitt Tory
administration in London. The corollary of this is that, with the waning of
Melville's political influence after 1805, Bank of Scotland was forced into a
more modest role, one for which it was ill-equipped and which carried with it
the additional problem of being tagged as the Tory landowners' bank.

The banking system was built between 1774 and 1778. It involved Bank
of Scotland and the Royal Bank adopting, in close co-operation, the joint
role of a quasi-reserve bank for Scotland. This did not prevent the entry of
new provincial partnership banks; however, it did ensure that their ability
to trade depended in the last resort upon their acceptance by Edinburgh,

78 and that in turn depended upon the new banks' acceptance of constraints on trading and note issue. It worked, precisely because the system permitted itself to expand rapidly enough to accommodate the financial needs of the expanding economy of Scotland. However, it would be difficult to argue that Scotland at this time possessed an unregulated banking system, as has been suggested by a number of twentieth-century free market economists.

Henry Dundas was the fourth son of Lord President Robert Dundas of Arniston, a family which had a long lineage as Edinburgh lawyers. Admitted to the Faculty of Advocates in 1763, he became Solicitor-General in 1766 and a Director (like his father before him) of Bank of Scotland in 1768. There is evidence that when the young Duke of Buccleuch returned from his continental tour, with Adam Smith as his tutor, Dundas had encouraged his participation in the Ayr Bank. Despite this, the two became friends and in 1774 Dundas was selected as MP for Midlothian, a seat in Buccleuch's gift. It is worth pointing out that Scotland's 36 parliamentary seats had a grand total of 2,660 voters, an average of 74 voters per seat. In 1775 Dundas was appointed Lord Advocate, an appointment which ensured that all Scottish parliamentary business passed through his hands and which by 1778, with the support of the Duke of Buccleuch allowed him to determine the choice of MPs in 25 out of the 36 Scottish seats in Parliament.

Within Bank of Scotland Dundas found willing allies. He supported the Governor, Henry, third Earl of Marchmont; the Deputy Governor, David, Earl of Leven; and Patrick Miller of Dalswinton, to push through the changes which Miller felt were necessary in 1771–72. The relationship between Dundas (Deputy Governor 1779–89, Governor 1790–1812) and Patrick Miller (Deputy Governor 1790–1812) seems to have been particularly close. The evidence of the minute books suggests that during the period up to 1793 this pair effectively decided the Bank's strategy with Miller supervising its execution. The Extraordinary Directorships of the Bank were used to ensure that there was little dissent. By 1775 the Duke of Buccleuch, who because of his parliamentary patronage saw himself as 'prime minister' of Scotland, and the Earls of Lauderdale, Panmure, Dalhousie and Hopetoun had all been added to the Board.

The target of this group in the 1770s was the lesser lairds, made prosperous by Government contracts after the Forty-five, who in the 1760s were Whigs and whose power was personified by Lawrence Dundas of Kerse, Governor of the Royal Bank of Scotland after 1764. The manner in which he was replaced in 1778 as Governor of the Royal by the Duke of

Buccleuch is not entirely clear, but it is known that it involved a complicated series of share transactions in 1775–76 which resulted in some 40 per cent of the Royal Bank's shares changing hands. A proportion of these transactions were a direct result of bankruptcies following the Ayr Bank collapse, but it is certain that a number of Edinburgh private banks, notably Sir William Forbes, James Hunter & Co., Mansfield, Ramsay & Co. (in which Patrick Miller was a partner), William Cuming and Thomas Kinnear were all active in buying Royal Bank stock which they then held as part of their reserve. In addition, several Bank of Scotland Directors (including the ubiquitous Patrick Miller) were directly involved in purchases. The upshot was that by 1777 Henry Dundas commanded a majority of Royal Bank shares, and the elections of 1778 completed the process with a change of Governor, Deputy Governor and six Directors.

From 1776 the thrust of Henry Dundas's policy towards the banks was public knowledge, and during the 1778 elections for Royal Bank directorships it was explicitly stated that, while it was important that the banks should co-operate on a larger scale than before, they would not be united formally into a single bank. Henceforth the two banks marched in step, with clearly delineated activities and spheres of influence, and the senior officials of each met regularly to iron out any differences which might have arisen. At a practical level, interest rates, regular exchanges of bank-notes, balances of notes held by each, the grant of facilities to provincial banking partnerships, and information about fraud and forgery were shared and acted upon in concert. The clear message which was sent to London was that the Government party in Scotland was supported by the most sophisticated and stable banking system in Europe and that there was no place for the Bank of England.

A simple measure of the pace of change in Scotland's economy is that between 1774 and 1804 the authorised capital of Bank of Scotland was raised from the £100,000 which had served since 1695 to £1.5 million by four separate Acts of Parliament, the last figure proving sufficient until 1873. The Proprietors' return on capital never fell below 6 per cent between 1775 and 1815. Between 1781 and 1790 it stood at 8.3 per cent and in 1799 an additional bonus of £90,000 was divided among them. Throughout the period, the Bank's stock found a ready market and shares traded well above their nominal value.

In most respects the fortunes of the Royal Bank of Scotland paralleled those of Bank of Scotland, but the third chartered bank, the British Linen Company, was on the sidelines. After an abortive attempt in 1781 to increase its capital from £100,000 it concentrated on steadily improving its existing business and on developing its local agencies, the earliest of which was probably Aberdeen, started in 1760.

Even a cursory glance at Bank of Scotland's ledgers demonstrates the great variety of projects and industries to which loans were made. There were two main methods of lending: the bill of exchange, which was in effect a loan with a fixed term; and the cash credit – what we would now call an overdraft. The bill of exchange business was the Bank's most traditional source of income, whose volumes varied with the seasons. Even allowing for this, income rose from around £100,000 in 1772 to £1 million in 1800, with a consequent rise in profits, even when the margins on loans were being squeezed by inflation during the 1790s. The cash credit was theoretically renewable each year, but this tended to be rolled over year on year and increased in line with a particular business's expansion. The evidence is not wholly clear-cut but there are strong indications that in many, perhaps most, businesses the cash credit was used to deal with day-to-day fluctuations in cash flow rather than for capital development. In most partnerships or single-owner firms this appears to have been achieved by reinvestment of profits. On the other hand, direct loans were made for infrastructure projects, for example £8,000 to the City of Edinburgh towards the building of the South Bridge, and £10,000 to the Leith Docks and Harbour development.

The clearest indication of the role the Bank played in Scotland is that it was able, and willing, to grant loans at little or no interest to burghs to buy grain or meal for distribution to the poor in years of bad harvests and high prices. The worst year was 1782, when Edinburgh received £5,000, Ayr £2,000, Aberdeen £3,000, Stirling £1,000, Dumfries £800, and Dunfermline, Kirkcaldy, Inverness, Kelso, Kilmarnock, Banff and Elgin £500 each, all interest free. Similar loans were made in 1795, 1796, 1799 and 1800.

Bank of Scotland's influence was increased by the spread of branches and agencies throughout Scotland. The first five in order of founding – Dumfries and Kelso in 1774 and Kilmarnock, Ayr and Inverness Union Street in 1775 – were all started in areas where the Buccleuch–Dundas influence was strongest.

The first agents – David Staig at Dumfries, David Ferguson at Ayr, Robert Scott at Kelso (he was Buccleuch's ex-chamberlain) and John Mackintosh in Inverness – were prominent local figures in their own right with extensive non-banking interests. Staig, for example, was responsible for the transmission of revenue funds from Dumfries and was involved in

Top: *Letter of agreement to co-operation between Bank of Scotland and the Royal Bank of Scotland, dated 1783*

Above: *Letter from the artist Sir Henry Raeburn requesting a loan of £600 on the security of his Bank of Scotland stock*

Right: *Private Act of Parliament to increase the capital of Bank of Scotland*

Inverness in the early nineteenth century by John Clark

Portable coin scales of c.1780

the purchase of the Dalswinton estate for Patrick Miller. In every case where a branch might be considered, it was essential that the agent be a man of local knowledge and standing. By 1778 the five branches plus Stirling, which was added in 1776, showed a total profit of £5,488. By 1795 some 27 branches had been opened of which only two, Paisley and Greenock, faced severe competition from local banking companies.

It is in the matter of a branch in Glasgow that the co-ordination of policy between the Bank and the Royal Bank can be shown most clearly. The main sources of the Royal's profits in the 1770s were the receipts of Customs and Excise, the Commission for Forfeited Estates, the Army and cross-border money transmission. Many of the new provincial banking companies were provided with cash credits by the Royal, which was both an indication of their standing and a guarantee in times of crisis. In Glasgow and the Clyde ports, 1782–83 was an important watershed. The activities of the French fleet in American waters disrupted the West Indies trade, and the surrender of the British Army under Cornwallis at Yorktown, Virginia, in 1781 (where the regimental bands played *The World Turned Upside Down*) effectively finished the Virginia trade. It appears that all the Glasgow banks, with the possible exception of the Ship Bank, required support and extended credit. To deal with this, the Royal opened an agency in Glasgow in 1783 under David Dale and Robert Scott Moncrieff. David Dale had set up the celebrated New Lanark Mills, which quickly became the largest water-powered spinning-mill in Britain, with 1,500 employees. In 1793 around £400,000 of bills were discounted, rising to £700,000 in 1810. Bank of Scotland did not open a Glasgow branch until 1802, by which time it had become obvious that most of the increase in capital of both banks would be required to underwrite the rapid industrialisation of the West of Scotland. At this stage the major contribution of the two Edinburgh banks was to provide a stable platform from which greater entrepreneurial enterprise could be launched. It was a role valuable in its time and place, but one which became unnecessary – or so it seemed – within a generation.

The very existence of a branch network brought the Bank a new series of problems, for which there were few precedents. In December 1784 agents were informed that 'the frequent robberies . . . make it necessary to have another armed servant on horseback added to the former guard, when remittances are sent from the branches'. A loaded pistol was a normal part of the equipment of any bank clerk accompanying remittances to and from branches. Many of these journeys have an epic quality, particularly in winter or early spring. (See page 102, for example.) Most journeys were made on horseback. Transmission of letters to and

84   from St Andrews, for example, required the messenger from the branch to meet the Edinburgh-Perth courier at Cupar in Fife. The exact timing varied according to the season and the weather on the stretch of the Forth Estuary between Leith or Granton and Burntisland or Kirkcaldy. The development of turnpike roads and stagecoaches improved matters, but at no point before the arrival of railways could timing be guaranteed.

In these circumstances there was little alternative to allowing branches a good deal of autonomy and relying upon the agents' indemnity bonds to limit harmful conflicts of interest. Agents were paid high salaries, but the Bank demanded proper security against losses and issued detailed instructions to branches as to the conduct of business (six pages in 1783; now, in 1995, a five-volume blockbuster). Agents were usually required to meet losses on bills of exchange and cash credits, and it was usual for each to be assisted by an accountant and teller. From 1783 branches were inspected by Head Office every eighteen months. These inspections concentrated on a limited number of objectives: that the cash and notes in hand matched the book balances; that all bills were properly listed; that the agents' private accounts were not mixed with those of the Bank; that the security for cash credits and other loans was up to date; and finally that current accounts were properly listed and the interest recorded. What, at this stage of development, the system could not deal with was systematic and deliberate fraud, where the agent's 'friends' were merely a front for manipulating the branch accounts. A case at Haddington branch, which came to light in 1801–2, taught many hard lessons, and although it increased the Bank's vigilance in such matters it could not eliminate the problem completely.

The third element of the Bank's business, and that of all the Scottish banks, was its relationship with its London correspondents. In general these were London-Scots houses; the two used by Bank of Scotland were Hog & Kinloch and Coutts & Co. The relationship was close enough for Coutts to handle secret business for Dundas. The bulk of the ordinary business of the London agents was handling and discounting bills of exchange which was, for all practical purposes, the normal method of money transmission between Edinburgh and London. During the 1780s the volume of this business quadrupled, in itself an indication of a developing, single, 'British' economy, but it became necessary for Bank of Scotland to create reserves in London. This took two forms: short-term cash deposits and longer-term investment in Government stock. The key to permitting the Scots bank to hold such stock was an unwritten agreement that they would be held to maturity and not traded for short-term profit.

The Falls of Clyde by Jacob More (National Gallery of Scotland).
The water of the Falls was harnessed to provide the motive power for
David Dale's cotton spinning factory at New Lanark,
pictured below by John Clark

Above: Letter from James Fraser to Henry Dundas about the crisis in the West of Scotland, 27 April 1793

Left: Letter from Sir William Forbes to Henry Dundas hoping that a naval force will be sent to protect Scotland, and discussing the Bank of England suspension, 4 March 1797

The net result of this was that Bank of Scotland built up very large reserves in London. The close co-operation of the various parts of the system was tested in 1789 in an incident which cannot be explained in any other way than to say that those involved chanced their arm. Public revenues in Scotland were sent to London jointly by the Royal Bank and Sir William Forbes Bank, which had also since 1749 dealt with the excise money of Scotland. The Royal Bank directors wrote to Dundas suggesting that they be given a monopoly in the matter and that Forbes be dropped. Unknown to both, Thomas Coutts, Bank of Scotland's agent in London, had laid claim to the contract for his own bank in a letter to Prime Minister Pitt. The toing and froing was considerable and it was not until 1796 that the whole matter was settled by dividing the revenue business into four and giving a quarter each to the Royal, the British Linen, Sir William Forbes and Bank of Scotland. This was the first time since 1727 that the 'Old' Bank had handled any Government revenues and it added to the feeling of success as the Bank completed its first century. The man who had for a number of years defended Bank of Scotland's interests in London was felt to be worthy of a present in addition to his normal fees and in 1797 the directors paid £127 for an épergne which was engraved and presented to the lawyer James Mansfield 'for his services'.

After 1791 Henry Dundas, now Home Secretary, was at the peak of his power and influence, but in Scotland itself the Government was unpopular with Whig and radical advocates of reform. The French Revolution of 1789 itself enjoyed considerable support from no less a person than the Earl of Lauderdale as well as from academics and the educated middle classes of Scotland. It is also tempting to conclude that Patrick Miller's offer of a farm near Dumfries to Robert Burns in 1788 and the latter's employment as an exciseman under David Staig was, if not an attempt to bribe Scotland's national poet, at least an encouragement to him to modify the criticism of Scotland's rulers which may be found in some of the poems he wrote between 1790 and 1792.

In 1791 the harvest was bad and, as the expansion of trade began to falter, the Bank began to draw in credit. The outbreak of war with France on 11 February 1793 precipitated a major crisis of confidence: bills were returned unpaid, goods and raw materials were

A late eighteenth-century flintlock pistol, originally from Kelso branch

88   hoarded, manufacturing orders were cancelled and Government stock fell sharply in value. From Bank of Scotland's point of view the problem was a sharp banking dilemma: it needed to realise a substantial part of its London reserves to support both the Royal Bank and its own operations, mostly in Glasgow, but did not want either to break agreements or to sell at the bottom of the market. In addition, a number of the provincial banks needed support from the chartered banks. Sir William Forbes's *Memoir* records the anxieties of the next two months. The scheme devised by the banks and presented to Dundas and Pitt was for the issue of exchequer bills against the security of goods already in warehouses via a small number of approved firms to restart the economy. For Britain as a whole, just over £2 million of exchequer loans were made, of which £404,000 was necessary in Scotland. Of this latter sum £350,000 went to Glasgow and Paisley, while only £54,000 was required for the rest of the country. In this situation it was the Royal Bank which suffered most severely, at one point requiring a loan of £150,000 from Bank of Scotland. The Government's action prevented a commercial crisis becoming a catastrophe, although there were inevitably a number of casualties among manufacturers and some of the lesser banks. On the whole, from the summer of 1793, businesses made a swift recovery, in part because the actual needs of war required continual Government spending.

As the war progressed, mostly on land and in France's favour, problems of disruption to export trade gradually accumulated and added to the strains of the Government's own borrowings of £100 million. One major consideration was the steady drain of gold from the Bank of England, partly sent abroad for payment or trade and partly hoarded at home. The crisis broke on 23 February 1797, when there was a French landing at Fishguard, in Wales. Panic ensued. Gold was withdrawn from circulation and on 26 February the Privy Council issued an order forbidding the Bank of England from issuing any more specie until further notice. The carefully nurtured paper currency system of Scotland was under severe strain. On 1 March the Court of Session passed a resolution supporting the suspension. However, public meetings were held in both Edinburgh and Glasgow to support the banks, which continued to receive each other's bank-notes. The crisis was contained but the real need was for small-denomination currency to replace silver, which had also disappeared. A variety of token coinages appeared for small amounts; and Bank of Scotland and other banks, whose notes were 'as good as gold', issued (contrary to the 1765 Act) a large number of five-shilling bank-notes, which had a very short life as they passed from hand to hand.

In spite of all this, the 1790s saw the fastest rate of growth in the Bank's history: net profits rose from £31,013 in 1791 to £89,200 in 1800, a figure which was sustained through 1801 and 1802. Over the same period, the value of bills on London increased four times, while the income from branches went from £19,580 to £68,215. By 1802 the Bank's business in Glasgow had even overtaken that of the Royal.

At the Bank's general meeting of 1796, on completion of one hundred years of trading, it was with great confidence that the Directors announced that they were to begin looking for a site on which to build a new Head Office. There were a number of considerations and constraints on the search. Firstly, the site had to be within the bounds of the Old Town, in part because property within the main area of Edinburgh's New Town contained covenants restricting usage to domestic occupation, and in part because the core business area of Edinburgh remained around Parliament Square and the Lawnmarket. Secondly, the property was to be free-standing and not approached through a vennel or court. The Bank's customers had ample experience of Edinburgh's method of waste disposal in Gourlay's Close: 'gardyloo' cost many a pair of silk stockings. The problem grew worse as the properties fronting the High Street degenerated into slums. Thirdly, there was an acknowledgment that the new Head Office should adequately reflect the prestige and central role of the Bank.

In 1800 a suitable site became available, the result of the Town Improvement Commissioners' demolition of tenements on the north side of the Lawnmarket from Lady Stair's Close to Dunbar's Close. The approach street had already been named Bank Street and seemed to bridge the gap between the Old and New Towns via the Mound, then known as 'Geordie Boyd's Mud Brig'. The land cost £1,350, and plans for the Bank House on the Mound were prepared by Robert Reid and Richard Crichton, two promising pupils of the architect Robert Adam. The plans were approved by the Dean of Guild in 1802 (hardly surprising since Crichton was Clerk) and excavations began. Because the new building was to be sited on the junction between the basalt rock of Edinburgh High Street and the travelled earth of the Mound (essentially the excavated spoil from New Town foundations), the footings were substantial. Excavations caused slippage of some properties in Bank Street and the collapse of a whole tenement, a matter whose financial implications were still unsettled ten years later. The building, which faced the Old Town and presented its rear to the New Town, was a late Georgian villa of four storeys with a shallow dome and the coat-of-arms of the Bank, carved by John Marshall, above the front door. The financing of

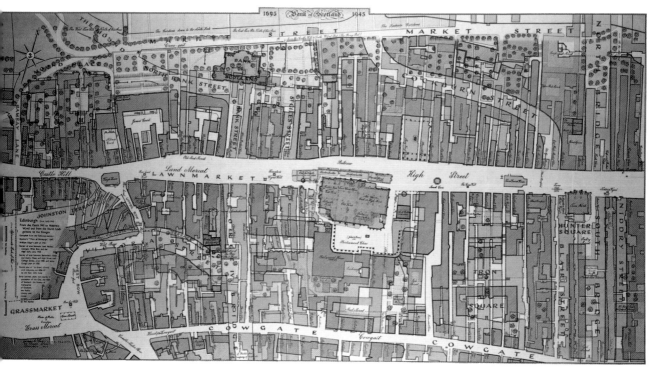

*Plan of Edinburgh Old Town redrawn in 1945 showing the locations of
the Bank Head Office, 1695–1995*

the building is in itself an object lesson, one to which the Proprietors were
never party. In each of the five financial years between 1800 and 1805, £5,000
was withdrawn from the Bank's undivided profits and placed in a separate
account which was reinvested, partly in the Bank's own stock. This had
accumulated to some £30,000 by 1819, when it was decided finally to apply
the sum to the building costs of £43,000. The Bank House was therefore
placed on the Bank's books as being 'worth' £13,000.

In many ways the Bank House provided the model layout for bank
houses erected in most of Scotland's towns during the succeeding century.
There was an impressive entrance which gave access to the telling room
and offices on the ground floor with some Directors' rooms on the first
floor, but above and below the business floors were domestic quarters. The
former were occupied by the Cashier and his family and the latter by the
bank messenger. There was no formal opening of the building, but on 12
August 1806 the staff of the Bank moved papers, ledgers and cash to the
new Bank House and opened for business. The whole process from
decision to occupation took ten years and six months. The architects each
received presents of £150, and a fire insurance policy worth £5,100 for the
building and £100 for the contents was taken out with the Edinburgh
Friendly Insurance Company.

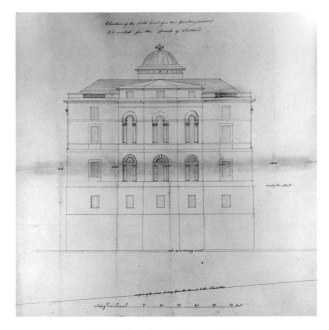

*North elevation and ground floor
plan of proposed Bank House by
Crichton and Reid*

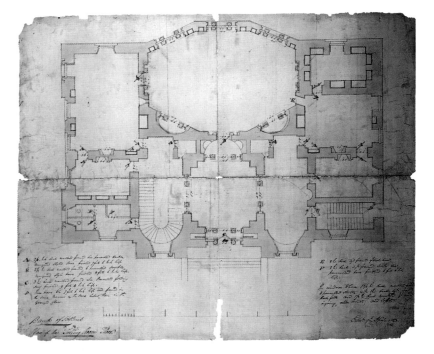

The Bank House on the Mound in 1809

While the Bank had been building, the world had moved on. By 1800, although the British fleet dominated the seas, French armies controlled mainland Europe and there was an effective stalemate. The Pitt–Dundas combination seemed to have failed and in 1801 Henry Addington became Prime Minister. The Treaty of Amiens, which temporarily halted the Anglo-French conflict, was accompanied by retrenchment in public expenditure and a decline in Dundas's control of Scotland. Peace lasted barely two years, and the threat of war in 1803 brought with it bankruptcies and speculation in commodities in Scotland of which, for once, the Bank had ample warning – one of the benefits of a branch network, namely better communications. Despite this, there was a major financial crisis for both the Royal and the Bank because the Government and the Bank of England refused to provide the support which would have produced confidence.

For Bank of Scotland, bad debt provisions rose sharply, and the return to power of Dundas, now first Viscount Melville, was only a temporary respite. His political enemies charged him with corruption, particularly over his handling of the Navy and Scottish revenue accounts. The two Scottish banks were not named but they were implicated in the charges. Although Melville was cleared at a trial before his peers in 1806, the system over which he had presided fell apart and many of Bank of Scotland's agents and contacts were tainted. As if to confirm the end of an old system, in 1806 the British Linen

Company had its authorised capital increased to £200,000, and in 1810 an entirely new co-partnery bank, the Commercial Bank of Scotland, was formed in Edinburgh from among the Whig interest, which included the advocate Henry Cockburn, better known in his later role as the judge Lord Cockburn.

The period after 1806 to the end of the war was profitable for many of the Bank's agricultural and business customers, and this is reflected in both the market price of Bank stock and the dividend paid, which averaged 7½ per cent between 1811 and 1815. At the close of a generation of war in 1815 the Bank was illuminated and the Directors made loans for the extension of Princes Street to the east, the streets known, appropriately enough, as Waterloo Place, Regent Road and Regent Terrace.

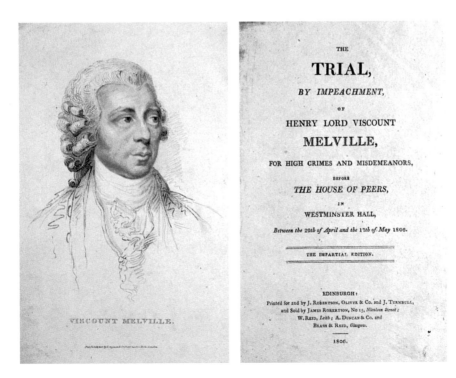

Two pages from a report of the trial of Lord Melville

—Lines Written on a Bank-note—

Wae worth thy power, thou cursed leaf!
Fell source o a' my woe and grief,
For lack o thee I've lost my lass,
For lack o thee I scrimp my glass!
I see the children of affliction
Unaided, through thy curs'd restriction.
I've seen the oppressor's cruel smile
Amid his hapless victims' spoil;
And for thy potence vainly wish'd,
To crush the villain in the dust.
For lack o thee, I leave this much-lov'd shore,
Never, perhaps, to greet old Scotland more.

R.B.
Kyle

This poem was written by Robert Burns on the back of a Bank of Scotland guinea note dated 1 March 1780, and the holograph is among the manuscripts preserved at the Burns Cottage at Alloway. The context of the poem is clear enough. In September 1785 Burns 'attested' his marriage to Jean Armour, but it was only revealed to Jean's father, James, when he discovered his daughter's pregnancy in February 1786. Burns was repudiated as a son-in-law by the Armour family and Jean was sent off to relatives in Paisley. About this time he began to contemplate emigrating to Jamaica but postponed a decision until after the first edition of his poems was published (the first Kilmarnock edition) in April 1786. In the meantime, Burns met Mary Campbell (Highland Mary) and they made plans to emigrate together. In June, Burns appeared before the Kirk Session at Mauchline and in July, still planning to emigrate, went into hiding after Jean Armour got a writ to 'throw me into jail till I find security for an enormous sum'. The poem seems to reflect his financial situation at this time, which was relieved by the success of *Poems, chiefly in the Scottish Dialect*, published on 31 July (at 3s.). Also written, and then included in the second edition, is the poem 'On a Scotch Bard gone to the West Indies'. The voyage to Jamaica was postponed during September, the month that Jean Armour gave birth to their twins, Robert and Jean. In October, emigration was abandoned after the death of Mary Campbell at Greenock, possibly in premature childbirth. It is from this point in time that Robert Burns begins to think of a career as an exciseman.

OPPOSITE PAGE:
Robert Burns in 1787 by Alexander Nasmyth (National Gallery of Scotland)
Holograph lines on a bank-note (Burns Monument, Alloway)

One Guinea! Edinr 1st March 1780.

The Governor and Comp...
of the Bank of Scotland prom...
...paper...
ONE POUND ONE SHILLING on de...
By order of the Court of Directo...

No 75
421

Wae worth thy pow'r, thou cursed leaf!
Fell source of all my woe and grief!
For lake o' thee I've lost my lass;
For lake o' thee I scrimp my glass;
I see the children of Affliction
Unaided, thro' thy curst restriction:
I've seen th' Oppressor's cruel smile
Amid his hapless victims' spoil;
And for thy potence vainly wish'd
To crush the Villain in the dust:
For lake o' thee I leave this much-lov'd shore,
Never perhaps, to greet old Scotland more.

R. B.

Bank of Scotland one guinea note of 1780

Drawing by Thomas Watling of a white-tailed warbler
(British Museum of Natural History)

—8—

BANK-NOTES AND FORGERY, 1780–1815

FOR a bank which issued its own bank-notes, detecting and stopping forgery was a normal part of the control of note issue before 1770. Forgery was on the whole quite small-scale and did not appear to pose a great threat to the acceptability of paper currency. Detection required alertness and a good 'eye'. In 1767 James Balfour, one of the Bank's accountants, requested permission to employ someone at his own expense temporarily because he had an eye problem which made it difficult for him to do his job, which included maintenance of the note-issue books. The Bank agreed and there was no shortage of applicants. With the development of a branch network in towns such as Dumfries, where Bank of Scotland notes predominated and were treated as part of other banks' reserves, the problem grew. The appearance of a forged note in a particular town did not necessarily mean that it had been manufactured there. In Dumfries during the 1770s and '80s there was a steady trickle of forged notes whose author escaped detection. There is now evidence to suggest that they were made in Belfast and shipped into various west coast ports – notably Dumfries, Ayr and Greenock – since they all appear to be from the same hand.

It was, however, the Bank's one-guinea note, designed in 1780, which attracted most forgery attempts. One of the more unusual concerned the artist Thomas Watling. He was born in Dumfries in 1762 and was a skilled artist and painter who started his own drawing academy. On 27 November 1788 he was arrested in Dumfries and charged with forging at least 12 Bank of Scotland one-guinea notes.

98

Dumfries, December 2

On Thursday last, after a long examination before the Sheriff Substitute of Dumfries, was committed to the prison of this place, a young man, for being concerned in forgeries on the Bank of Scotland and British Linen Company.

The Sheriff Substitute, in seaching the young man's lodgings, found in a drawer a half-finished guinea note, in imitation of the Bank of Scotland's notes, which left no doubt of his guilt. This young man endeavoured to criminate another person of this town; but the account given being so very contradictory, and totally unsupported by the evidence he condescended on, and the other person's innocence having appeared to the entire satisfaction of all concerned in the investigation, the Sheriff Substitute dismissed him.

Dumfries Weekly Journal, December 1788

Watling was described as a 'young man of unripe years', and although he attempted to implicate a Dumfries engraver, John Roberts, as the principal, he was found guilty and on 14 April 1789 sentenced to transportation for 14 years to the colony founded just a year earlier, Botany Bay. After two years in the prison hulks in Plymouth Harbour he finally reached Port Jackson, Australia, on 7 October 1792, the first professional artist to reach the colony. He was placed in the charge of the surgeon general, John White, and began to record in descriptions and drawings the flora and fauna of the continent. In Penrith in 1794 his *Letters from an Exile to his Aunt in Dumfries* were published and in them he gives a vivid account of the countryside and climate and of the customs of the native inhabitants. Watling seems to have got on well with the aborigines, and his extensive collection of paintings and drawings is the main visual record of the earliest decade of British settlement in Australia.

Sydney Cove, from where I write . . . is the principal settlement, and is about one third part as large as Dumfries. . . . When you write to me, be so kind as to inform me of every little incident in Dumfries. Your new bridge and theatre I have already heard of . . .

In 1796 Watling was conditionally pardoned and on 5 April 1797 this was made absolute and he left Australia. He returned home via India and by 1803 was back in Dumfries, where he became art master at the academy at a salary of six guineas a year. Clearly this was not enough and he was tempted into making new bank-note plates. In 1805 he was arrested and again charged with the forgery of seven Bank of Scotland £5 notes. Three were passed by him, and both the teller and David Staig, the agent, gave evidence against him. The jury found the charge not proven, however, and he was freed. His later years were penurious and he appears to have died of cancer in 1814–15.

Between 1811 and 1814 a series of forgeries of £1 and one-guinea notes was discovered, not only those of Bank of Scotland but of the other banks as well. These were eventually traced back to French prisoners-of-war held in Edinburgh Castle and in the camps at Penicuik, the largest complex of its kind in Scotland and second only to the cage at Norman Cross in Northamptonshire. The forgery was a large-scale effort requiring the active co-operation of outsiders. It is more than likely that forgeries were commissioned by the guards in return for small favours or improvements to the conditions, which for most prisoners were decidedly spartan. At first the majority of prisoners were seamen, but by 1810 a large number of soldiers began to appear as a result of Wellington's successes in Spain and Portugal. For officers who were prepared to be paroled and live quietly in the neighbourhood, life could be pleasant, if dull. The British Linen Company's agent in Cupar was responsible for handling the parole of officers in central Fife. The parole book (see illustration) records the physical appearance of each prisoner, whose description would have been circulated had there been any attempt to break parole and escape. For the majority of ordinary prisoners, camp life was monotonous and at times distinctly harsh. It is estimated that in the three camps around Penicuik between 1803 and 1814 there were some 11,000 prisoners; and although described as 'French', they included many nationalities, particularly Danes and Swedes among the seamen. As so often happens, the gap between the rations officially supplied by the War Department and what the prisoners actually ate was a large one. Food was always meagre and scarce and, as in many similar circumstances, the guards encouraged trading and private enterprise. Activity was a necessary antidote to despair and lassitude, and on 25 September 1811 the Edinburgh *Evening Courant* reported that three prisoners from Greenlaw camp in Penicuik were in the Tolbooth, the city's main prison, on suspicion of forgery. The outcome of this incident is not known, but combating forgery became a regular feature of the Bank's concerns over the next three years. The Bank published advertisements offering a reward of £100 to anyone who could provide information leading to the conviction of the perpetrators within three months. The forged notes were normally made by hand with pen and pencil, without any engraving. 'In most of them the body of the notes has the appearance of foreign handwriting. The names of the bank officers, though common and well known in this

*Parole book for French prisoners-of-war 1808-15, maintained by
the agent of the British Linen Company in Cupar, Fife
Below: Description of the elements of forgery which would
permit their detection*

country, are in the forged notes most illegible or wrong spelled.' In fact they were easy to detect because of a variety of imperfections, but that they appeared in circulation at all was worrying to the Bank. A steady trickle of prisoners were detected as forgers and a number were sent to the hulks at Chatham, Portsmouth or Plymouth, but none was ever formally tried and convicted. In retrospect perhaps this was fair enough since the real culprits were the members of the Aberdeen or Kirkcudbrightshire militia who guarded them and 'the riff raff of Edinburgh who came to see the prisoners and to profit by their illicit activity'. One case which was defended by Lord Cockburn concerned Thomas Gray, a soldier in the Kirkcudbrightshire militia, who was found to be in possession of £33 of forged notes. Gray was sentenced to 14 years' transportation in 1814 but this was reduced almost immediately by the Prince Regent to six months' imprisonment. Others were not so lucky. Nathaniel Blair was sentenced to death, and cheated the executioner only by hanging himself in his own cell.

The most surprising souvenir of these events which the Bank possesses is a set of mutton and rabbit bones carved by hand to provide instruments of forgery. Some at least seem a little unlikely since if ever used they would have reproduced the Bank of Scotland's name as mirror writing!

Bones carved by French prisoners-of-war in the camp at Glencorse,
Penicuik, for forging Bank of Scotland notes

— The Pursuit of Forgers from — Dumfries

It was rare for the Bank's clerks to have an opportunity of chasing and capturing forgers of the Bank's notes. Yet there were two occasions in 1779 – in September and October – when the staff at the Dumfries branch had to prepare for the capture of two separate gangs. On September 5 James Graham and William Macdowall, pistols primed, took seats in a post-chaise and set out to arrest three men – David and William Reid and William McWhirr, whose physical appearance was known and who were implicated in the forgery of the Bank's pound notes. After many days' travel the clerks were successful, two of the culprits being caught in Stranraer, the third in Portpatrick.

ACCOUNT
of expences laid out in detecting DAVID REID'S forgery upon the Bank of Scotland

Mr James Graham and William Macdowall left Dumfries in pursuit of the forgers the 8th day of September 1779 and apprehended Willm Reid and Willm McWhirr at Stranraer, and David Reid at Portpatrick, whom they lodged in Dumfries-prison after 5 days absence.

THEIR EXPENCES

Hire of two horses 83 miles @ 3d. p. mile	£2	1	6
ditto of two chaises back to Dumfries with the 3 prisoners 83 ms. @ 11d.	7	12	2
ditto of a chaise from Stranraer to Portpatrick after David Reid		7	0
ditto of a saddle horse for one of the Soldiers doun to Dumfries		18	-
paid two chaise drivers for 7 stages each	1	-	6
paid hostlers for chaises and saddle horses going and coming		12	9
Maintenance of ourselves and horses going up when we called at every alehouse upon the road to make enquiry	3	12	11
Bill at Taylor's Stranraer for ourselves and some friends who sat up all night with us taking the precognition	1	1	4
ditto at Alexander's Stranraer for the Prisoners and Military and charge for confusing and taking up the house on the fair day	1	16	10
ditto at Portpatrick for constable and military		5	-
Maintenance of ourselves, the prisoners, military, constable and saddle horses from Stranraer to Dumfries-prison	4	17	7
Paid two men as Scouts at the fair of Stranraer		7	6
Paid Serjeant and party for guarding the prisoners part of two days and a night at Stranraer, there being no prison	1	7	-

Paid Corporal two soldiers and Constable for attending the prisoners to Dumfries	4	5	-
Paid Jail-ffees etc. at imprisoning the prisoners in Dumfries		7	8
Paid Express from Stranraer to Provost Fergusson at Ayr		8	-
Paid Sundry Incidents particulars for which are forgot	1	3	10

Mr Graham and W. Macdowall set out for Kendal fells 15 September 1779 to search for the plates hid there by David Reid, they travelling at night and the weather being rainy took chaise and were absent five days.

THEIR EXPENCES

Hire of a chaise for 182 miles @ 11d. p. mile – having gone twice from Penrith to the 11th mile stone beyond Shap	8	6	10
Chaise-drivers being rainy and often under night	1	5	-
Paid Tollbars, Waiters, Hostlers and Chambermaids		19	2
Paid labourers for digging near two days for the plates		8	-
Maintenance going and coming and at rendering account to the Sheriff of our proceedings	3	11	-

Mr Graham and William Macdowall set out for Mochrum in the shire of Galloway to have John Stewart apprehended on suspicion of his being either an accomplice of or useful witness agt. D. Reid, and were absent three days.

THEIR EXPENCES

Hire of two horses to Newton Stewart 48 miles @ 3d. p. mile	1	4	-
ditto of a chaise from ditto to Mochrum		17	-
Hire of a horse for Stewart to ride to Dumfries upon		10	6
paid a Constable for going from Wigtown to apprehend Stewart		6	6
Maintenance of ourselves, Stewart and 3 horses till our return to Dumfries including waiters &ca.	2	18	3
paid Stewart's expences being 8 days detailed in Dumfries till instructions came from Edinburgh and his bail bond was executed	1	19	11
paid expences of his horse for same time		9	4
paid express to Wigtown with Stewart's bail bond for execution		15	-
paid Constable for 5 days attending Stewart in Dumfries		7	6
paid Sheriff's Officer for ditto		4	6
paid Stewart in order to carry him home		10	-

22 November 1779 William Macdowall set out upon a journey through the different places the forgers had been in order to take precognitions and discover who would be useful evidence upon David Reid's trial, which took 13 days in March 1780. The whole cost to the Bank of pursuing the forgers and a successful prosecution totalled £128 17s. 11d.

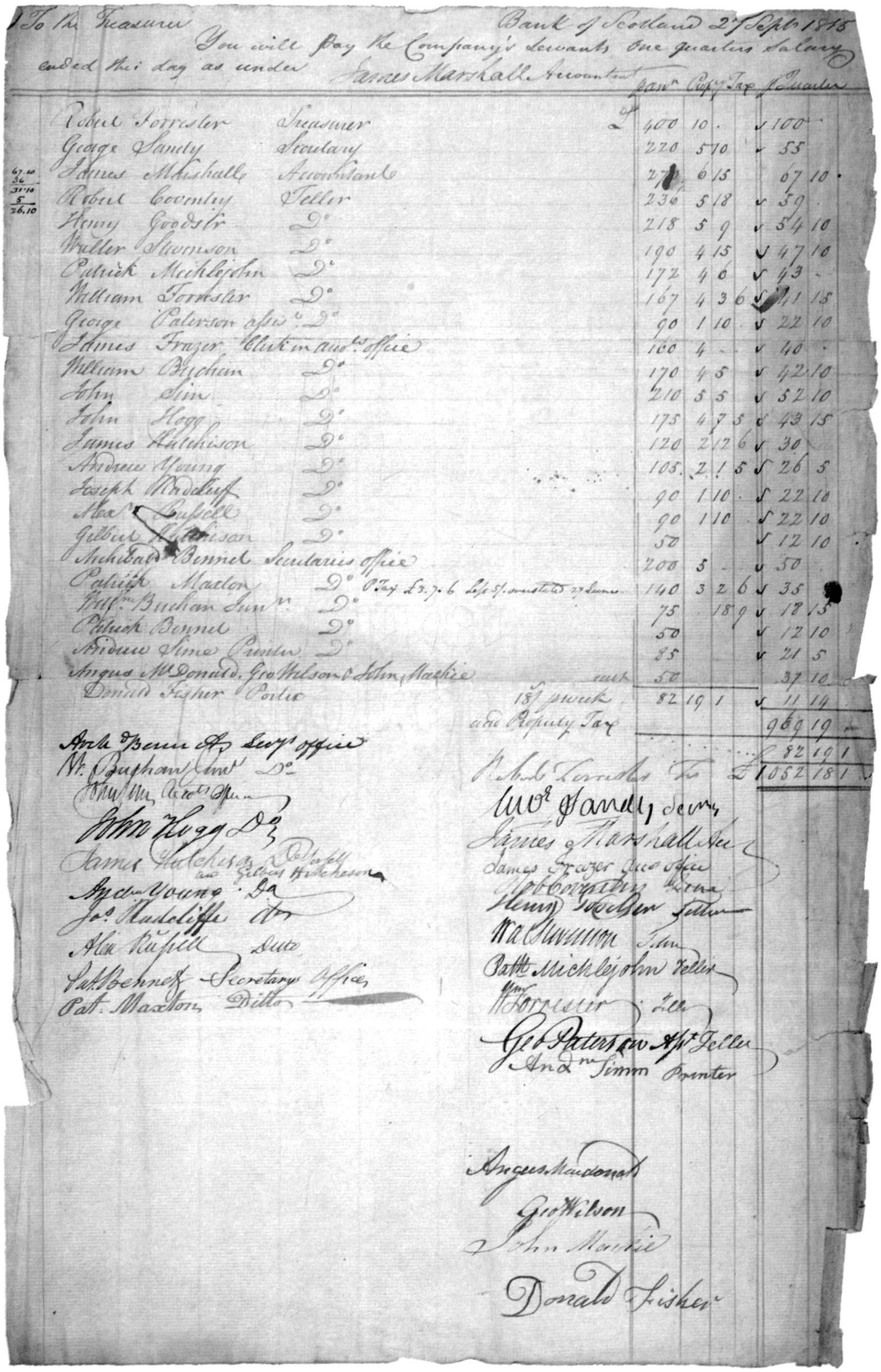

—9—

DOLDRUMS AND UNCERTAINTY, 1815–55

THE two decades after the Battle of Waterloo saw a reversal of the Bank's fortunes and the slide into a trough from which it took nearly a generation to recover. Although after the death in 1812 of Henry Dundas, first Viscount Melville, the governorship was offered to and accepted by his son, the second Viscount, the Bank was no longer able to rely on political management to protect its interests. The low point was 1831–32, and recovery was only achieved by the application of strict banking principles. Part of the problem, which was not unique to Bank of Scotland, was that the second phase of industrialisation in Scotland produced a much more demanding and complex banking environment. This in its turn required a substantial shift in policy-making within the Bank from the Board of amateur (if enthusiastic) Directors to professional managers. One consequence of the Bank's difficulties was that in the 1830s and 1840s it was in no position to take full advantage of the opportunities generated in the West of Scotland. It also had to face the full impact of competition provided by the new Glasgow-based joint-stock banks, most notably the Glasgow Union Bank (later the Union Bank of Scotland) in 1830 and the Western Bank in 1832. By 1850 the paid-up capital of these new banks together amounted to some £5,663,700 as against £3,500,000 for the original three public banks in Edinburgh. In rank order, Bank of Scotland declined from first position to sixth in terms of liabilities and deposits and to fifth in terms of advances. It is ironic that this should have been the underlying reality of Bank of Scotland's situation precisely when it was enjoying its greatest reputation furth of Scotland.

106   In 1815 demand for the war effort had been the source of prosperity for many of the Bank's customers in the iron-founding and textile industries. Peace reduced opportunities for firms like the Carron Iron Company, whose chief product, light cannon, was no longer in demand. The expansion of such companies had been achieved during a period of inflation, when borrowing was relatively cheap, a situation which changed as prices stabilised and then fell during the 1820s. It was the Bank's farming constituency which had to make the greatest adjustments. During the Napoleonic Wars, Britain's farmers had a virtual monopoly over agricultural products in the home market. By 1814 the boom in agriculture which had been the reason for 'improvement' on many estates was over, and the price of oats, barley and wheat fell steadily, discouraging new investment. Some of the changes were permanent. Much of the land in Buchan and the north-east had been won for agriculture, planted for the first time, and the landscape of fermtouns with its bothies created from scratch. But on West Highland estates the fall in the price of cattle and kelp produced a financial crisis for many landowners. For example, between 1799 and 1811 the rental income from Lord Macdonald's estate on Skye rose from £5,500 to £14,000. Attempts to maintain these income levels between 1815 and 1830 meant that new sources of income were needed and he began the process of replacing people with sheep in the clearances on his Skye and Uist estates. The price of kelp had risen from two or three pounds a ton in the 1780s to £20 a ton just after the turn of the century as a result of the war with France. Then the kelp-burning industry collapsed quickly after the removal of duties on Norwegian kelp in 1813. The price of the alkali created by kelp-burning fell by two-thirds between 1817 and 1827, despite the fact that it was of prime importance in the soap and glass industries, both of which were expanding. Applications for loans from Mackenzie of Seaforth, the principal landowner on the Isle of Lewis, appear in the Bank records in the 1820s, couched in terms of greatest optimism about the benefits of 'development' on his property. In all cases these were rejected because the extended cash credits simply added to the indebtedness of the estate, which Mackenzie was already having difficulty in servicing.

The route to survival often involved leasing out part or all of the estate to successful industrialists or southerners, while attempts were made to rebuild family fortunes in public service or commerce in the colonies. This was the route chosen by the Grants of Rothiemurchus and the Macleods of Dunvegan. Others, like Archibald McNab of McNab, spent years trying to keep one step ahead of the bailiffs; when that failed in 1822 he attempted to relaunch his fortunes by a fraudulent settlement scheme at the junction of the Ottawa and Madawaska Rivers in Upper Canada (modern Ontario Province).

Between 1813 and 1820 the Bank's net income from its branches, mostly in rural areas, fell sharply from £61,363 to a mere £859. As a result, the branches in Tain, Huntly, Montrose and Wigtown were closed, while the branch in Greenock was closed because it was losing business to the Greenock Banking Company. The Edinburgh private banks, which provided a number of Bank Directors, were particularly badly affected by these changes, since all were heavily involved in agricultural lending and, as a result, during the 1820s they stopped being a major part of the general banking scene. The East Lothian Bank, which had been founded on the premise of agricultural prosperity and engaged in speculation in wheat and barley prices (what would now be called trading in agricultural futures), went bankrupt in 1822. The private banks were forced to sell their shareholdings in the Bank and to reduce the quantity of Bank of Scotland bank-notes held as part of their reserves. The situation was such that even Sir John Sinclair of Ulbster, the foremost advocate of agricultural improvement, was forced to sell most of his Bank shares to pay off his overdraft.

The Bank had two methods of dealing with this situation. The first and most obvious was gradually to contract its agricultural lending and switch it into more profitable areas, particularly new industries or companies, which were by definition more risky investments. The second, seen as vital by the Directors in view of the sales of Bank stock, was to ensure that there was no crisis of confidence among the Bank's Proprietors. Stock was bought in and released gradually to flatten out short-term fluctuations in the price and to discourage speculation. (This is now illegal in the UK.) It was also seen as important to maintain the dividend paid out to Proprietors so that the shares continued to trade at a premium. After the immediate post-war slump in 1815–17, business began to pick up. In 1818, buoyed up by the windfall profits made on handling coin for the reminting of the United Kingdom coinage in 1816–17, a special bonus of £200,000 was paid out of reserves over and above the £95,000 declared as the 'normal' dividend, a total return on each share of 29.5 per cent. Between 1819 and 1824 the normal dividend was maintained at 9.5 per cent. From 1824 it was reduced to 8 per cent and then in 1827 to 6 per cent. The dividend reduction in the financial year 1824/25 was softened by a further special bonus of £200,000 which was taken from reserves. These bonuses were crucial to maintaining the share price, particularly in 1818 when £31,784 had to be provided for bad and doubtful debts, as against a previous ten-year average of around £1,800. Between 1810 and 1814 the

108

Paisley in the 1820s by John Clark

price of £100 of Bank stock had stayed at around £170. In 1817 it stood, before the bonus, at £174. The price leapt to £254 in 1818 and stayed above £235 until 1824. It looked as though the price would fall, but the second bonus pushed the stock to an all-time high of £276 in February 1825, after which it fell away steadily to stand at £198 in 1831 and continued to slide during the 1830s until January 1841, when it sold at £162, the same price as in 1809.

In 1824 the policies with which the Directors charged William Cadell of Tranent when they appointed him Treasurer, with additional powers as General Manager, were as follows:

(1) to enlarge the branch network wherever an opportunity presented;
(2) to look for new investment opportunities;
(3) in co-operation with the other banks, to attempt to control or reduce the price paid for deposits; and
(4) to use the reserves in difficult times to maintain the dividend to Proprietors to counteract speculation in Bank stock.

William Cadell faced a major national crisis within a year of taking office. By the summer of 1825 there was high confidence in the national economy. A boom was fuelled by the repeal of the South Sea Bubble Act of 1720, which had contained specific restrictions on speculative share dealing. There were many new company formations, particularly in ventures associated with the cotton trade and those involved with newly independent states in South

St Andrews in the 1820s by John Clark

America. The problems had become obvious by the late summer. In Scotland, particularly in Paisley and the west, speculators used funds, including bank loans, to hold large stocks of cotton in warehouses, raising the price to the mill owners. Spinners wanted higher wages, and many mills went onto half-time working. The net result was that the Bank of England, fearing a balance of trade deficit and the loss of gold overseas, contracted credit and precipitated a full-scale monetary crisis. Sixty banks failed in England, compared with only three in Scotland – the Stirling Banking Company, the Falkirk Banking Company and the Fife Banking Company – which retired or failed in the subsequent five years. The crisis did not have the same devastating impact north of the Border as it had in England. Although it was regretted in London that the Royal, the British Linen Company and Bank of Scotland did not have confidential understandings, the three agreed to raise interest rates to prevent the outflow of funds. All the five major Scottish banks (the Bank, the Royal, the British Linen, the Commercial and the newly founded National) provided funds to hard-pressed customers and extended overdrafts to customers and other banks. There was no panic in Scotland, because paper currency had been around for so long that there was little temptation to demand specie in exchange.

The most famous casualty of these events was Sir Walter Scott, author and impresario of George IV's visit to Edinburgh in 1822, an event which the Bank celebrated with fireworks and by illuminating the Bank House on

110   the Mound. Sir Walter was a partner in Ballantyne & Company, which became involved in the bankruptcy of the firm of Constable & Company, and was relying on this plus the income from his novels and from investments to underwrite the costs of building his house, Abbotsford. In 1818 Bank of Scotland had granted a cash credit of £1,000 to James Ballantyne and Company towards the purchase price of £1,850 for the *Edinburgh Weekly Journal*. It was assumed, although it was not then revealed, that Scott was a partner in the company. Another member was Robert Cadell, brother of the Bank's Treasurer, William Cadell. When the latter's stewardship of the Bank's affairs came under scrutiny in 1830, he was fiercely criticised for having allowed his brother to clear his deposit account the day before the collapse. At the time of the collapse of Constable & Company Sir Walter's debts amounted to £104,082, of which £40,000 consisted of short-term bills payable on London. There were additional publishers' debts, for which the author felt morally bound if not strictly liable. Sir Walter's largest creditors were Sir William Forbes and Bank of Scotland, although his day-to-day accounts were held at the British Linen Company branch, first in Jedburgh and then in Selkirk. The second Sir William Forbes was the prime mover in putting together the rescue package for Scott in January 1826. The London bill brokers who would not agree were bought off. Abbotsford and all Sir Walter's debts were placed in a trust guaranteed for his lifetime but into which all his earnings would be paid. So faithful was he to his friends that his efforts almost certainly hastened his death. It is a matter of record that Scott's debtors had received 13s. in the £1 by 1832 and that full repayment was completed with Lockhart's edition of his works in 1837–38. It is small wonder that at a public meeting to raise subscriptions for a memorial in Scott's honour it was minuted that:

> The sum of £500 should be subscribed by the Bank of Scotland, the Royal Bank, Sir William Forbes and Company, the British Linen Company, the Commercial Bank, the National Bank and Ramsays, Bonar and Company in token of their admiration of those honourable feelings which induced the late Sir Walter Scott at the time of his embarrassment in 1826 to dedicate his life to insuring [*sic*] full payment to his creditors . . .

To members of Parliament and the public at large the causes of the crash of 1825 seemed clear enough: small-denomination bank-notes and English country banks. An Act was passed which prohibited the issue of bank-notes under £5 in value in England and Wales. Lord Liverpool's Government, perhaps following the advice of Adam Smith fifty years earlier, proposed in February 1826 to extend the Act to Scotland, ironically

Above: *Sir William Forbes of Pitsligo Bt by Sir Henry Raeburn. Forbes was Scott's school and university companion. Their friendship cooled only temporarily in 1797 when they competed for the hand of Elizabeth Belches of Fettercairn. Scott lost.*
Right: *Sir Walter Scott drawing, as prepared for the 1971 series Bank of Scotland notes*
Below: *Cheque signed by Sir Walter Scott drawn on the British Linen Company branch in Selkirk*

The last of the old-style printed bank-notes
for £5 dated 4 March 1824

The first of the Lizar steel-engraved bank-notes.
This technique permitted much finer and more exact
designs to be used to challenge the forger

a move approved of by Lord Melville, the Bank's Governor. This was in spite of the fact that Scots banks seemed to have escaped unscathed; and although it appeared to be little short of a miracle, there were plenty who thought it a conjuring trick. When the proposal became known, Parliament was deluged by petitions from Scotland, from all sectors and interests in society. The arguments were encapsulated in *The Letters of Malachi Malagrowther*, a thinly disguised but well-argued polemic from the pen of Sir Walter Scott, which appeared in March 1826. A Parliamentary Committee sat from March to May of that year taking evidence from Scots bankers on the efficacy of the £1 note. They were virtually unanimous in supporting the Scottish system of banking. For English members the problem became not how to 'tame' the Scottish system, but how to prevent its spread to England, where it would have challenged the Bank of England's monopoly and taken over most of the provincial banking companies. In the end an Act was passed prohibiting the issue of Scottish notes under £5 in England after 5 April 1829.

William Cadell's policy of expansion began to come into effect during 1825 and 1826. Branches were opened or reopened at Fort William, Leith, Stonehaven and Falkirk. New lending to new industries began to appear on the Bank's books, but lending to untried prospects led inevitably to a large and growing bad debt provision. There was also an overhang of irretrievable debts and past-due bills from the 1825-26 crisis which were not provided for. In 1829 two Directors reckoned that in total these stood at £193,293. Many famous names of Scottish industry appear as borrowers at this time, including cotton firms such as Locke and Dunlop, Bogle, and Haddens of Aberdeen, and shipping companies such as the Clydesdale Steam Boat Company. In 1828 the chemical manufacturers Charles Tennant and Company of St Rollox in Glasgow were granted a cash credit of £10,000, which was increased to £40,000 within a decade and at various times reached £100,000. The sheer complexity of the new businesses, for example in distilling, is well illustrated by the relationship between William Haig and the Bank's branch in St Andrews. William Haig was the son-in-law of John Stein, whose family had brought the continuous still to Scotland and which had set up distilleries at Leith and Alloa. William Haig's distillery was established at Guardbridge in Fife at the high point of the tidal estuary of the River Eden. His two farms, Seggie and Monksholm, initially supplied the grain, but as the business grew, more grain had to be imported. The records make it quite clear that the bulk of the grain distillate (hardly whisky) was shipped by sea to London, where it was rectified into 'London' gin. The returning ships picked up grain from East

114 Anglia and coal from Tyneside. To keep up a continuous production, grain had to be stored between harvests. As a sideline, a tile drain and pantile manufactury was set up, whose products are to be found in many fields and on many houses in East Fife to this day. The financial complexities of such a business, dependent on the London market, were considerable. The gap in time between purchase of raw materials and payment for the product could be a year or more. The Bank's role was to finance the stocks and the trade. By 1833 this one account represented 45 per cent of the total lending of St Andrews branch. The local shipowner, John Patterson, who was the carrier, was also on the Bank's books. It gradually became clear that Haig had over-reached himself, and in 1835 over-production and the defalcations of his London agent brought a crisis. The result was a leaseback arrangement of the works to Haig. The Bank took over direct management of the farms of Seggie and Monksholm and brought the account into Head Office. For a generation thereafter, the profits of these two farms appear in the Bank's annual balance. In due course the distillery was taken over by William's son John, who continued until the 1860s. Eventually the site was sold and became the basis of the Guardbridge paper works.

It is easy to overlook the fact that the Bank's business in any town depended crucially upon the character and abilities of the agent. One outcome of the duel in Kirkcaldy (described on page 124) was that the Bank's business among the town's linen manufacturers faded away. When Walter Fergus, a linen manufacturer and shareholder in the Glasgow Union Bank, decided to open a Union Bank branch in 1834, he took most of these accounts out of Bank of Scotland. Even Head Office acknowledged that little could be done until the agent, David Morgan, was gone and that new accounts would depend on new industries. It was the growth of the jute trade, the harbour development and the invention of the linoleum manufacturing process in the 1840s and '50s that gave the Kirkcaldy branch a second lease of life.

A more general and perhaps surprising problem was that despite loans and investments the Bank was actually taking in deposits faster than it could arrange for these to be employed profitably. All the Scottish banks paid interest on deposits, and it required agreement among the Edinburgh banks before the rate could be lowered. In May 1827 it was reduced from 4 to 3 per cent, in May 1828 to 2.5 per cent, and a year later to 2 per cent for sums above £500. It became increasingly clear in the late 1820s, and was commented upon by a number of the Directors, that the accounting systems then in existence did not give a true reflection of the

Bank's position. Between 1827 and 1831 the Bank made an apparent profit of £65,000, enough to cover the 6 per cent dividend paid to shareholders, but this masked inadequate provision for losses and the run-down of the Bank's reserves. When a Directors' Committee began to examine the problems in detail in the summer of 1829 they reached the startling conclusion that virtually *no* profits were made between 1824 and 1829 and that average yearly provision for bad and doubtful debts should have been set at about £50,000. None of this became public knowledge and Cadell was given time to try to change the Bank's course. During 1830 matters got worse, partly but not wholly as a result of uncertainties surrounding the change of regime in France. It was only the threat by a number of the Directors to 'go public' that persuaded the Governor, Lord Melville, both of the seriousness of the situation and that action was required. Negotiations were begun with the Bank of England for a credit of £200,000 on the security of £50,000 of Bank of England shares and £200,000 of 3.5 per cent Government New Annuities.

At the Annual General Meeting in March 1831 the Bank revealed the worst set of trading figures for over a century. There was loud criticism of the management of the Bank, as £30,000 of bad debts had been written off. Resolutions of the meeting included a proposal, which was passed, that the stock qualification for Directors be doubled and that no one who had been a Director within the previous five years was to be eligible for a Bank appointment. In 1832 Lord Melville again reported heavy losses and in July of that year William Cadell resigned. The anger felt at his stewardship of the Bank is illustrated by the fact that consideration of a pension was delayed for a whole year and its payment was nearly blocked by the Annual General Meeting of 1833.

These events severely damaged the reputation of Scots bankers in London, particularly among English politicians. They also demonstrated clearly that the days of amateur, part-time direction of a complex organisation such as a bank were past. Professional skills were needed and every aspect of the Bank's internal control systems and management needed to be overhauled. One of the more important resolutions of the General Meeting was that private bankers should no longer be eligible for election as Directors. There was a strong suspicion – unproven – that such Directors used their position to influence lending policies and provide opportunities for their own banks. In brief, in 1832–33 the last vestiges of Henry Dundas's system of control by the Directors was laid to rest.

From July 1832 the full management of the Bank was given to the newly appointed Treasurer and General Manager, Alexander Blair, who quickly

Edinburgh from the Mound

The Bank House on the Mound from (the present-day) Mound Place, 1830

118   identified two able lieutenants, Charles Campbell, the Bank's agent in Glasgow, and Archibald Bennet, the Bank Secretary. Under Blair's direction this trio dominated the Bank's affairs down to the late 1850s. The Bank was exceptionally fortunate in its choice of Treasurer. Alexander Blair was a classics scholar who read both Greek and Hebrew; and he was a close friend of Thomas Tooke, the celebrated contemporary banking theorist. He began his career with the British Linen Company, first as confidential clerk, then as assistant secretary and secretary, until in 1828 he was appointed joint manager with Thomas Corrie. By the time he was appointed to Bank of Scotland he had already developed a coherent view of sound banking principles which he could apply to the situation he found. His first innovation was to collect – in a monthly return of deposits, loans, cash credits, outstanding bills, note circulation and bad debts – the detailed information necessary for hands-on control of the Bank. This permitted adjustments to be made quite quickly and allowed an accurate overview of the Bank's trading position to be given to the Directors every six months. It also enabled him to estimate how much of and where the Bank's reserves and investments could be redeployed. It also allowed the Bank, for the first time, to calculate the relationship between profits and share dividend. Charles Campbell was appointed the first Superintendent of Branches, responsible not only for the audit of their books but also for assessing the quality of the Bank's business in any town: its viability and prospects, accounts which might cause or were causing problems, the competition, and the efficiency or otherwise of any particular agent and his staff. Campbell's detailed reports form the first entry in a new series of record books, known as procedure books, one for each branch. These were maintained in the Superintendent's office and were log books of recommendations or instructions about the conduct of business. Archibald Bennet, who had hoped to be made Treasurer, seems to have accepted the situation and concentrated on the day-to-day management of Head Office and all legal matters. It was Bennet who introduced the practice of retaining a law firm to act as the Bank's long-term legal advisers, one in Glasgow and one in Edinburgh.

    During the 1830s a new round of branches opened: Duns in 1832; Dundee and Lauder in 1833; Fraserburgh, Greenock and Montrose in 1835; Ardrossan and Paisley in 1836; Banchory, Cumnock, Kilmarnock, Strathaven and Whithorn in 1838; and finally Blairgowrie, Castle Douglas and Callander between 1839 and 1842, giving the Bank a total of 31 branches by 1845. The strategy of branch opening was dictated by a need to increase the Bank's lending business in new areas, ahead of the Glasgow banks. Both the Western Bank, founded in 1832, and the City of Glasgow Bank, founded in 1839, were particularly active in branch formation. For Scotland as a whole, the 1830s was a period of recession, and the additional competition meant that the Bank's profitability continued to decline. During 1840 Alexander Blair conducted an extensive review of the Bank's operations to explain to Directors and dissatisfied Proprietors why, in spite of a great increase in total business, the profits struggled to cover a 6 per cent dividend. Blair argued that there were four reasons for this:

(1) the extensive growth of joint-stock banking: in the 15 years from 1825, 16 new banks had been formed, nine of them between 1838 and 1840. The most important were Glasgow-based, operated on smaller reserves, offered higher rates on deposits and tended to invest in riskier ventures. For the old banks this meant a narrowing of the margin between interest rates on deposits and the yield on Government investments, where most reserves were placed;

(2) the traditional sources of Bank profits, bank-note issuing commissions, and Government revenue handling had all declined in value;

(3) attempts to establish agreed interest rates with other banks and a system of bank charges on customer accounts had failed; and

(4) the creation of branch offices often led to short-term losses.

Western Bank of Scotland specimen £1 note

120   What Alexander Blair did *not* say on this occasion was that his own conservative attitudes to banking, honed by the events of 1830–32, led him to believe that a proven profit of £65,000 should be earned before a 6 per cent dividend was paid and that as a matter of course banks should carry between 25 and 30 per cent of the sum of note issue and deposits as negotiable securities. With these parameters established, Blair could consider diversification of the Bank's investment portfolio and this was precisely the story of the 1840s.

The 1841 Parliament, in the aftermath of a number of English bank failures in 1839, appointed a Select Committee on Banks of Issue; and Blair, as the foremost advocate of classical Scottish banking principles, was invited to give evidence. Once again the suspected culprit was bank-note issue. The immediate motivating force was that the Bank of England's charter was due for renewal in 1844 and Sir Robert Peel, the Home Secretary, saw this as an opportunity for limiting the ability of banks in England and Wales to issue bank-notes. The Committee of Scottish Bank Managers (at first an informal organisation whose existence was not acknowledged publicly) commissioned Blair to deal with the Government, and then orchestrated a stream of protest and petition to prevent the extension of the 1844 Act to Scotland. A compromise was reached in the 1845 Banking Acts, which permitted each bank which issued bank-notes to continue to do so freely up to its average circulation for 1844. Thereafter, if a bank wished to exceed this authorised issue, the excess was to be backed pound for pound in gold and silver in no more than two offices of the bank. For most of the major Scottish banks this meant their Edinburgh and Glasgow offices. No new banks of issue were to be permitted. One important concession made to the Scots was that if two banks merged, their note issue should be combined, rather than – as with English bank mergers – that the note issue should lapse. In fact, the three Edinburgh chartered banks were displeased that no distinction was made between them (in view of their 'tried prudence, usefulness and high respectability and the confidence of the country placed in them') and the joint-stock banks, whose shareholders did not have limited liability. This was special pleading which the Government ignored. The average bank-note circulation at 1844 of the 19 Scottish banks was £3,087,209, of which Bank of Scotland's share was £300,485. By 1865 the Bank was issuing £553,160 in bank-notes, which had risen to £1,079,044 by 1896. Despite the fuss, the blunt fact of the matter is that by 1844 bank-notes were a less important liability for the Bank than deposits. This change in emphasis had occurred within fifty years: in 1802 notes equalled approximately half of total deposits and in 1825 a quarter, but by 1850 the ratio was nearly 1 to 10.

One immediate result of the 1845 Bank Act was that Bank of Scotland had to buy £50,000 of gold from the Bank of England to bring its reserve up to the required balance. In exchange, the Bank of England agreed to receive the transmission of the Bank's remittances of the Scottish Revenue without fee.

The years 1842 to 1844 were years of good harvests and prosperity for the Bank's agricultural customers. This, with the careful watch kept on branches since 1833, had returned the whole system to profit, with only two branches – Kilmarnock and Castle Douglas – showing a small loss. The most volatile business was experienced by the Bank's branches in Airdrie and Paisley which, along with Glasgow, were the only ones in which the amount lent was larger than the sums of money deposited. The Bank's Glasgow business was in the hands of a distinguished series of managers: Charles Campbell was succeeded in 1833 by W.J. Duncan, who resigned from the Bank in 1843 on his appointment as general manager of the National Bank of Scotland; his successor was Andrew Neilson, the fourth generation of his family to serve the Bank. At that time the Bank's office in Glasgow was in cramped premises in Ingram Street at the easternmost end of the city's new business district.

The years 1845 and 1846 were peak times of railway promotion and building. The Bank made numerous loans to Scottish railway companies and authorised its Glasgow manager to lend up to £50,000 for railway building, but it was well aware that much of the money was going directly into share speculation. (Keen as the Bank was to promote the railways, it was less enthusiastic about a railway in its own backyard in Edinburgh. It opposed the construction of the North British Railway Company's lines through Princes Street Gardens and sold land for the purpose only when forced to do so.) The Directors became very concerned during the latter half of 1845 at the outflow from reserves and asked Andrew Neilson to provide them with a detailed report of the situation in Glasgow. His comments are worth quoting in detail.

> As desired by you we beg to report that the manufactures of this district during the whole of 1845 were generally speaking in a very sound and healthy state: the cotton spinning trade being particularly prosperous. The only exception which might perhaps be made to this observation is that of handloom manufacturers and calico printers in the export trade and in regard to them we doubt whether their foreign consignments would yield a return adequate to the increased price of the goods.
>
> The railway speculation which existed here as in every other part of the Kingdom was certainly an unfavourable feature in the transactions of the

year, but it had this effect that prices of raw productions and manufacture were generally kept low and production more moderate than it would otherwise have been. The article of iron was the only exception – in it prices vibrated greatly and much money must have been made and lost in it by speculators.

Our working population were very well employed, their wages were good and provisions cheap, their power of consumption had therefore a very favourable reflex influence upon the internal trade of the country.

As to the position of matters now, they are in several respects less favourable than they were; confidence has been so checked that the regular demand for manufactures has been much interfered with, the foreign markets are not generally in a better state, and though labourers in the formation of railways and in some other branches are well employed and at good wages, we think that the home trade generally cannot be in as favourable a position as it was twelve months ago. Add to this the rapid advance in the value of money and that at a time when railway calls and outlays otherwise arising out of the prosperous trade of last year are just beginning to operate most powerfully.

In these circumstances and with the belief that the value of money will continue high for a considerable time forward, we do not think the position of matters here so favourable as it was; at the same time we are not aware of anything in our own position involving undue risk. We have lately waived anything of this character as also transactions in which we thought the parties were too much dependent upon facilities of Banking Accommodation.

To-morrow the 3rd of March is one of the heaviest days of bill payments throughout the year and being followed by the 4th of the month (always a heavy day) we anticipate that the strength of the mercantile community will be severely tested. If the payments be well got over we think it will be a favourable feature in our prospects for some time to come.

We think the chief danger at present is with houses who are widely extended or whose paper requires to be kept uniformly up or to be turned over by extended transactions. There are few accounts in our books which seem to answer this description.

The bubble burst on 18 October 1847. Alexander Blair revealed to the Directors that to sustain the Bank's position between 1845 and 1847 it had been necessary to sell, usually at a loss, some £1,198,000 of its reserve stock, which was equal to the whole of the undivided profit. If the Bank was to continue to support lending at the same level it would be necessary to sell a further £600,000 of Government securities. The alternative was to contract credit and thereby give a further downward twist to the collapse. Glasgow was particularly badly affected and it was reckoned by one of the Directors that the crash cost £4 million, which represented 10 per cent of the banking capital of Scotland. Part of the story for industrial firms in Glasgow and Paisley was wage demands to meet rising grain prices, itself one outcome of the failure of the potato crop in Ireland and the West of

Scotland. The period of panic did not last long. The Government allowed the Bank of England to make loans freely and all the Scottish banks to exceed their authorised issue without penalty. Bank of Scotland's comparative caution in railway lending meant that the Glasgow agency suffered a loss of only £15,000 and was obliged in its central accounts to make further provision of some £12,800. Total losses of £30,000 in 1847 were very small compared with those of other banks. But events did demonstrate very clearly to Blair that the capital of the original three Scottish chartered banks would be more effective if they could combine to create a specific reserve bank for Scotland. Soundings at both the Treasury and the Bank of England produced no insurmountable obstacles to the idea, so negotiations were opened with the Royal Bank and the British Linen Company to create a single chartered bank with a combined capital of £3.5 million, a note issue of £979,483, deposits of £14 million and a network of 74 branches. The prize was a large one. The restructured Bank of Scotland would have had unrivalled leadership over the Scottish banking system; it would have yielded greater profits to the shareholders of the original three banks by restraining competition; and it would have allowed Blair's ideas about correct banking principles to be imposed upon the whole system. It would also have created one of the biggest banks in Europe and made it one of the largest players in the City of London. The project excited Government interest and in 1850 the Treasurer received a surprise visit from Sir Charles Wood, Chancellor of the Exchequer, who wished to inform himself about the Scottish banking system. In fact the idea of a combined bank faded away, probably killed in 1851 by the British Linen Company, which was 'not prepared to consider further the state of banking in Scotland till after the meeting of Parliament'.

The years between 1848 and 1854 were lean ones for business. Trade reports emphasise general caution and a lack of demand for loans. As a consequence, branch profits slumped and general policy was dictated by a need to rebuild the London reserves. Money loaned to railway companies was not withdrawn: in 1850 the Edinburgh and Glasgow Railway, for example, had its loan facility renewed for £50,000, the same amount as had been lent in 1843. In 1853 Bank of Scotland took its first steps towards 'new technology'. Head Office in Edinburgh was connected to the London agent by electric telegraph, and London Stock Exchange prices became instantly available. It was the announcement of war with Russia in 1854 which restored confidence to industry, with a huge increase in demand for the products of the Scots burghs.

—The Last Duel in Scotland,—
23 August 1826

The protagonists in the last duel fought in Scotland were the Bank of Scotland's agent in Kirkcaldy and one of the Bank's customers. David Morgan, who became the Bank's Kirkcaldy agent in 1816, was also a prominent lawyer and conducted both his own and the Bank's business from Pye's House in the Kirkwynd. In 1820 he was joined as co-agent by his son George, who was a half-pay lieutenant in the 72nd Regiment. George Morgan was an arrogant and irascible man who failed to honour customer confidentiality and publicly queried the credit-worthiness of David Langdale, a linen merchant, bleachfield owner and prominent 'Auld Lichter' in the 'lang toun'. Whether by malice or stupidity, the quarrel was allowed to grow until Morgan challenged Langdale to a duel. This was fought at Cardenbarns on 23 August 1826 and Morgan was killed. At the trial before Lord Cockburn at Perth in September, Langdale was acquitted on the grounds that he had done everything to avoid a quarrel and had therefore acted in self-defence. Among those appearing for Langdale were Archibald Bennet, the Bank Secretary, and Walter Fergus, the town's former Provost. As a result, Kirkcaldy linen manufacturers felt they were no longer well served by the Bank and transferred their business to a branch of the Union Bank of Scotland which opened under Walter Fergus in 1835. It is pleasing to record that the quarrel between the Langdales and Morgans was not long-lasting. In 1839 Alexander G. Morgan joined his uncle in the Bank agency and subsequently married David Langdale's daughter. Out of this came Langdale, Morgan & Co., jute manufacturers of Calcutta, and the beginnings of Kirkcaldy's linoleum industry.

David Langdale's duelling pistols, now in Kirkcaldy Museum

—10—

WIDER HORIZONS AND DOMESTIC PROBLEMS, 1850–95

O N 10 June 1851 the Governor – Robert, second Viscount Melville – died, breaking 75 years of continuous family service to the Bank. He was 80 years of age and had, since the events of 1832, largely withdrawn from daily and active involvement in the Bank's affairs. Lord Cockburn provided a fitting epitaph:

> After holding high offices and performing their duties well, he retired from public life about twenty years ago and has ever since resided quietly at Melville Castle. But though withdrawing from London and its great functions, he did not renounce usefulness, but entered into every Edinburgh work in which it could be employed with respectability . . . He deserved this unanimous public trust by plain manners, great industry, excellent temper, sound sense and singular fairness. There could not possibly be a better man of business.

It is a measure of the change in the management style of the Bank since 1832 that Melville's successor, Lord Dalhousie, was Governor-General of India and therefore not resident in Scotland. As President of the Board of Trade in Peel's administration he had coped well with the consequences of railway 'mania' in 1846–47. His task in India was to modernise the administration and improve communications. The grand design was to build a railway network on the subcontinent. This was to be financed by stock offering a guaranteed interest rate above British Government stock with identical security, which it was hoped would limit the opportunities for speculation. Lord Dalhousie's role was to encourage the Bank to take

James Alexander, tenth Earl and eighteenth Marquess of Dalhousie, Governor 1851-60, in the uniform of the Royal Company of Archers, by Sir John Watson Gordon (Scottish National Portrait Gallery)

investments in Indian stock and play a more active part in foreign capital investment. In one sense he was pushing at a half-open door. Bank customers in Dundee and Kirkcaldy were already becoming heavily involved in the jute trade and needed more knowledge of trading conditions to support this. Bank of Scotland's main problem was that, unlike most other Scottish banks, it had no foreign correspondents and sub-contracted all work of foreign remittance and letters of credit to Coutts or Smith, Payne and Smith in London, who found the business very profitable. In such circumstances the Bank could build up no foreign investment expertise. Alexander Blair remained sceptical about the merits of foreign correspondents in India, USA, Canada and Australia, so the matter was allowed to rest during the rest of his Treasurership.

By 1854 the Bank's now traditional views about the extension of credit and liquidity began to look seriously outmoded, and even Alexander Blair believed that a more adventurous investment and lending policy was justified. The reasons for a change of direction were presented in 1855 in a report to the Directors, who were most impressed by the fact that a bank with a capital base similar to that of Bank of Scotland (unnamed, but probably the Union Bank of Scotland) could create profits of £130,000, some £40,000 more than the Bank's profits for 1854. This difference was the direct result of using £1 million of deposits to discount commercial bills in Glasgow. The Board also noted that the Bank was at a disadvantage in attracting Glasgow business because it had no resident support among merchants and manufacturers, and they seriously considered setting up a Glasgow board of directors. The final decision was that there should eventually be three new branches in Glasgow, with new loans being negotiated either by the Glasgow manager or by the agent of the new branch at Laurieston, the only one which was actually opened in 1855. These were to report to Edinburgh and be inspected in the traditional way. This expansion required £500,000 in extra deposits and permitted additional loans of £850,000 while still allowing £3,505,000 for the Glasgow bill trade. Business expanded rapidly among West of Scotland manufacturers and traders and this was also extended to England. All the Scottish banks, with the exception of the British Linen Company, pursued a similar course of action.

The backcloth against which this happened was a very rapid growth in the British economy and in overseas trade. Between 1845 and 1855 British manufactured exports rose by some 62 per cent. Both self-confidence and pride in achievement were boosted by the success of the Great Exhibition at London's Crystal Palace in 1851; and the feeling of general prosperity

Dundee, weaving at Mid-Wynd Jute Works, 1850 (Dundee Museum and Art Gallery)

was enhanced by the discovery of gold in California in 1849. Although Alexander Blair was uncertain about the effect of an increased gold supply on commodity prices in Britain, it was a matter for regular review rather than serious worry.

In the first four months of 1857 the general economic position began to deteriorate and the Bank began to draw back on its lending for fear of becoming over-extended. The twenty-five years of Blair's stewardship had shifted the balance of the Bank's business very significantly. In 1832 deposits in the Bank had been £3,188,000, advances in Scotland £1,970,000 and reserves in London £2,035,000. In 1857 deposits were £5,327,000 and advances £4,390,000, while London reserves stood at £2,140,536. After certain allowances were made, this gave the Bank a convertible reserve of £1,530,536. If Blair's own principles about reserves had been followed, the convertible reserve in 1857 should have stood at £1,800,000. The ratio of reserves to liabilities had been set at 1:3 at a Board meeting of 30 November 1840, and so there was a shortfall of some £269,464. In other words, the structure of the Bank's business was increasingly similar to that of its competitors, from which followed the obvious corollary that it was no longer in a position to act as a quasi-reserve bank for the whole Scottish system. That opportunity had been lost with the rejection of Blair's amalgamation plans in the 1840s. In view of what was to follow, it was ironic that the public perception of Bank of Scotland's

Photograph of Head Office, the Mound, c.1850, from Waverley Station

proper role remained that of an earlier generation.

The crisis gathered momentum during the summer of 1857. News of the mutiny of a number of regiments in the East India Company in northern India and the subsequent massacres of British subjects reached London in July, and a number of small American banks began to close. By mid-October the trickle had become a flood: all but one of the 63 New York houses closed; and trade to the USA was severely curtailed. Prices of manufactured goods awaiting shipment from Britain began to fall and the Bank of England added to the problem by raising its discount rate from 5.5 to 8 per cent within a period of ten days in October. There were even more bank failures in the USA: some 1,415 banks were shut during October, with total liabilities of $299,810,000. By early November many industrial companies and merchant houses, particularly in Liverpool and Glasgow, suspended payments and laid off workers. Crucially, the Dennistoun business, with interests in Glasgow, Liverpool, London, New York and New Orleans, stopped payments. There was a crisis of confidence in Glasgow, leading to runs on the Western Bank, the City of Glasgow Bank and the Union Bank of Scotland; but all Scottish banks were affected, apart from the British Linen Company and the Dundee Banking Company. On 9 November the Western Bank and the City of Glasgow Bank closed their doors.

The Western Bank had, since its founding in 1832, been consistently

Panoramic view of Edinburgh, 1868

opposed to the sound banking principles advocated by Blair and had considered that £20,000 to £25,000 in London reserves was more than sufficient for the conduct of its business. There had been problems in 1834 and 1847 and from these the Western carried an overhang of bad and doubtful debt for which no provision had been made. In 1854 this was estimated to be £420,000, equal to four years' annual dividend. This was not publicly known. By July 1857, after writing off £125,000 of bad debts, £327,000 of debts remained as 'hopeless'. If US debts and their impact on the Glasgow scene were taken into consideration, the total problem was believed to amount to £1,603,726. During October the Bank and the Royal, together with the Union, Commercial and National banks, put up £600,000 as an initial safety net, but on the 19th news of this was leaked to *The Times*, and customers' deposits were withdrawn from the Western. The Bank of England refused to intervene and would not suspend the Bank Charter Act to permit Bank of England notes to circulate in Scotland. On 10 and 11 November £1 million of gold was moved north and the military placed on full alert. Bank of Scotland has consistently received a bad press for its actions during this crisis. In fact, the books reveal that its support for the Western Bank cost £413,500 which, when added to support for other banks in difficulty, amounted to a total support operation costing £874,000 by the first week of December 1857.

Predictably, the Bank's own customers had problems and they had first call on its resources. It has been calculated that by the end of 1857 Bank of Scotland had moved a total of £2,173,000 from its reserves to increase liquidity. Had not new deposits of £500,000 been forthcoming during November and December 1857, total Bank reserves would have shrunk to £300,000 at the start of 1858, a dangerously inadequate base for sound banking. Support from the Edinburgh banks was sufficient to allow the City of Glasgow Bank to reopen on 14 December, while both the Union Bank and the Edinburgh and Glasgow Bank were helped to weather the storm. So far as the Western Bank was concerned, the funds of depositors were guaranteed, and by January 1858 all business accounts and loans had been honoured. Even so, the shareholders forfeited the whole of their capital and Glaswegians felt that Bank of Scotland could have done more.

The entire episode revealed brutally to the Scottish banks that they were now regarded as bit players on the financial scene, particularly since it demonstrated to English commentators the value of the 1844 Act. Scots ideas about banking were unreliable and their behaviour un-British. *The Times* spoke for most articulate judges south of the Border on the Western Bank: 'An attack upon our currency system from representatives of a concern which with eight millions of British capital entrusted to its care has brought itself to bankruptcy by fostering a set of fraudulent traders to the damage of legitimate merchants . . .' Public opinion in Glasgow preferred to believe that the whole episode was yet another example of Edinburgh mean-spiritedness, determined to do down the entrepreneurial skills of the city. Bank of Scotland's accounts reveal that the Western Bank's collapse came closer to pulling down the entire banking structure in

Left: *Silver arm-plate worn by the Bank messenger, 1840-60*
Right: *Photograph of Alexander Blair, Treasurer 1832-59*

Scotland than could be publicly admitted.

The events of 1857 took a heavy toll on Alexander Blair, although their immediate effects were by no means as bad as he had feared. He was in declining health for most of 1858. After preparing the Bank's submission for the Parliamentary Inquiry into the Western Bank he had to be content to sit on the sidelines while the Deputy Governor, Sir George Clerk of Penicuik, made the presentation. No new initiatives resulted from the Inquiry and in the eyes of the Board of Trade, presided over by W.E. Gladstone, the Scots system was discredited. It was a severe blow to Bank of Scotland's morale. The Bank had to rebuild its reserves and public trust in the banking system; yet at the same time Blair knew perfectly well that there was no legislation or group sanction in place which could prevent any other bank from operating in precisely the same way as the Western.

Alexander Blair died in office in February 1859 and was succeeded as Treasurer by John Mackenzie, who had previously been manager of the Scottish Widows Fund. Blair's efforts brought the Bank through the crisis in good shape, and recovery was rapid. By 1860 Bank of Scotland possessed some 43 branches, of which only five had been taken over from the Western Bank, and deposits rose rapidly. The Earl of Dalhousie's interests in India bore fruit in 1859, when the Bank tendered for £150,000 worth of British India debentures. It was during this operation that John Mackenzie began to look hard at the commission taken and at non-interest-bearing cash deposits carried by the Bank's London corresponding banks, Coutts and Smith Payne's. He reckoned that in total this cost the Bank £5,256 a year. One particular area for concern was that all Scottish banks were finding it increasingly difficult either to lend money or to obtain first-class secure bills in London.

Although Britain was not directly involved in any major wars during the 1860s, the export business was affected by a number of changes in Europe. The Franco-Austrian War of 1859–60 began the process which was to lead to Italian unification. The German empire, dominated by Prussian interests, was created in a series of wars with Denmark and Austria and finally in 1870 with France. It was, however, the American Civil War, with its consequent restriction of raw cotton exports from the Southern States, which hastened the decline of the cotton industry in the West of Scotland. Its eventual replacements – modern steelmaking and shipbuilding – were in their infancy. Bank profits fell from £150,000 in 1861 to £115,000 in 1862 and 1863. By 1865 they were down to £80,000.

It became clear to the Directors that if lending opportunities in the West of Scotland were to become more restricted, new outlets for

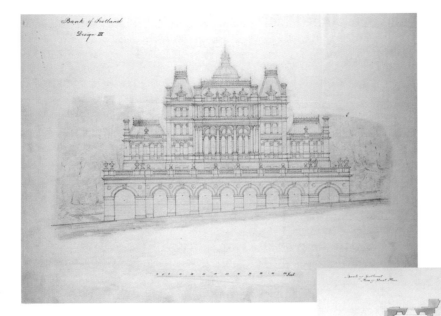

Above: *One of Peddie and Kinnear's alternative treatments for the north elevation of Head Office, the Mound, 1859-61*

Right and below: *David Bryce's plan and south elevation for Head Office, the Mound, 1864-70*

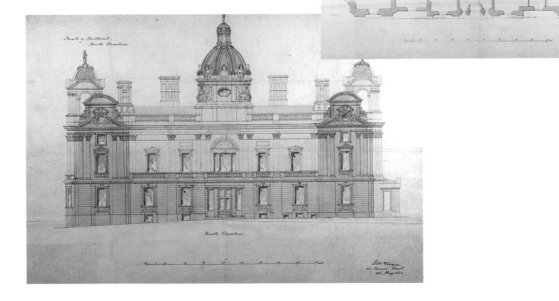

134   investment were required. This was a direction in which the Treasurer, John Mackenzie, felt his inexperience, and the pressures of the situation aggravated his ill-health. He wisely decided to step down in 1863 on health grounds, although he was to live until 1901 and serve as a director of the Union Bank of Scotland from 1887. His successor was David Davidson, who after apprenticeship in Scotland had become manager of the Bank of Montreal, a 'Scots' bank very familiar with the activities of Scots in Canada's West and North West Territories. His experience of land settlement and investment in new territories was invaluable to the Bank, and his period of office to 1879 signalled an advance of the Bank's efforts on every front.

The most obvious change was that work began almost immediately on extending the Bank's Head Office on the Mound in Edinburgh. This was a project which had been under consideration for over fifteen years. In 1850, in response both to criticism from Edinburgh residents that the Bank presented its ugly back to the New Town and to the need for additional accommodation, the Bank had commissioned drawings from the architect Thomas Hamilton. His proposal was to extend the Bank sideways to the east and west with a pair of pavilions linked to the earlier building and to place the main entrance of the Bank on the north side facing the New Town. Architecturally the main problem was that Hamilton stuck to a 'Georgian' appearance, and although he could get the building to look balanced from either the north *or* the south side, his design did not allow both to appear in proportion. In fact the project was abandoned after preliminary discussions and was never costed. In 1859–61 the Edinburgh architects Peddie & Kinnear prepared a portfolio of alternative treatments of the exterior, based on a near-identical ground plan. These varied from Greek temple, through French château to Victorian Gothic railway station. It is probable that the Directors and Treasurer took fright, but in 1864 the architect David Bryce was commissioned and his designs were carried out between 1864 and 1870. His solution was neat and very satisfying. In effect he encased the original building in a new shell and added two new wings, which emphasised the vertical lines of the Old Town building but broke up the sheer mass with horizontal elements of decoration. Internally, a two-storey entrance and banking hall were created with offices and two domestic flats. The original dome was extended upwards and topped by a statue of Fame, balanced by two smaller, lower cupolas, also with statues.

For the whole period of the remodelling, the Head Office staff worked on in the middle of a building site. When the building account was closed in 1875 some £43,500 had been spent on the alterations, but at the Annual

General Meeting of 1870 Davidson had told the Proprietors that Head Office on the Mound would not stand in the Bank's books at more than £30,000. The way in which this was done is an interesting example of the attitudes to property values in the Victorian age compared with the present day. In a Board minute of 28 December 1858 it was agreed that a general property account would be created in which rents received for the Bank's let property would be set against expenditure, with only the balance being carried to the general accounts. The other decision was to take a sum of money out of the net profit each year before the declaration of the Proprietors' dividend, to 'the reduction of the heritable property in the occupation of the Bank'. Between 1861 and 1891 this amounted to £5,000 a year and tended to be set against the costs of new or refurbished buildings. In other words, property values were depreciated each year. Up to 1880 the Bank Head Office on the Mound had cost £96,229 to build. By 1910 it had no value as an asset in the Bank's accounts.

This was not the only building work carried out. In 1860 the Bank had 43 branches, but by 1880 this had risen to 106. Of this additional number only 15 were taken over from other banks. Even with a policy of writing down costs, the value of property recorded on the Bank's annual balance sheet rose from around £83,000 in 1860 to £249,021 in 1880, a three-fold increase in just twenty years. As a proportion of the Bank's total assets it rose by 50 per cent, a clear indication of the speed of expansion under

Central Bank of Scotland £1 note
'pull' from a steel-engraved plate

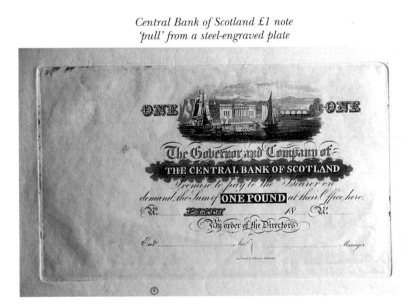

Left: *David Davidson, Treasurer 1862-79*
Right: *James Wenley, Treasurer 1879-98, taken about 1881*

Above: *Bank of Scotland notes of the 1860s and 1870s*
Foot: *Experimental £100 note of 1880 (never issued)*

David Davidson. In addition to changes at Head Office other major building works were carried out at Beauly, Falkirk, Aberdeen, New Cumnock, Oban and St Andrews, while in Glasgow a new principal office was built between 1865 and 1869 at 1 St Vincent Place at a cost of £48,654.

The expansion of the Scottish banks into England began when the National Bank opened an office in London. The problem remained the Bank of England's charter; and during 1865 Bank of Scotland, the British Linen Company, the Clydesdale and the Union Bank of Scotland prepared a scheme for a jointly owned bank, the London and Scottish Banking Association, with a capital of £3 million and limited liability. The intention was to channel all Scots investment business through the new bank. The project collapsed in 1866, and Bank of Scotland decided to establish its own London office. Premises were leased at 11 Old Broad Street at an annual rental of £3,430 and opened for business on 16 April 1867. To the surprise of the Bank's Directors, the London branch had taken over £400,000 of deposits by 1869, and a move to new rented premises at 43 Lothbury in 1870 provided much-needed business space. By 1871 London deposits had reached £900,000 and the potential for lending to London Scots was very large. The net profit of the London branch had reached £3,500 after only three years of business.

The success of the London office both justified and confirmed David Davidson's instincts about the disabilities that Scots banks faced in London if they operated through agents. First, with the growth in the social importance of the London 'Season', aristocratic customers preferred to deal with a London-based bank, even if the bulk of their income was derived from Scottish estates or businesses. Good business was being lost. Secondly, the Scottish banks were only getting access to London bills and lending after others had taken first pick. Thirdly, they were paying handsomely for the privilege of being second-best in London. Finally, it was clear that there was a strong latent demand among London Scots for Scottish banking facilities.

In 1868 the Bank took over seven of the branches of the Central Bank of Scotland, a Perth-based concern founded in 1834. At various times of crisis during the 1840s and '50s it had been assisted by Bank of Scotland and by 1868 owed a total of £52,000. The solution was to buy the bank outright by offering Central Bank shareholders Bank of Scotland stock held either in reserves or in the pension fund. A minority of the shareholders were reluctant to sell, so the Central Bank had a nominal independence for a further 12 years, when those surviving were bought out by a payment of £2 3s. per share. It was a good purchase, with large

138   deposits, and gave Bank of Scotland a secure footing among the farmers and landowners of Perthshire.

In 1873 it began to seem probable that the Bank's expansion would be restricted by its authorised capital, which had been set at £1.5 million in 1804, although up to 1872 only £1 million had been called up. The new Act of 1873 authorised a capital of £4.5 million, which appeared to meet needs as far ahead as anyone could see. In fact, only £250,000 was called up from the Proprietors in 1876 and the Bank's paid-up capital remained at £1.25 million until 1907. Unlike the Union Bank and the Clydesdale, Bank of Scotland was able to support its continued expansion from within its reserves without making calls on its Proprietors.

In 1875 Scottish banking faced a serious challenge to its intention to expand into the English market. The Chancellor, Sir Stafford Northcote, was determined to remove existing Scots banks from England, and a Parliamentary Committee of Inquiry was set up. There were several threads to his thinking. Firstly, the Scottish banks tended to work together, and with their large capital funds they provided increasingly strong competition in London. Secondly, there had been a steady stream of complaints that the 1845 Act had given the Scots banks an unfair advantage. Thirdly, from 1874 the industrial boom of the previous decade was over and all banks and bill brokers were looking for good, secure investments. The desire of Scottish banks (and English joint-stock banks) to move into the profitable 'acceptance' business challenged the role of city brokers and bankers, who presented this expansion as a direct challenge to the authority of the Bank of England. It is notable that among the chief advocates of restricting the Scottish banks was the South Essex MP, Thomas Charles Baring, in a happy coincidence of private interest and public duty. George Joachim Goschen, MP for the City of London, emphasised the point that Scots banks moving to London could keep their bank-note issue in Scotland, but that English banks moving to Scotland could not issue Bank of England notes 'because people will not take them'. In fact, for once, the Scots banks underestimated the eagerness of London interests to expel them. The Scots case was not presented with sufficient robustness and clarity. One of the features which most strongly told against them was that they appeared to be operating in concert, as a cartel, with agreed rates of interest and terms of trade. Recalculations of profit presented to the Committee suggested that loss of London business would not be a severe blow to the Scots. In the end no final report was issued and no legislation enacted on these matters, but the Scottish banks in effect gave an undertaking that no new branches would be opened in England. The quid pro quo was that English banks would not open in Scotland. This understanding stood for a century and can be identified in retrospect as one of the key elements that shaped Scottish banking in succeeding years. It came as a shock to David Davidson to realise the depth of hostility in London to Scottish banking methods.

One initiative with which Davidson was associated has remained of lasting value. In 1875 the Institute of Bankers in Scotland was founded, the first of its kind in the world, and a system of professional banking examinations began. Banking apprenticeships were long established but common standards of practice and ethics were felt to be the best guarantee of the quality of Scottish banking.

The views of Londoners about the unsoundness of Scottish banking seemed amply justified when the City of Glasgow Bank closed its doors in 1878, with liabilities amounting to over £6 million. There was a great difference in the perception of the City Bank between the public in the West of Scotland, who saw the bank as sound and go-ahead, and the other banks, particularly Bank of Scotland, which had watched its activities apprehensively for over twenty years. The possibility of a rerun of the Western Bank crisis of 1857 was reported privately to the Treasurer as early as 1871 by the then Glasgow manager, James Wenley. If Bank of Scotland

Telegrams announcing the closure of the City of Glasgow Bank and instructions for immediate business conduct

Robert Salmond (left) *and Lewis Potter,*
two directors found guilty of fraud at the City of Glasgow Bank trial,
and an unused City of Glasgow Bank cheque

was prepared for trouble, it was not prepared for the extent of mismanagement and fraud uncovered by the accountant George Auldjo Jamieson. The story which emerged deserves more detailed treatment than can be given here, but the salient features are as follows. In 1857 the City of Glasgow Bank had lost £700,000 and had only been kept going by loans from other banks. Thereafter it expanded rapidly and by 1877 had 133 branches with deposits of £8 million, while the published annual accounts indicated a flourishing loan and investment business. In fact, the accounts had been falsified and control of the bank was vested in a small group of directors. It was ironic that the branch staff of the bank were considered to be well trained and of excellent probity and skill. The fraud centred on a huge discount and loan scam operated on only eight accounts, most of which were involved in either the Indian trade or land purchases in New Zealand and Australia. The bank's total liabilities amounted to £12,723,822 and the eventual loss to £5,190,983. Since the shareholders did not have limited liability they had to find £4.4 million and lose the whole of their capital. For each £100 shareholding £2,750 had to be found. Of the 1,819 shareholders only 254 remained solvent. The fact that a number of directors served prison sentences was no great consolation to a swathe of investors, mostly in Glasgow, who were made bankrupt. James Wenley was the Bank of Scotland's main representative in the subsequent clear-up. As in 1857, the prime consideration was the banking system as a whole. Deposits and loans were honoured, and the bulk of the branch system, with its existing staff, was taken over by the Royal Bank. Bank of Scotland acquired just eight branches. One additional complication was that many of the City of Glasgow Bank's agents had also been shareholders and a number were personally bankrupt. In one or two cases Bank of Scotland could help. The manager of the Edinburgh branch in Hanover Street was appointed Cashier of Bank of Scotland, which gave him a flat in the Bank House on the Mound, and his salary was publicly designated as 'allowances'. The collapse of the City of Glasgow Bank scarred a generation of Scots bankers and was the worst crisis to hit the Scots business community in the second half of the nineteenth century. One long-term consequence of these events was that over the next ten years there was a raft of legislation limiting the personal liability of shareholders and dealing with company structure and bookkeeping. In banking the 1882 Cheque Act and the Bankers Book Evidence Act 1881 are still extant in 1995 and dictate record-keeping practices. Independent auditing of company accounts, registration of companies, and publication of annual results in a standard form were required by the 1879 Companies Act. It is interesting to note that the names of the Bank's auditors appear in the Annual Report for the first time in 1879. That year's Annual Report is also unusual in that it contains two pages of remarks on the crisis by the Governor. The Annual Report reverted the following year to a simpler format which was basically unchanged until 1946, when a profit and loss account was added for the first time.

When David Davidson retired in May 1879 in ill-health, one major effect of the worries of the previous year, the clear choice of Bank of Scotland's Directors as his successor was James Wenley. Many of Davidson's initiatives in colonial business were steadily bearing fruit. Important companies became customers, and a series of corresponding agents was established in Canada, Australia, New Zealand and South Africa. Increased knowledge of conditions made it possible for the Bank to widen the scope of its investment book, and in 1878 US government bonds and New South Wales government debentures were bought for the first time.

James Wenley's 19 years as Treasurer were very mixed ones for the Bank. On the one hand it regained its position as Scotland's first bank, a matter which owed much to David Davidson's groundwork. On the other hand the general economy of Scotland remained in depression during

142 much of the 1880s and the collaboration which had been a normal feature of Scottish banking became a rigid system in which banks did not poach customers from each other, matched interest rates and were in general very cautious. The changes in the Bank's business were the subject of a detailed report prepared by James Gourlay, the Bank's Glasgow manager, for James Wenley in 1894. His summary was as follows:

> The above will show that the conditions under which business is conducted in Glasgow are much more difficult now than they were twenty years ago, and that the profits of banks show a downward tendency . . .

In fact he was describing what had emerged during the 1860s and 1870s as a distinctive geographical pattern in the Bank's business. The spread of branches into new middle-class suburbs and country towns, 123 by 1895, meant that in Scotland most were taking in deposits almost twice as great as the sums of money lent. The significance of the Glasgow and Laurieston branches was that they were the prime channels through which the Bank's lending business was conducted. After 1889 the surplus on this process had to be placed in bills and securities through the London office. The difficulties of finding profitable opportunities for lending is a constant theme of the 1880s and 1890s. In 1883 the Bank contemplated, in defiance of the 'agreement' of 1875, opening a second London branch in the West End. It was hoped that this would become a channel for lending, but in fact the idea was dropped when it became clear that it too would become a channel for deposit-taking rather than lending. The question must be asked whether the Bank was over-cautious in its lending policies. The whole underlying theme of Gourlay's report is a defence of the role of the Glasgow office, which over the 15 years since 1879 had resulted in some £102,000 being written off the Bank's lending book. The view from the Mound suggested that a cavalier policy was in place rather than the reverse. Some detailed figures illustrate the crucial points better than many words.

		1869	1894	Increase
A	**Deposits** (Bank)	8,400,000	14,700,000	6,650,000
	Deposits (Glasgow Chief Office)	650,000	2,000,000	1,350,000
	Deposits (Glasgow and Glasgow Branches)	1,000,000	2,750,000	1,750,000

Some Bank of Scotland Agents in the 1880s and 1890s

144   B   **Loans at Glasgow Chief Office**

	On Bills	On Cash Credits	On Overdrafts	Loans on Stock	
1869	1,250,000	350,000	150,000	-	1,750,000
1894	1,450,000	500,000	1,300,000	500,000	3,750,000
				Increase	2,000,000

It can be seen that in 1869 Glasgow Chief Office's deposits covered only 30 per cent of loans, but by 1894, if the other Glasgow branches are taken into consideration, they covered 73 per cent of lending. Most significant of all was the change from lending on a bill with a fixed time limit to lending on overdraft, in theory instantly recoverable but in practice a running account whose limits were adjusted according to the business concerned. The implication is clear and fits with the deposit evidence. During the 1880s and '90s most of the Bank's large business customers in the West generated their capital requirements from internal profits and looked to the Bank to cover cash flow variations. Gourlay also stated that the cash credit had simply become unfashionable among customers and there were fewer bills because people preferred to pay cash and take an extra discount on their purchases. There is very little doubt that most of the Bank's new connections in the period came from Glasgow and were widely spread across the whole range of business in the West of Scotland. Of its rivals only the National Bank came close, while of the two Glasgow-based banks the Union Bank of Scotland slipped in rank order and the Clydesdale maintained its 1869 position. The outcome of the Board discussions which followed Gourlay's report was to keep the policies in place but to be on the look-out for new businesses and industries which might offer increased lending opportunities.

Between 1891 and 1893 the focus of the Bank's concerns shifted to London. The business of the London branch was very distinctive. Such advances as were made were to corporations, public bodies, other bankers, bill brokers and stockbrokers. Private customers were Scottish firms which preferred to pass their bills via London. In other words, it was a specialised business which did not rely on private customers.

In 1891 the lease on the Bank's premises in Lothbury expired and it was made clear that the landlord required possession of the property. Several sites were reported on and the Bank's architect, G.W.T. Gwyther, suggested that offices at 'Bishopsgate within' be bought for £120,000. The earlier buildings on the site had included Crosby Hall, occupied for a number of years by Sir Thomas More, Henry VIII's Chancellor. In one of those curious circles in the Bank's story this had been the meeting place in

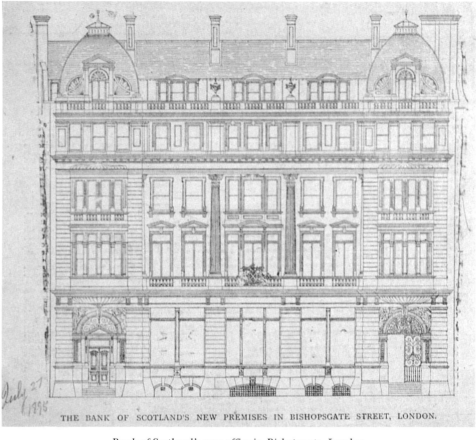

THE BANK OF SCOTLAND'S NEW PREMISES IN BISHOPSGATE STREET, LONDON.

Bank of Scotland's new office in Bishopsgate, London,
as illustrated in a newspaper report

the eighteenth century of the East India Company. In 1894 the building was demolished and a new office erected, now known as 30 Bishopsgate, which opened its doors on 25 April 1896. The London manager tended not to follow the traditional banking career of most Scottish bankers because the skills were specialised and the business unusual. From 1873 to 1899 the London manager was Robert Davidson, who had been trained in the Bank of England and who was able to build up good relations within the City and to handle the investment business.

The relationships between the Bank, the Bank of England and the City were severely tested during the Baring crisis of 1891. News was received that the City house of Baring Brothers & Company was unable to meet its liabilities, amounting to £21 million. The Scottish reaction was to treat the crisis as an English matter which the City should be left to sort out in precisely the same way that the Scots had had to sort out the City of Glasgow débâcle in 1878. Robert Davidson made it clear to the Board in Edinburgh that much more was at stake. A great swathe of investment in

146 South America was at risk, as were the City of London's credibility and the Government's own international standing. A parochial attitude would not be tolerated by the Bank of England. By the time Barings was reconstituted in 1894, each of the Scottish banks had guaranteed £300,000, while the Government provided £2 million and the Bank of England £1 million. Three London joint-stock banks provided £750,000 each, and two others £500,000. It is a measure of the changes in English banking since the 1860s that the available resources of Bank of Scotland, biggest in its own kailyard, were overtaken by no fewer than five London-based banks.

The years from 1891 to 1894 continued the depression in the coal, iron, jute and sugar industries. The Bank made two large loans to cane sugar producers in Trinidad, and from time to time an official was sent out to report on progress, a pleasant change from the normal routine of branch banking.

It looked as though trade, on the domestic front at least, would begin to improve during 1894, and the Treasurer hoped to signal better times at the Bank's bicentenary by increasing the dividend to shareholders and providing a bonus for all staff. Towards the end of the year there was a further downturn in trade, however, with a number of major customer losses being written off. In the words of Charles Malcolm, 'The 200th anniversary had thus to pass unhonoured and unsung in a year that was worse than any for a decade.'

—11—
THE UNION BANK OF SCOTLAND, 1843–1914

OF all the banks which were to become part of Bank of Scotland's twentieth-century inheritance, the Union Bank of Scotland was the most unusual in the manner of its formation. It represented the amalgamation or absorption of no fewer than 12 separate banks in different parts of Scotland, each with a distinctive history and place in its respective community. The core around which the bank developed was the Glasgow Union Banking Company, Glasgow's first joint-stock as distinct from partnership bank, which opened for business in 1830. The prime mover was the merchant Robert Stewart who, with a number of like-minded Glasgow businessmen, proposed a joint-stock bank with a nominal capital of £2 million, divided into 8,000 shares of £250 each. Their motives are made crystal clear in the first paragraph of the prospectus, which was issued on 1 January 1830:

> Seventy years have elapsed since a Native Bank was first established in this City, and during the long interval between 1760 and 1829, the population of Glasgow has increased from 25,000 to 200,000 souls; while its Manufactures, Shipping, and General Trade have increased in a much higher ratio. Accordingly, the three local Banking Establishments of this City (which have in all not more than thirty Partners) have proved so inadequate to answer the demand for Bank accommodation, that, no fewer than nine Branches of Banks, not indigenous to Glasgow, have been introduced to supply the deficiency, and are now in such active operation, as to engross a very large proportion of her Banking business. Thus have *others* been allowed to reap those profits, which, had her own citizens been more active, and more alive to their own interests, would have been realised by themselves.

Panorama of Glasgow Trongate in 1839 (Glasgow City Libraries)

Not only, however, are the citizens of Glasgow excluded from participating in the *Bank's Profits* created by their own trade, and in a great measure at the mercy of strangers for their bank accommodation, but they have, besides, been for some time back, subjected to great inconvenience, and very many of them to great loss, by the removal of almost all the Branch Banks, from the Eastern and Centre to the Western portion of the City. The waste of time thus occasioned to Merchants in the Middle and Eastern Districts, by being compelled to proceed to Virginia Street, Queen Street, or the New Exchange, to transact their Bank business, is a very serious evil, and one universally felt.

Despite the rigours of New Year, the issue was oversubscribed, so that the bank was able to pick and choose its shareholders. By 21 January, with 4,221 shares subscribed, including 1,000 which had been allocated for distribution in Edinburgh, the list was closed and the Interim Committee of Management was able to confirm that the bank would commence trading as soon as possible. A series of meetings at the beginning of February in the Tontine Building at Glasgow Cross settled the details of staffing, bank-note production and premises, and the first formal directors' meeting took place on 16 February. The first appointment was James A. Anderson as general manager. This caused some misgivings because he was a merchant, not a trained banker, but it was balanced by the appointment of William Mitchell as his deputy and cashier who *was*. The bank opened for business in premises in Post Office Court, 14 Trongate, Glasgow, in October 1830. That

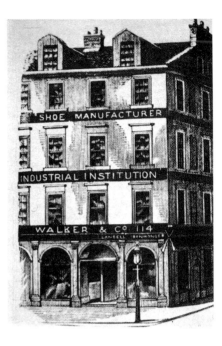

Office of the Glasgow and Union Bank, 114 Trongate, Glasgow

One of a set of late eighteenth-century boardroom chairs, used by the Thistle Bank and then by the Union Bank of Scotland

same month the management was completed by the appointment of John Smith of the Aberdeen and County Bank as secretary. Perhaps the two most important decisions taken by the directors were, first, to establish a branch in Edinburgh and, second, to institute an Edinburgh committee of shareholders to supervise operations. Another innovation was a standardised five-tier system of designating customers from 'very bad', through 'bad', 'very fair', 'very good' to the supreme accolade, 'undoubted'. In their first report the directors were able to report that with a number of minor exceptions the bank had been favourably received in both Glasgow and Edinburgh. During the 1830s and unlike its younger competitors, the Western Bank and the City of Glasgow Bank, it concentrated on steady growth: by 1836 14 branches had been established compared with the 30 or so set up by the Western Bank between 1832 and 1838. The published results suggest the careful addition of new business, and lending was cautious. It was rare for a credit of more than £1,000 to be

Union Bank of Scotland Main Office, 1841-43, fronting Virginia Street,
by David Hamilton

sanctioned. It was 1838 before the bank had sufficient confidence to lend £28,000 to a railway company. The first lending on overdraft to John Leadbetter, one of the bank directors, was not agreed until 1841. As with the business, so with the return to shareholders. The dividend was increased from £7.50 to £12.50 per share over the same period. The original prospectus had stated that the bank would remain in the Trongate area of Glasgow. It was therefore with great heart-searching that in 1833 the Union Bank followed the westward march of Glasgow's business district to new premises at the head of Virginia Street.

In 1836 the Union Bank began what was over the next twenty years to become a habit of absorption and amalgamation. During the course of three weeks in June, with three meetings and two exchanges of letters, the assets and liabilities of the Glasgow-based Thistle Bank were taken over at valuation. During 1838 two additions were made: the Paisley Union Bank and Sir William Forbes and Company, Edinburgh's last surviving private banker. In the former case the partners were eager to retire and the terms agreed revolved around the size of annuities and the issue of Union Bank stock. There were only three partners, and the settlement gave each an annuity of £2,500 for ten years and 50 Union Bank shares.

In many ways the most significant takeover was that of Sir William Forbes and Company. The great days of private bankers were past, and the firm had been steadily losing its traditional business to either the National Bank of Scotland or the three chartered banks. The basis of negotiation was the net profit of £16,000 made during 1836. A close examination of the books indicated that this was an above-average year for profits, and the figure was reduced to £10,666, which was accepted by the Edinburgh partners, provided that it was guaranteed. The remaining un-issued Union Bank stock was given to them, and the remaining sum was made up with annuities. The partners undertook to continue the management of the Edinburgh business for six years (when their own co-partnery agreement would expire), and Charles Forbes, grandson of Sir William Forbes of Pitsligo (see Chapter 6), undertook to live in Glasgow to work towards the full integration of the two banks.

151

At no point were Union Bank shareholders permitted to know the exact terms of the agreement and they were barely content with the assurance that discussion would be 'highly inexpedient and objectionable'. When during 1843 it became clear that both the Glasgow and Ship Bank and Hunters and Company of Ayr were to be amalgamated with the bank, it was decided that a new company structure was required. The actual document forming the Union Bank of Scotland in 1843 is one of the most extraordinary in all Scottish banking. It is in the form of a roll nearly 15 metres long, one-third of which contains the articles of agreement and the remainder the signature of every single shareholder. Being no longer 'a local bank in the City of Glasgow', the Union Bank

Banking Company in Aberdeen bank-note after amalgamation with the Union Bank Below: *Castle Street, Aberdeen, in the 1820s. The Bank is on the right of the picture*

established two head offices, one in Glasgow and one in Edinburgh, with six directors resident in each city, a system of regional organisation which, suitably modified, persists into the 1990s and is one of Bank of Scotland's legacies from the Union Bank. The paid-up capital of the older Glasgow and Union Bank stood at £500,000, although the nominal capital stood at £2.5 million. Since the paid-up capital of the Glasgow and Ship Bank also stood at £500,000, a decision was taken to keep the paid-up capital of the Union Bank of Scotland at £1 million divided into £50 shares, while the nominal capital was set at £2 million.

The combined effect of these amalgamations is best illustrated in a table prepared by the Japanese scholar Norio Tamaki, which is reproduced in simplified form on page 158.

Seven years of amalgamations resulted in the creation of a formidable bank with a national spread of branches, a large fund of goodwill and a wide range of business. The full absorption of Sir William Forbes & Co. into the Union Bank did not take place until 1846, when the original Edinburgh partners retired. The new Edinburgh manager, Samuel Hay, appointed at a salary of £800 a year, was quickly accepted as an honoured and trusted member of the Edinburgh financial community. The Edinburgh office became the base for control of circulation and coin.

Between 1844 and 1857 two further takeovers gave the Union Bank its final shape; and there were two attempted takeovers, of the Dundee Bank in 1849 and of the Caledonian Bank in 1851 and 1856, both of which failed.

The Aberdeen Banking Company, which agreed to be taken over in 1849, was in very poor shape. It had a large overhang of bad and doubtful debts, the largest of which was the Banner Mill, alone estimated at £35,340. This bank had had a chequered career over the previous twenty years which had reduced its capital to £7,047, divided into 34,235 shares. It has to be said that the Union Bank mounted a rescue operation. Shareholders were offered £2 per Aberdeen Banking Company share in Union Bank stock priced at £80 a share. That is to say, 40 Aberdeen Banking Company shares were exchanged for one Union Bank share. An attempt in 1849 to bid for the Perth Banking Company was rejected. But by 1857 the Perth partners had changed their minds and come to the conclusion that increased competition for business forced them to look for a marriage with a larger bank. The paid-up shares of £100,050 were valued at £2 each and were once again offered in exchange for Union Bank stock. With a number of minor financial adjustments the terms were accepted, and on 27 February 1858 the Perth Bank name disappeared from the office in St John Street, Perth and from 11 other branches in Perthshire.

During the 1840s and '50s the Union Bank of Scotland, despite policies that were very much in the spirit of Glasgow enterprise, never attracted the criticism of its peers. Between 1844 and 1858 the bank's total liabilities grew by *140 per cent*. Two arms of business distinguished it from the Edinburgh banks. First, it moved into 'acceptances' (bills of exchange) in the late 1840s and became heavily involved in the American and Australian trade of J.A. Dennistoun and Company, whose trade account stood at £400,000 in October 1853. Word of mouth ensured that the international business connections of Dennistoun's also provided new business, and it has been calculated that this was one of the main engines of the Union Bank's expansion in the period. Loans were made to the Tennants of St Rollox Chemical Works in Glasgow, and to the Monkland Iron and Steel Co.; and in 1855 a credit of £20,000 was granted for the first time to J. & G. Thomson, Shipbuilders, a firm which under various names was to feature regularly in the Union Bank's lending book down to 1955. The second area was railway finance, where loans were made almost entirely on the security of railway stock or debentures. These loans were usually for six months, but could be for up to two to three years.

The early years of the 1850s saw the Union Bank open an account with the Bank of England, develop a portfolio of railway stock and commit itself to foreign trade financing. Accounts were opened with Dennistoun contacts in New York, Paris and India. A significant proportion of the bank's 'formal' portfolio was invested in its own stock, and indeed the directors were encouraged to buy up stock whenever the price showed any signs of decline. In parallel with this development, branch formation accelerated

Glasgow in the 1860s

154 and by 1858 the network contained 99 branches: this was part of the policy of James Robertson, who succeeded James Anderson as manager in 1852, and it meant that the Union Bank topped the league table.

In 1857 the crisis which led to the closure of the Western Bank also severely affected the Union Bank. The failure of Carr, Josling & Co. of London had a severe knock-on effect and the firm of Dennistoun & Co. collapsed and had to stop business. Dennistoun's had a widespread international business, particularly in America, and had over-extended its trading. Alexander Dennistoun was a director of the bank and, as indicated earlier, the firm was almost certainly its largest customer. There was a run on the Union Bank during 10 and 11 November, but the Bank of England and the Edinburgh banks were able to provide help. Despite this, the price of Union Bank stock plummeted as the public perceived just how completely the Union was thirled to Dennistoun's. In the event, and with a little help from its friends, the Union Bank survived, but the experience provoked an examination of its policies and a change of direction.

In the eyes of the Edinburgh directors, James Robertson had been largely to blame for the near disaster of 1857. A young accountant called Charles Gairdner, who had been assistant liquidator of the Western Bank and a founding member of the Institute of Accountants and Actuaries in Glasgow in 1855, was asked in 1861 to carry out an investigation and to report on the Union Bank's structure and balance sheet. This revealed a range of problems and in 1862 Gairdner was appointed joint general manager, becoming sole manager in 1865 when James Robertson retired. He joined the bank board in 1865 and remained until his retiral in 1895. Quite apart from the performance of his duties as general manager, he was one of the foremost writers on banking theory in nineteenth-century Scotland and therefore had an influence on banking far beyond the confines of Glasgow.

Charles Gairdner's period at the Union Bank saw the implementation of cautious lending policies and much tighter management of the bank. The most significant change of all was the outcome of a review of investments which resulted in a much higher percentage of assets being carried as Consols and other Government securities. The consequence of all this was that between 1866 and 1879 the Union Bank fell continuously in ranking among the Scottish banks in terms of total liabilities, deposits and advances; even its branch network was overtaken by others. The policy of caution in these years was reinforced by two major failures which impacted on the bank's assets. The failure of the bank Overend, Gurney and Co. in 1866 led to an eventual loss of £26,000; although worrying, this was not serious. The fraudulent collapse in 1875 of

Charles Gairdner, General Manager of the Union Bank 1865-95
Staff of the Law Department, Union Bank, c.1900

Alexander Collie and Co., one of the largest East India merchants, with debts of £3 million, was an entirely different matter. The Union Bank was the only Scottish bank involved, and this also affected other bank customers such as Alexander Dennistoun, Finlay Campbell & Co., and Smith Fleming & Co. Losses of £150,000 were sustained, which required a reduction of £120,000 in the bank's reserve and money to be earmarked from the 1876 profits. The Collie fraud seriously damaged both the Union Bank's business and its public image.

The events of 1878 and the City of Glasgow Bank affair gave a further downward twist to public confidence in the Union Bank. Gairdner, the general manager, with the full support of the bank's Edinburgh and Glasgow boards, issued the following statement:

> The Directors deem it right to make a Special Report to the Proprietors on the extent to which their interests have been affected by the suspension of the City of Glasgow Bank and subsequent failures, and this more particularly as four months must elapse before the Annual Meeting is held.
>
> The amount due to the Bank by the City of Glasgow Bank, exclusive of the Notes retired in the public interest, is only £4,000. These claims, it is believed, will be paid in full; and the Directors have the satisfaction of informing the Proprietors that, on a careful estimate of all other bad and doubtful debts, the provision required from the profits of the current year is under £3,700.

156
The Directors believe it will also be satisfactory to the Proprietors to receive at this time an explicit assurance that the Accounts of the Bank are closely and constantly scrutinized by them; that the Advances are safe and well distributed; that losses are invariably provided for as they arise; that the Securities and Investments are of greater value than they stand at in the Books; and that the Bank's Capital of £1,000,000, and Rest of £330,000 are intact. The Proprietors will have observed that an unusual fall has recently taken place in the market price of the Bank's Stock. In connection with this, it is right to mention that a considerable amount of the Stock offered for sale belongs to Proprietors who, unhappily for themselves, are involved as Shareholders in the City of Glasgow Bank. The Bank sustains no loss from this circumstance; and as sales are effected, this depressing influence will, no doubt, pass away.

The Directors have delayed issuing this Report until the effects of the commercial and financial disorder of October have been so far developed as to admit of the Board reporting with confidence on their bearing on the Bank.

The selling price of Union Bank stock stood at £270 in November 1875; a month later it was only £160, a figure at which it remained for most of the succeeding year. Two measures were taken to try to restore confidence. In 1879 a full external audit of the bank's affairs was undertaken and, when published, was on the whole favourably received. Only *The Economist* struck a sour note with a judgment which the 1995 business editor might endorse: 'a good set of accounts may exist with bad business'.

The most important step of all was that the bank took advantage of the Companies Act of 1879 to register, and thereby secured limited liability for its shareholders. One of Charles Gairdner's very strong beliefs was that where a bank had limited liability it should have a reserve capacity of capital immediately available to protect the note issue. Thus a special meeting called in February 1882 agreed to increase the nominal capital of the bank to £5 million, while the paid-up capital was to remain at £1 million.

In addition to difficulties created by the general conditions of the 1880s the Union Bank had a continuing problem with its share price and continued to lose out to the other Scottish banks in the proportion of its advances to its deposits. The geographical flow of business noted in Bank of Scotland was repeated almost exactly in the Union Bank. In most branches 30 to 40 per cent of deposits could be lent, and money flowed therefore to Glasgow and London. Throughout the whole period, the affairs of J. & G. Thomson required major nursing. In 1874 the firm had moved from its shipyard at Finnieston to new works at

Union Bank Office, George Street, Edinburgh, by David Bryce

Dalmuir, Clydebank. By 1881 the advances stood in the books at £124,000, but a bad fire and delay in commissioning put the firm's future in jeopardy. Careful examination of the books led to a restructuring of the firm, which was relaunched as a public company in 1889. The background against which Thomson's emerged in 1889 as the most modern yard on the Clyde, and Clydebank itself as a 'new' town, was the phenomenal growth in iron shipbuilding on the Clyde after 1860. In the 1880s mild steel replaced iron in hull construction, and Clydeside yards built one-third of all British merchant tonnage, which was 18 per cent of the world total. By 1885 the Union Bank had declined from second place to sixth in the ranking of Scottish banks and there can be little doubt therefore that Charles Gairdner's legacy was a mixed one. To the outsider he was a formidable intellectual figure who appeared to devote himself to writing papers on banking and economic subjects. Within the bank he was an austere, autocratic manager who increased the bank's investments and maintained a tight discipline on banking policy. His shortcomings as a banker are reflected in the fact that at his retiral in 1895 the advances of the Union Bank were the smallest in Scotland at precisely the time that Glasgow was developing into a world-class industrial centre.

From its establishment in December 1877 the Union Bank's London office became the main channel for translating deposits into profitable investment, mostly in colonial government or railway bonds.

Charles Gairdner's successor was Robert Blyth, who had been manager of the Scottish Amicable Life Assurance Society. He was general manager until 1910, when he retired. The most notable domestic change of these

158   years was the reconstruction of the Union's London office on the corner of Cornhill and Bishopsgate in the City of London. In 1910 Arthur C.D. Gairdner (nephew of Robert Blyth and grandson of Charles Gairdner) was appointed general manager, and in the four years before the outbreak of the First World War he began to develop new business and once again to increase the level of profitability. There was one innovation in those years for which the staff of the bank felt profoundly grateful. In 1911 the sum of £10,000 was applied to a pensions and allowances fund which was translated into a fully-fledged and funded pension and superannuation scheme. It was contributory, and from the outset included bank officers among the trustees.

	Glasgow and Union Bank	Thistle Bank	Sir William Forbes &	Paisley Union Bank	Hunters & Co., Ayr	Glasgow and Ship Bank	**Union Bank of Scotland**
	1836	1836	1838	1838	1843	1843	
paid-up capital	287,050	–	–	24,000	18,000	500,000	1,000,000
total liabilities	1,284,072	468,604	1,580,835	447,099	–	2,414,665	6,294,782
advances	480,812	213,088	824,057	137,233	–	1,789,799	4,669,414
reserve	1,344	3,300	91,500	–	–	50,030	100,000
profits	16,844	–	16,000	–	2,650	55,000	82,623
no. of partners	517	8	6	3	10	36	–
branches	14	–	4	5	8	3	29

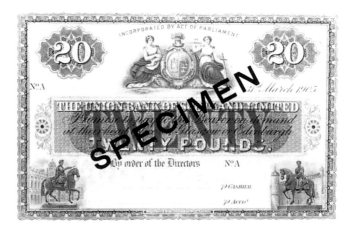

Union Bank of Scotland £20 note of 31 March 1905

—12—

EDWARDIANS AND THE FIRST WORLD WAR, 1895–1918

W HEN James Wenley retired in 1898 he had been in the service of Bank of Scotland for over fifty years, nearly twenty of them as Treasurer. His influence within the Bank, and in the wider banking community, was such that it seemed only appropriate that it should be recognised. A subscription was therefore raised during 1896 and the artist Sir George Reid was commissioned to paint his portrait – the first Treasurer to be honoured in this way. The Directors appointed George Anderson, general manager of the North of Scotland Bank, in his place. The latter had begun his banking apprenticeship at the age of 12, and for him the call to the Mound represented the highest possible pinnacle of a Scottish banking career. In many ways he exemplified the rise of the 'lad o' pairts', who is such an important symbol in Scottish lowland culture. It was his obvious energy and his success in rebuilding the North of Scotland Bank's fortunes during the 1890s which recommended him to the Governor, the Earl of Stair, and to the Directors.

George Anderson had definite views about the significance of the office of Treasurer of the Bank. In 1899 work began on a new villa, called Beechmount, on Corstorphine Road in Edinburgh. Built as a private house for Anderson, the long-term intention was that it should become the Treasurer's official residence. A copy of the pediment over the main entrance to Head Office on the Mound was created and included in the structure. At the coronation of King Edward VII in 1902, the Treasurer acted as Deputy Usher of the White Rod. This hereditary office had been vested originally in the family of Cockburn of Langton, to which James

Portrait of James Wenley by Sir George Reid

Cockburn, the Bank's second Treasurer, belonged. Later it was sold to Sir Patrick Walker of Dalry, one of the Bank's Proprietors. On the death of the last male heir, the whole estate was left in trust, the main condition of which was that an episcopal cathedral be built for the diocese of Edinburgh. St Mary's, Palmerston Place, designed by George Gilbert Scott, was the very tangible result. The trustees were the Lord Provost, the Dean of the Faculty of Advocates, the Bishop of Edinburgh and the Treasurer of Bank of Scotland. An inquiry by the Committee of Privileges ruled that in future the office of Deputy Usher of the White Rod would be performed by one of the trustees. In 1905 George Anderson received the honour of knighthood.

Behind the pomp and circumstance there were both hard work and great confidence in the Bank's underlying strength. In its way this was the best memorial to George Anderson's predecessors, David Davidson and James Wenley. Between 1896 and 1914, with the notable exceptions of 1898 and 1899, the trend of the Bank's business was upwards. The dip in 1898 coincided with and was caused by the uncertainties surrounding the start of the Boer War, but as it progressed and the Bank's customers became involved as suppliers of goods and services for the war effort, there was a rapid recovery. Similarly, the increase in naval shipbuilding after 1902 was of great benefit to the Clyde shipyards. The establishment between 1910 and 1912 of a naval dockyard for the North Sea fleet at

Rosyth, with its related destroyer base at Port Edgar, impacted strongly on the economy of southern Fife.

The published annual accounts for those years show some interesting changes. The following table extracts some of the salient features:

	Balance Sheet Total	Note Circulation	Reserve Fund	Government Securities	Overseas Investment	Net Profit	Proprietors' Dividend
1896	18,920,369	1,012,494	800,000	4,377,843	1,406,779	161,003	12 per cent
1904	20,180,997	1,111,531	900,000	4,362,619	2,897,137	202,053	13 per cent
1914	26,777,850	1,238,666	1,350,000	5,788,118	3,855,448	321,000	20 per cent

There are a number of general observations to be made on these figures. The nominal capital of the Bank was set at £4.5 million by the 1873 Bank Act, but up to 1907 the paid-up capital stood at £1,250,000 and was only increased to £1,350,000 in 1907 to deal with the absorption of the Caledonian Bank, about which more will be said below. It must also be remembered that these figures are to be seen against a backdrop of stable or declining prices. If the Retail Price Index is set at 100 in 1880, then it stood at 84 in 1914, a 16 per cent gain in value over the period. Perhaps most strikingly of all, the reserve fund, which had been instituted by Alexander Blair nearly eighty years previously, by 1914 matched the value of the paid-up capital. The relative importance of both note circulation and Government securities declined, but the Bank's overseas investments increased by a factor of 2.74.

There were two major problem areas which affected all banks: the fall in value of first-class securities, particularly Consols; and the continued difficulty of finding profitable new lending opportunities in Scottish industry. In the former case the figures in the table reflect not a reluctance to purchase Government securities – London branch was as busy as ever in this respect – but a fall in their market value. In the latter case the Glasgow office continued to be of crucial importance. In 1896, with a total of 117 branches, lending through the Glasgow office far outstripped the rest at £4,047,000, ten times that of its nearest rivals – Dundee with £472,000 and Greenock with £374,000. Within Edinburgh, New Town branch under Charles Bruce had the fastest-growing business, although it was still beaten by Head Office with £348,000. By 1914 the rank order remained unchanged, although Glasgow's lending had declined to £3,192,000 and other branches were narrowing the gap.

Commemorative medal struck by Hamilton & Inches, Edinburgh, 1897

The Bank Rifle Club on parade for Queen Victoria's Diamond Jubilee
Left: *Martini-Henry single shot lever-action rifle used by the Rifle Club, 1885 pattern*

James Gourlay's efforts resulted in lending to some of the light-engineering and other industrial firms which were beginning to prove of importance in the 1890s. Just three examples will have to serve as an illustration for a much wider spectrum of businesses. The only common connecting link was that each began from scratch and grew rapidly without the long development typical of the established heavy-engineering firms. In short, it was riskier lending, in which the parameters for success or failure were difficult to assess.

In 1896 the Bank became involved in the affairs of the British Aluminium Company, formed in 1894 with Lord Kelvin as scientific adviser. The first step to establishing the hydro-electric power necessary for the manufacture of aluminium was the purchase by the company of the Foyers Estate, which included the Falls of Foyers on the eastern side of Loch Ness. In 1896 the total world output of aluminium was 2,000 tons, but by 1903 the Foyers plant had 700 tons in stock, while costs fell by 25 per cent. By 1904 world demand for aluminium had almost doubled and British Aluminium felt confident enough to embark on a second and much larger scheme at Kinlochleven, harnessing the water power of the Blackwater group of lochs and lochans at the western end of Rannoch Moor. It was a civil engineering project matching the scale of organisation of any British railway project and took four years to complete. The pressure on the company's capital was very great and required its recapitalisation in

1910. It was estimated that the Kinlochleven works cost around £620,000 between 1906 and 1910. However, work proceeded steadily, with the running costs met by the Bank's lending system. The flavour of working conditions is captured in the atmospheric novel, *Children of the Dead End*, by Patrick McGill. It was the outbreak of war in 1914, with the upsurge in demand for aluminium for – among other uses – aircraft engines, which finally put the viability of the industry and company beyond doubt.

It was in 1895 that Messrs Barr & Stroud were granted their first overdraft facility (ever cautious, they had also secured a facility of £30,000 from the Clydesdale Bank). The success of their optical rangefinders, developed for and used primarily by the British Navy in their large warships and adopted by the Imperial Japanese Navy after 1900, required the firm to expand very rapidly. The prime requirement was not outside capital but funds to cover the cash flow of their expansion. Since in virtually every case their major customers were governments, eventual payment was more secure than most. Early premises in and around Byres Road in Glasgow, added to piecemeal, proved unsatisfactory, so in 1903 a decision was taken to build a factory on a greenfield site close to the new residential and business community developing around Anniesland Cross. The Bank sought to cement the relationship by opening a new branch at Anniesland in 1904 to service the area.

By contrast, the story of the Bank's relationship with the unsuccessful

Left: *Jute ships in Dundee harbour, c.1905 (Dundee Museum and Art Gallery)*
Right: *The battle-cruiser HMS* Indomitable, *built at Fairfield's Yard, 1908*
(Strathclyde Regional Archive)

The Earl of Stair, Governor 1870–1903, by Sir George Reid

Argyll Motor Company offered an antidote to any easy complacency about lending to new industries. It began in 1901 as Hozier Engineering, a private company with an issued capital of £8,785 and a connection formed with the Bank's Glasgow manager, first James Gourlay and, after his retiral in 1903, A.C. Robertson, his successor. The business grew steadily, but in 1905 it was decided to subsume Hozier Engineering in a newly created public company, Argyll Motors Limited, with an authorised capital of £500,000. The prime aim of the company was to build a new factory at Alexandria in Dunbartonshire with a production capacity of 2,500 cars a year. The plans were over-ambitious, the project under-capitalised, and the working money borrowed from the Bank for cash flow was being used for construction. In retrospect the financial controls and costing of the whole scheme were inadequate. In all these matters A.C. Robertson's inexperience showed, as well as the Bank's lack of experience of such ventures. Overdraft and borrowing limits were breached consistently and allowed more latitude than would have been the case for a traditional industry. In 1907 Robertson was transferred to New Town, Edinburgh, and his place in Glasgow taken by the more hard-nosed James Bissett. It is clear that the Alexandria factory never reached its planned output; at most, 1,000 cars were produced in 1907, and with the downturn in the motor trade at the beginning of 1908 many of these were unsold. The company was forced into liquidation, and it is a measure of Bissett's thoroughness that the Bank's final losses were only £50,000, despite the fact that 18 months previously overdrafts and borrowings had stood at £200,000.

It would be a mistake to draw too many rigid conclusions from comparing just three examples. All they had in common was that each was involved in the new technologies of the early 1900s. The problems of the British Aluminium Company were essentially those of funding and building a large-scale civil engineering project and then matching the outcome to successful industrial production. Barr & Stroud were selling patented products which, once their worth was proven, had an assured, Government-backed market with no British competitors. Argyll was selling a consumer product into a market in which it had many rivals. Reliability, manufacturing quality, design, fashion and cost were all elements in a complex equation for which there was little precedent for the Bank's managers to call on. What was different was the sheer scale of the financial resources required to bring such projects to completion.

It was such considerations, coupled with the decline in value of reserves held in Government stock, which told most severely on the Caledonian,

166 the smallest of the Scottish banks. By 1900 the bank was in decline, unbeknown to the public in the Highlands. It had been founded in 1838 in Inverness with a nominal capital of £125,000, of which one-quarter was paid up. A network of some 20 branches was created between 1838 and 1845 in the towns around the Moray Firth and in the main settlements of Caithness and Wester Ross. As the Caledonian expanded eastwards into Buchan it came into dispute with the Aberdeen-based North of Scotland Bank. Despite raising its capital to £75,000 it was able to maintain its business but not to expand beyond its geographical core. Its main shareholders and customers were to be found among Highland gentlemen and farmers. Its business was among farmers, fishermen, grain factors, whisky distillers and summer visitors. Anyone attempting to trace its interconnections in detail needs a Highland appreciation of the ramifications of the various Grant, Gordon and Ross family trees. The bank's head office was built in Inverness High Street in 1847 to the design of Mackenzie and Matthews. It is a splendid building with huge urns at either side of the building with garlanded portraits of Queen Victoria and Prince Albert. The tympanum, carved by A. Handyside Ritchie, has allegorical figures showing the wealth of land and sea. Its authorised note issue was set at £53,434 by the 1845 Act and throughout its life there was only one design type, engraved on steel by W.H. Lizars. The Gaelic motto round the border reads 'Tir nam Beann, nan Gleann, s'nan Gaisgeach' (Land of Mountains, Glens and

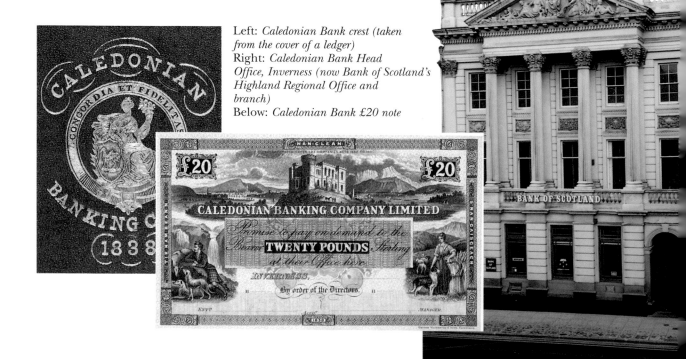

Left: Caledonian Bank crest (taken from the cover of a ledger)
Right: Caledonian Bank Head Office, Inverness (now Bank of Scotland's Highland Regional Office and branch)
Below: Caledonian Bank £20 note

Barr & Stroud's new factory at Anniesland Cross, c.1910 (Messrs Barr & Stroud)
A 1907 Argyll motor car with Aberdeen owners (Aberdeen Press and Journal)

Heroes). Until the collapse of the City of Glasgow Bank in 1878 there appear to have been no major problems, and its network expanded to 34 branches, including Portree and Stornoway. The possible extent of the bank's liability, as a result of taking £400 of City of Glasgow Bank stock on security, caused a panic among the shareholders, and it was forced to close its doors on 5 December 1878. Bank of Scotland loaned money to tide it over; and this, with the realisation that the extent of liability would be only £11,000, allowed it to reopen in August 1879. In 1882 the bank registered under the Companies Act but it was permanently crippled. By 1896 its total capital and reserve stood at £222,000, with deposits of £1,065,000, liabilities of £1,223,000 and a net profit of £14,000. By 1907 reserve and profits had declined to £195,000 and £12,000 respectively. Problems with Government securities have been mentioned already, but the other major problem was that investment and lending controls were very lax. It has to be said that a number of famous Highland distilleries would not have been built had the attitudes of Glasgow or Edinburgh prevailed. Most seriously, one-third of the bad debt of head office, Inverness, was the result of just one investment, the Scottish India Coffee Company. This project began in the early 1870s to develop tea and coffee plantations in virgin jungle in Madras province. The problems were huge, the major one being that the cost of developing the infrastructure to get the product out had been seriously underestimated. During the 1880s and '90s money was poured into the project without profit and finally, in 1902, the company went into liquidation, leaving the Caledonian Bank with a debt of £300,000 on its books. In 1906 the Caledonian directors approached Bank of Scotland to

168   ask for union. Caledonian Bank stock was exchanged for Bank of Scotland stock after approval of the Proprietors at a special meeting in 1907.

The contrast with Bank of Scotland's confidence could not have been greater. At the Annual General Meeting of 1905 the Governor, Lord Balfour, declared the 1904/5 results to be the 'best the Bank has ever had'. The dividend to Proprietors was matched by a 10 per cent bonus on salaries to all members of staff 'down to the youngest apprentice'.

Although there is a photographic record of all Bank officials from the 1870s, it is only from around 1900 that they begin to emerge as something more than simply names in a salary book. In 1897 A.W. Morton Beveridge (later Treasurer) and a group of like-minded young colleagues formed a debating and discussion group which met in a flat in Marchmont, Edinburgh, to consider the important issues of the day. The minutes of the Seven Club reveal that the range of interests was very wide: politics, theology, art and literature all appear among the topics prepared for discussion. By 1914 the membership had changed to include as secretary John Duncanson; and the last recorded meeting was in October 1914, two months after the outbreak of war. Annual dances, Burns suppers and the very popular 'smokers' were among the events in many of the larger offices. At most of these even the manager was called upon to do a turn. It was well known that the then London manager, Thomas Aitken, was a devotee of Burns songs and could always be relied upon for such occasions.

In 1908 Andrew Shirlaw, a clerk in the Ledger Department, began to caricature his colleagues in the London office in a volume which was known as Ledger 99 and whose existence was an open secret. They provide a running commentary on the personal characteristics of his immediate colleagues and on themes well known to any banker: late-night work trying to find the difference when posting the ledger, the lost deposit receipt, and the office manager's lectures on procedures (and personal conduct). The outbreak of war in August 1914 gave an edge to the cartoons which had been missing before. Leo Spaeth, who had worked in the Bank's investment department since 1887 and was meticulous (Germanic) in his habits, received more than his fair share of comment. The period was in any case a difficult one for adjustment within the office since the new London manager, appointed on 11 February 1914, was William Smiles, a name belied by nature (to his juniors at any rate). He had come up through the ranks, and doubts existed about his abilities.

It may seem churlish to criticise the Bank at a time when its success was assured and seemed comparatively easy, but the records and correspondence of the years between 1910 and 1914 convey an impression of increasing complacency. There was a growing lack of direction from the Treasurer, whose hunger for business had been sapped by the civilities of Edinburgh life. At the start of war on 4 August 1914 the Governor, Lord Balfour of Burleigh, was one of two Scottish bankers who went to London to explain to the Treasury the significance of the Scottish note issue. The Treasurer, on the other hand, dealt with the details of financial policy with the Bank of England. The Annual Report for 1914, presented to the Annual General Meeting in April 1915, showed just how quickly the situation had changed. There was a decline in profits which, although unstated, was due to diminished business volume in the London office and some particularly bad debts. The decline of Consols was continuing and some £70,000 was taken out of the declared profit and £200,000 from reserves to be put in the investment account to counteract depreciation. On the bonus side, both the volume of deposits and the note issue had risen sharply and the Bank had subscribed (as it was bound to do) some £2 million to the first War Loan in November 1914. The net result was a reduction in profits and a reduction in the Proprietors' dividend to 16 per cent with tax deducted. The major problem for the future was seen to be the decline in business lending and the rapid accumulation of deposits for which a 'safe and profitable' home had to be found.

The trends noted in 1915 continued throughout the war, the most dramatic change being in the proportion of Government stock held as investment. In 1913 it had stood at between 25 and 30 per cent of the total, by 1916 at over 50 per cent, and with the sale of dollar-based and Latin American stock, and losses in Russia as a result of the 1917 Revolution, it was over 90 per

Right: *Programmes for Dinners and Entertainments from towards the end of the nineteenth century*

Below: *William Smiles and Leo Spaeth, Bank of Scotland's London Investment team, 1910-14*

Bank of Scotland £1 note, January 1914
(this design remained substantially unchanged
from its introduction in 1885 until 1963)

The first women employees . . .

cent by 1919. Continued depreciation meant steady transfers from reserves into the investment account. In all of this, Bank of Scotland's story was no different from that of every other bank.

In spring 1916 John Rae was appointed Assistant Treasurer and became Treasurer later in the year. It was quickly established that a special fund, which was not revealed to the Proprietors, had been created to cover the bad and doubtful debts of the London office. In 1915 this stood at £1,460,000. John Rae's task was to get a grip on all the Bank's business and get it back on course. If London was the main problem area, Glasgow was another worry. The heavy industries on Clydeside prospered, but the Glasgow office was not able to increase lending on overdraft, which remained at around £1.4 million throughout the war.

For the Bank staff the war years produced steady reductions in their numbers. Among the first to go to war were members of No. 7 Company, the 4th Battalion the Royal Scots, before 1908 known as the Bankers Company, the Queen's Edinburgh Rifle Volunteers. Many of these men were sharpshooters (one result of Bank rifle clubs and competitions) and they covered the retreat to Mons. At the beginning, volunteering meant resigning from the Bank's service with no guarantee of re-employment. However, this was quickly changed. When compulsory registration for military service was instituted in 1915 there was still sufficient enthusiasm for the war effort for men of military age to hope that their services to the Bank would not be declared essential. The prospect of being left among the old men was not an attractive one. Women first appeared on the Bank staff during the spring of 1916. For the men who had not gone to the war the appearance of women provoked a mixture of hopes and fears. Initially women were employed in the correspondence department, and in the larger offices were supervised by a formidable school-marmish figure or, in the case of Glasgow Office, a minister, to ensure suitable discipline. The London Office, which contained a number of elderly bachelors, provided much material for Andrew Shirlaw's pen. The head of ledgers, Edmonstone Smith, became positively skittish and gallant. Leo Spaeth, on the other hand, pretended that nothing had changed. So far as the war itself was concerned, in 1916 few could foresee its end. Shirlaw was convinced that it would still be going on in 1940, and that the Bank would by then have female bank managers. In fact, the Bank was extremely reluctant to employ women. Gaps in the staff were filled in the first instance by under-age apprentices, but this merely postponed the problem as these boys became eligible for military service. Even by Armistice Day in 1918 there were only 39 women employees out of a staff total of 804. The many gaps in the ranks of friends and colleagues are commemorated in the war memorials in Edinburgh at Head Office, the Mound, and 38 St Andrew Square and in Glasgow at 110 St Vincent Street, while those returning in 1919 tried to readjust to the business of being a bank clerk once again.

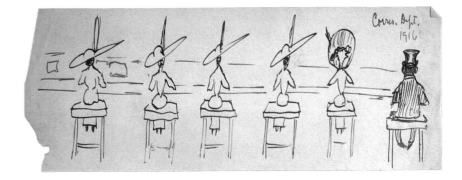

. . . as seen by Andrew Shirlaw

The architect James Miller's designs
for the exterior and banking hall of the Union Bank Head Office,
110 St Vincent Street, Glasgow, built 1925-27, now Bank of Scotland's Glasgow Chief Office

—13—
BETWEEN THE WARS, 1918–45

HE return to 'normality' after the war, which was the expectation of British business and the strongest hope of ordinary people, proved to be a will o' the wisp. Bank of Scotland found that peace brought a new situation, one which was less comfortable and required new solutions. Its very place in the Scottish banking firmament had changed. The Clydesdale Bank's lending in Glasgow had expanded and overtaken that of Bank of Scotland. By every other banking measure the Royal Bank of Scotland had moved into pole position. Both the Governor, Lord Balfour of Burleigh, and the new Treasurer, John Rae, were well aware of all of this. They knew (and persuaded the Board of Directors) that their prime tasks were to overcome the inertia which had developed; to eliminate by new legislation some of the constraints imposed by the Bank of Scotland Acts of 1695 and 1873 on the Bank's approach to business; to reshape both the lending and the investment books; and finally to conduct a detailed review of the Bank's management. From this period major internal policy decisions were taken jointly by the Governor and Treasurer outwith the formal structure of the Bank's governance and presented to the Board only as a matter of report. Any attempt therefore to write the Bank's history solely from minute books would be drowned in a slough of detail, with few indications of major strategy or decisions. What neither Governor nor Treasurer could control were the external circumstances in which the Bank was operating.

One striking feature of pre-war German banking which recommended itself to British bankers was the close link between German overseas trade, foreign policy and banking support. This gave a unity of purpose to

*1920s branch interior, 191 Ingram
Street, Glasgow
John Rae, Treasurer 1916-20
(National Westminster Bank)*

foreign ventures such as the construction of the Berlin to Baghdad Railway
between 1890 and 1910, and to the national prestige involved in the setting
up of Banco Aléman Transatlantico in South America by Deutsche Bank.
By contrast, Britain's efforts were much more piecemeal. The Farrington
Commission of 1916 recommended that British banks take joint action to
secure a higher proportion of foreign trade finance. James Tuke of The
British Linen Bank and Arthur Gairdner of the Union Bank proposed a
Scottish Foreign Exchange Bank, based in London, in which all the
Scottish banks would participate as shareholders and which could provide
a full foreign service for all. The proposal came to nothing, in part because
the National Bank and the Clydesdale had already received approaches
from Lloyds Bank and the Midland Bank respectively which were to lead
to amalgamation in 1918 and 1920. Similarly, The British Linen Bank
became a subsidiary of Barclays Bank in 1919. Each of these large English
banks was in the process of developing its own foreign department and was
not particularly interested in a joint venture which might prove to be a
competitor. For Bank of Scotland the problem related directly back to its
Founding Act and to regulations which effectively debarred the Bank from
taking a direct shareholding in another trading venture.

The takeovers of Scottish banks between 1918 and 1922 did not
contravene the guidelines laid down by the Colwyn Committee of 1918, of
which the Bank's Treasurer, John Rae, was a member. The main purpose
of the Colwyn Report was to limit amalgamations in both England and
Scotland which might tend towards a monopoly. In future they would

require the approval of both the Treasury and the Board of Trade. It was for this reason, and seeing the way in which the banking world appeared to be moving, that Bank of Scotland and the Union Bank did no more than skate around the possibility of a merger in 1919–20.

In fact the Bank's response to all of this was the Bank of Scotland (1920) Act. This was a major reordering of the Bank's structure and an extension of its powers. It was not necessary to increase the Bank's nominal capital, which remained at £4.5 million. The equivalent of the articles of association of a limited company were adopted, bringing the Bank into line with UK company law. For the first time the Bank was permitted to open branches in other countries, take a direct share in public works, conduct the business of any of the Bank's debtors and act as trustee for any bank customer who wished to make use of the service. Other clauses and rights were abolished, most famously the final clause of the 1695 Act which allowed those becoming Bank Proprietors to acquire Scottish nationality. This clause had not been invoked since 1822, and a century later it was simply an anachronism. Ironically, the most significant item for the Bank's future customer base was contained not in the Bank Act but in the Married Women's Property (Scotland) Act of the same year, which for the first time gave married women equal legal status with men and unmarried women in contractual agreements.

Behind the scenes serious efforts were made to remedy the deficiencies of the London management and bring one vital area of the Bank's business into good order. William Smiles, the manager, retired in 1918 and was succeeded by William Whitelaw Johnston. Although he had been in the London office since 1900, Johnston had served his apprenticeship in the Airdrie branch and was schooled in the Scottish banking tradition. In this he was unlike the earlier generation of London senior management, who had mostly been recruited locally from other London-based banks and businesses. The major tactic was to increase the unpublished fund for losses from £1,307,000 in 1916 to nearly £3 million in 1921 to permit all irretrievable loans, mostly in Latin America and Mexico, to be written off the books by a target date of 1922. Thereafter the fund would be required to deal only with a current year's problems, not with an historical overhang of debt. The continuing decline in value of Government securities required steady transfers from the published reserve fund between 1918 and 1922, which in 1921 fell to an all-time low of £550,000, less than half its 1914 amount.

As is often the case, neither Lord Balfour nor John Rae saw the results of their efforts. In April 1920 Rae accepted an offer to become general

176 manager of London, County Westminster and Parr's Bank, one of the most important of the English amalgamations, which had taken place in 1918. Rae's services and advice to Bank of Scotland were so valued that he was invited to become a Director, a position which he held until his death in 1932. Lord Balfour, the Governor, died in 1921. His successor was William J. Mure, WS, who had been a Director of the Bank since 1887, Deputy Governor since 1917, and who had played a large part in the actual drafting of the 1920 Bank of Scotland Act. Mure's period of office was short; he died in 1924 and was succeeded by the Deputy Governor, Lord Elphinstone.

The pattern of care and caution is also apparent if the structure of the Bank's major lending is examined between 1919 and 1922. The relative dominance of the Glasgow office continued to decline and there is little evidence of large-scale lending into the staple industries of Clydeside – coal, steel and shipbuilding. On the contrary, there is strong evidence of a deliberate attempt to spread lending, both geographically and by sector, to produce what John Rae described in 1919 as a 'balanced' loan structure. Among the Bank's most prominent borrowers of this period were: the Airdrie Savings Bank; the Burmah Oil Company; Barry, Ostlere & Shepherd of Kirkcaldy, linoleum manufacturers; Stoddards of Paisley, carpet manufacturers; Glasgow's *Daily Record*; the Highland Railway Company; Tate & Lyle, sugar refiners; the Clyde Navigation Company; and the New Zealand and Australia Land Company Limited. One large group of loans, £3.5 million in total, was made to the Canadian Bank of Commerce for Canadian railway development. These loans were secured against the stock of the Canadian Northern Railway Company and the Canadian Northern Pacific Railway Company. The single largest facility, granted on 10 January 1922, was £4.5 million to Standard Life Assurance Company of Edinburgh. Perhaps the most forward-looking, if ultimately unsuccessful, was a loan of £5,000 to Hamilton's Aerial Railway Syndicate Limited to build a test installation for a propeller-driven overhead railway. The result of these experiments (more usually known as George Bennie's Airspeed Railway) stood abandoned in a field, visible to all into the 1950s.

When George John Scott, who had been general manager of the Union Bank of Scotland for barely a year, accepted the treasurership of Bank of Scotland in 1920, much of the groundwork for recovery had been laid. This showed through on the balance sheets from 1923, when profits for division among Proprietors began to climb slowly from a low of £144,400 in 1919–22, but even by 1939 they had still not reached their 1912 level. It must also be remembered that the inflation rate reached 20 per cent in

1920 before being sharply dragged back with the onset of the post-war depression. The year 1920 was also notable for being the last in which the Bank's reserves in gold were actually held at the Mound. The sums of money held by the Bank against the non-authorised note issue were thereafter held in the Bank of England in the form of currency notes and currency note certificates.

Within Scotland there could be little real competition between banks, since the meeting of general managers in 1924 effectively agreed deposit and lending rates and renewed the 50-year-old agreement not to poach each other's customers. That said, it was hoped that when George John Scott was appointed Treasurer of the Bank in 1920 he would bring with him contacts from the heavy industries in the West. His correspondence certainly indicates assiduous cultivation, but no success. In fact, for most of the 1920s, retrenchment, reduction of loans, and reorganisation were the order of the day for most shipbuilders and the industries which depended upon them, steel-making and coal-mining. The only possible room for Bank expansion was in new deposit accounts, an area in which Bank of Scotland was in direct competition with the municipal savings banks. There was therefore a direct push to establish a more comprehensive branch network. In 1920 the Bank had 179 branches, only five more than in 1910. By 1930 this had grown to 240 branches and sub-branches, and the total reached 266 in 1939. Since the prime purpose was to attract savings, many of these offices were based in the new residential suburbs of Scotland's cities or in areas where the Bank had not previously been represented. This was backed up in 1927 by the introduction of an interest-paying savings account with passbooks for the convenience of small-scale depositors. Not all branches achieved the Bank's hopes for them. In 1924 the Bank opened a sub-branch at Leverburgh in Harris, the site of Lord Leverhulme's plans for helping to revitalise the Outer Hebrides. While a permanent site for the Bank house was being considered, the Bank rented a small piece of ground at ten pounds a year and erected a wooden hut there (at a cost of £583) as a temporary measure. Leverburgh never fulfilled Leverhulme's visions for it, and the Bank's sub-branch remained in its temporary hut, the smallest branch building of all, until it finally closed in 1994.

One other possible way of increasing the Bank's business was by amalgamation with other banks in Scotland which had a complementary spread of branches, provided the result did not contravene the Colwyn guidelines. In 1924 George John Scott opened preliminary negotiations with the Aberdeen-based North of Scotland Bank. When this came to

178 nothing, negotiations were begun with a bank Scott knew a great deal about, the Union Bank of Scotland, whose general manager, Norman Hird, had been Scott's deputy at the Union Bank's London office in Cornhill. The discussions went on, with varying degrees of intensity, up to 1930, when they were finally abandoned. It was in June 1927 that the boards of both banks had been closest to agreeing terms for merger. There was, however, one part of the price that Bank of Scotland was not prepared to pay: Norman Hird as Treasurer of Bank of Scotland, not then . . . or ever.

This reaction, which was little short of personal antipathy, requires some explanation. Norman Hird, appointed general manager of the Union Bank in 1920 at the age of 34, was both the dominant, and in many ways the most forward-looking, of the Scottish general bank managers of his generation. Apart from his youth, a fault which only time could remedy, the impression which comes down the years is of a man sure of his own abilities, who saw no reason to temper his views either for other general managers or for directors. He was also impatient and imperious with his own senior staff and, like all general managers of his time, Olympian to lesser mortals. Apart from a brief period in the Inspection Department between 1911 and 1914, almost all his career had been spent as an investment banker in London, and the evidence suggests that he was uncomfortable with the routine elements of retail banking – deposit-taking and lending. The minutes of the Union Bank board and the large loan book make it clear that it continued to lose ground to its rivals during the 1920s and '30s. On the other hand, it was Hird's investment abilities which prevented any greater crisis. Once again this has been quantified by Norio Tamaki in the following table which is derived from published annual accounts:

Money-box from Bank of Scotland Young Persons advertising of the 1930s (children hated the boxes as they could only be opened by the Bank)

Comparisons of Asset Management under Three General Managerships

Advances, Investments and Liquid Assets as Percentages of Deposits

	(1) *Advances*		‡(2) *Investments*		(3) *Liquid Assets*	
	(a)*	(b)†	(a)	(b)	(a)	(b)
Blyth (1895-1910)	63%	72%	23%	25%	36%	29%
Gairdner (1910-19)	62	57	29	35	31	31
Hird (1920-45)	40	42	56	53	24	26

*Union Bank   †Scottish total   ‡Figures are average of each tenure

Investments were actually five times greater in 1939 than in 1920, but advances as a percentage of deposits were never more than 40 per cent and had slipped to 16.6 per cent by 1945. Hird's technique was to explore new services and areas for expansion. The Union Bank was the first Scottish bank to establish a foreign exchange department and an independent trustee department; and it was the first to establish a bank nominee company. His attempts in 1924 to make the services of the Union Bank more widely known were regarded by the other banks' general managers as little better than competitive advertising. It followed therefore that the Union Bank was allowed little leeway by them.

Norman Hird's lasting memorial was the building of a new head office for the Union Bank in St Vincent Street, Glasgow (now Bank of Scotland's Glasgow Chief Office). The design was the result of an architectural competition, won by the Scottish architect James Miller, who submitted it as his diploma work for the Royal Scottish Academy in 1930. The brief, in which Norman Hird had a very large hand, was prepared as the result of a three-month fact-finding trip which he made to the United States during 1923, and incorporated the latest American thinking in bank design. Both architect and general manager had a clear idea of what they wished to achieve, and on the whole they worked harmoniously. On 17 March 1926 the foundation stone was laid by Viscount Novar on the site of the former St Mary's Buildings at the corner of St Vincent Street and Renfield Street. The design, usually described as American classical, could stand comparison with banks in New York or Chicago. It was in fact derived from York and Sawyer's 1913 Guaranty Trust Building in New York. The massive Ionic columns give an impression of elegant solidity, while the banking hall, with *forêt de brousse* marble and top-lit atrium, is handsome and spacious. On 4 November 1927 the building was visited by the Prince of Wales, and business was transferred from Ingram Street in December.

Union Bank of Scotland advertising of the 1920s and 1930s

179

180   The final cost of £232,000 was well within the acceptable margins of the original estimate of £215,000. The building was a massive public statement of confidence in the bank's future. A cynical comment would be that it contained a larger than usual amount of Glasgow window-dressing, whose consequences reverberated on the rest of the bank's property. Few branches were permitted to receive more than distress maintenance before 1955.

If there was one matter on which, even in 1930, Bank of Scotland and the Union Bank were united it was the need to maintain the Scottish independence of the two banks. This is explicit in a letter written by the Governor, Lord Elphinstone, to Viscount Novar, chairman of the Union Bank, in 1930:

> It is, I think, very important that we keep constantly before us the main object sought to be gained by the amalgamation of the two banks, viz. the formation of a large institution which, both from the size of its resources, and from the widespread network . . . would appeal to the Scottish people as in every sense a national institution.

The character of the Scottish banks' lending and investment policies was the subject of inquiry by the Macmillan Committee of Parliament in the 1930s. Among those serving on the Committee were John Maynard Keynes and Ernest Bevin. The major issue of the inquiry was whether bank lending policies in general had stifled investment in British industry and had therefore played a large part in the general depression of the second half of the 1920s. George John Scott appeared for Bank of Scotland. Reading through the printed reports of the proceedings it is difficult to escape the conclusion that the Scottish financial orthodoxy propounded by Scott in many cases missed the whole point of the inquiry. The Scottish bank-note issue was raised and defended. Scott pointed out that one of Bank of Scotland's problems, one which he believed it shared with most Scottish banks, was the difficulty of finding safe industrial investment. One of the ironies of the concentration of British industry into larger conglomerates might well be that it restricted the ability of smaller banks to provide the total level of investment required. Although not known to Scott, this was the experience of the Union Bank when it lost most of the Tennant family's business accounts in the creation of ICI in 1926–27.

It was also unfortunate that the Bank should create such a poor impression of itself and its relations with Scottish industry in the very year that John Craig, chairman of Colvilles the steelmakers, joined the Board, to be followed in 1934 by Samuel C. Hogarth, the Glasgow shipowner. John Craig joined the Board at the point at which Colvilles Ltd was created to

Norman Hird, General Manager of the Union Bank of Scotland 1920-45

Below: *The corner of Renfield Street and St Vincent Street, Glasgow, pre-1920 (Strathclyde Regional Archives)*

hasten the concentration of the Scottish iron and steel industry. Thereafter the affairs of Scottish shipbuilding and steelmaking companies were never allowed to stray far from Bank of Scotland's attention.

As if to consolidate the Glasgow connection, when in 1934 George John Scott announced his intention of retiring, he was succeeded as Treasurer by Alexander Morton Beveridge, who prior to being Deputy Treasurer had spent four years as manager of the Glasgow office. Scott's parting legacy to the Bank was to print privately *The Valley of Enchantment,* a collection of papers he had written on literary subjects over the years. The Directors, staff and pensioners each received a copy. It is a measure of the total size of the Bank in the 1930s that 1,366 copies were sufficient.

At the Annual General Meeting of 1933 Lord Elphinstone's statement to the Proprietors produced a summary of Bank of Scotland's situation and attitudes. The depression in the world economy and the abandonment of free trade meant the return of economic nationalism. As with all banks, deposits showed a substantial increase and, equally predictably, lending was down. Put simply, there was more credit available for investment than most companies wished to use. The only real sector for improvement was agricultural lending, which began to pick up from 1930. For the first time the Proprietors were presented with details of the Bank's lending, as set out in the table below.

Bank of Scotland Advances, Year End 1933
in £s sterling

Designation	Total Amount	Portion of Advances Unsecured
	£	£
Farmers and Livestock Salesman	1,202,000	340,000
Timber and Fishing	168,000	33,000
Produce Import, Grain, etc.	277,000	22,000
Iron, Coal, Steel, Quarrying; Engineering, Gas, Electricity, Motors; Shipping and Shipbuilding	1,379,000	287,000
Textile, Jute, Leather, Chemicals, etc. Manufacturers	574,000	93,000
Merchants, Distillers and Brewers	1,359,000	230,000
Stockbrokers, Insurance and Investment Companies, and Advances on Stocks and Shares	3,158,000	232,000
Public Accounts	197,000	54,000
Those not classified:		
(a) for general business purposes	862,000	264,000
(b) for private purposes	1,231,000	229,000
	10,407,000	1,784,000
		to 5,448 borrowers

Source: Bank of Scotland, Annual General Meeting of Proprietors, 1933

The overall impression is one of cautiousness and no change in the policies which had been put in place in 1920. They produced average annual net profits of £300,000 in the second half of the 1930s.

High policy and Government committees were very far removed from the hopeful 17-year-olds who began their apprenticeships, usually at twenty pounds a year, during the 1920s and '30s. Within every branch the inspection system ensured a large emphasis on the accuracy and elegance of routine work. In many branches the conditions of work were spartan or worse. But the purpose of apprenticeship was to admit the newcomer into the arcane mysteries of banking. It involved tasks like filling coal buckets, sweeping steps, polishing brass, filling ink-wells, putting new blotting paper in blotters, and making sure that there was an adequate supply of pen-nibs for making up the journal and eventually balancing the ledger. There was great pride in the appearance of a branch's books, and many a Glasgow or Edinburgh apprentice attended handwriting classes at Skerry's Commercial College. Each branch was usually presided over by an agent, who had an independence of action which the modern bank manager does not, and who was assisted by an accountant and a number of tellers, dependent upon the size of the branch. Their habits and eccentricities have formed a vital part of the memories recorded in the Bank's oral history programme, which was begun in 1987 to supplement the formal records with the reminiscences of former Bank staff. Charles Tennant recalled that on the first day of his apprenticeship he had to cross by ferry from Rhu to Greenock, climb the hill and present himself to the Union Bank agent. He was kept waiting for over two hours and received only the briefest of introductions because on a Monday morning the branch 'was a financial Niagara' with money pouring in. Timid enquiry revealed that the cause was the Saturday takings from Greenock and District Co-op, and that the total on this occasion was £173-odd. Despite the public image of po-faced sobriety, behind the scenes there was a good deal of fun among the younger members of staff. The lunch-break provided the opportunity for playing football or 'keepie-uppie' with a paper ball, using the manager's door as goal-posts (washing marks off the wall was also part of the apprentice's lot). The technical innovation of the pass-book and the replacement of Victorian whale-back counters with flat ones allowed shove ha'penny to be played, and table tennis using the pass-books as bats. When comparing various accounts of those days the overwhelming impression is of the sheer volume of routine clerical drudgery which was part and parcel of branch banking. For all Bank of Scotland staff, the last two weeks in February are particularly remembered as a fraught and tense time. The requirements of the annual balance ensured that most people worked well into the late evening, and midnight was not unknown for the final return home.

It is perhaps too easily forgotten that banks could pick and choose their staff and that throughout the inter-war period the rapid expansion of branch networks relied upon cheap clerical labour. In 1921 Bank of Scotland introduced a Joint Council of Staff and Directors, which evolved into the Staff Association, whose purpose was 'to secure co-operation in the domestic affairs of the Bank'. Retirement pensions and widows' funds were placed on a more independent and secure footing in 1926, when a staff assurance scheme was introduced. The Bank's contribution was 30 per cent of the life policy premium. The Staff Association was a direct response to the British Bankers Association, founded in 1919, and to the

184 spread of trade unionism among Scottish bank clerks. Discontent with conditions of service built up during the 1920s and '30s and came to a head in the bank strike of 30 April 1937. It had collapsed by 10 a.m. in Glasgow, largely as a result of the hard line taken by Norman Hird with Union Bank staff, and throughout Scotland it was all over by lunch-time. The strike cost the Union Bank one of its major customers. The Scottish Co-operative movement had warned Norman Hird that they would move all their accounts if the strike was broken. Hird believed that no other Scottish bank would accept them. He was wrong. It is a measure of his unpopularity with fellow general managers that the Commercial Bank welcomed the Co-op without hesitation. On the afternoon of the strike Bank of Scotland responded by raising general salary levels and relaxing the rules on the age and salary at which a banker might be permitted to marry. To modern eyes this is a very curious restriction. Initially, it had grown out of the formal apprenticeship contract, which specifically debarred the Bank apprentice from marriage until his indentures had been completed. In the twentieth century this became generalised into a principle that a banker should not marry until there was little possibility that his family and business obligations would produce conflicts of loyalty.

For most men in the 18 to 30 age group within the Bank the period of the late 1930s was one of not 'if' war returns but 'when'. Re-armament had

John Brown's Shipyard, Clydebank, c.1939 (Evening Times)

been taking place in Britain since 1936, and in the aftermath of the Munich crisis of 1938 many joined the territorial battalion of their locally recruited regiment. By the spring of 1939 the general managers of the eight Scottish banks had finalised their war plans. Account balances were to be carried in duplicate, air raid precautions were taken, and staff were trained in fire drill. The banks agreed that no new branches would be opened and, where appropriate and by mutual agreement, sub-offices would be closed. Moreover, for the duration of the war, branches would lend cash to each other and all banks would reissue each other's notes. Bank of Scotland negotiated additional borrowing rights of £700,000 with the Bank of England. The Currency Defence Act made Scottish bank-notes legal tender and Bank of Scotland became the most important note issuer in Scotland: in 1939 the Bank's total had been £23.7 million; by 1945 it had gone up to £65.9 million. This arose partly from firms wishing to hold larger than normal cash balances and partly from the increased demand for notes to pay weekly wages. Government regulation, in the form of control of lending, exchange control and the absorption of deposits into the overriding priority of the war effort, was in place by July 1940. There was little leeway for discretion. By far and away the largest loans made by the Bank were to Barr & Stroud. By 1945 these stood at over £1 million, split between the Piccadilly and Anniesland branches, while other support was available to the company as necessary. The second major area of investment was in agriculture, which, with the high demand for home-produced cereals and animal products, boomed. This rapidly became a vital element of the Bank's lending book, an element of great importance for the next four decades.

In 1938 Morton Beveridge retired as Treasurer and his place was taken by his deputy, J.W. Macfarlane, who had also served a period of time in the Glasgow office. He in turn retired in 1942, to be succeeded by J.B. Crawford.

The war experiences of individual members of the Bank varied greatly, and most were reluctant to give details for the oral history project. Experience depended on being in a particular place at a particular point in time. For some of the 1938 Territorials the story included St Valery and German prisoner-of-war camps; for others, Singapore and Changi; for yet others with the Highland and Lowland Divisions, it was North Africa, Tobruk, Italy and France. Some members of the Bank served on the Murmansk or North Atlantic convoys or saw action with the RAF. Unlike those in the First World War, many Bank staff left behind were also in the front line: a number of Clydeside offices were damaged in the Clydebank blitz, and the London office only just escaped. As men were called up, their duties were taken over, as in the First World War, by women, at first

186 on temporary employment. There was, however, an increasing recognition that, whatever the outcome of the war, female employment within the Bank was likely to be a permanent fact of life.

Napier Street, Clydebank, after the Blitz of 13-14 March 1941
(Clydebank District Libraries)

—14—
BANK OF SCOTLAND,
1945–58

BANK of Scotland's 249th Annual General Meeting fell on 3 April 1945. When he presented the Annual Accounts to the Proprietors, the Governor, Lord Elphinstone, was optimistic. The war in Europe was coming to an end, and although few could have foreseen the atomic bombing of Hiroshima and Nagasaki which ended the war with Japan in August 1945, the task ahead for the Bank was clear. The mistakes of 1919–20 were not to be repeated. The high level of wartime savings in the country seemed to indicate that with prudence the reconstruction of industry and the recovery of the country could be achieved within five years. The key themes were a determination to avoid in future the unemployment of the 1930s and the waste of resources which that represented, and a conviction that co-operation between industry, unions and finance offered the best way forward. During 1944–45 the Bank had participated in the creation of both the Finance Corporation for Industry and the Industrial and Commercial Finance Corporation. These had been devised, as a direct result of criticism levelled at the banks by the Macmillan Committee of 1931, to provide medium and long-term assistance to industry in situations where ordinary bank loans or advances would not be appropriate. Lord Elphinstone revealed that the Bank's 250th anniversary on 17 July 1945 would be celebrated by an additional 2 per cent dividend on the half-yearly payment to Proprietors; that a history of the Bank had been commissioned from Charles Malcolm, the Signet Librarian, to be published in 1946 (because of the paper shortage it did not appear until 1948); and that a silver casket of Celtic design had been commissioned

Sidney Herbert, sixteenth Baron Elphinstone, Governor 1924-55,
by P.A. de Laszlo (1931)

from the Edinburgh silversmiths Hamilton & Inches, paid for by contributions from the Bank's staff. The casket still occupies pride of place on the mantelpiece of the main dining-room at Head Office. Of the Bank's 1,263 permanent staff, 623 were on war service: there were 47 deaths; two were 'missing' (of whom one eventually returned); and 14 were prisoners-of-war, the majority in the Far East, whose fate was then unknown.

The return in July 1945 of a Labour Government committed to the establishment of a welfare state and to the extensive nationalisation of industry transformed both the political and the economic climate for the Bank. At its 250th Annual General Meeting on 2 April 1946 Lord Elphinstone struck a more pessimistic note. It had become clear that wartime controls would remain in place and might even be extended. The death of the Deputy Governor, Lord Henry Scott, who had been a Director since 1901, seemed to confirm the end of an era. His successor was James Gourlay, the fourth generation of his family to be associated with the Bank, his grandfather having been the first agent at Laurieston branch in Glasgow and his father manager of the Glasgow office from 1878 to 1904. Another new name on the Board of Directors was William Watson, a chartered accountant by training, but then investment partner of the fund managers, Baillie Gifford & Co., and a director of Standard Life Assurance Company. He was to become Treasurer of the Bank in 1952 and chairman of Standard Life from 1966 to 1969.

In many ways the Bank's business was radically altered by the war years. The funding of the war had required that all savings be channelled into public funds and that loans regarded as non-essential be refused. National Savings Certificates, War Bond Issues and Tax Reserve Certificates, all offering a guaranteed rate of interest and a fixed redemption date, were part of the Treasury's armoury. There was little room for manoeuvre. The effect of all this on Bank of Scotland's accounts can be seen by comparing elements from the Annual Accounts (the Bank's financial year runs from 1 March to 28 February) of 1939/40 and 1945/46.

[All figures to nearest £ sterling]	Year to end February 1939	Year to end February 1946
	£	£
Capital and Reserves	4,500,000	4,650,000
Deposits/Credit Balances	37,851,691	76,781,160
Loans	4,448,119	3,387,592
Cash and Credits at the Bank of England	3,507,518	11,746,691
Treasury Deposit Receipts	-	10,000,000
British Government Securities	24,738,089	48,727,205
Balance Sheet Totals	50,829,397	96,766,182

190   In 1939/40 loans represented 8.75 per cent of the Bank's liabilities; in 1945/46 they were 3.5 per cent. Conversely, in 1939/40 Government securities and Treasury and Bank of England deposits represented 55.6 per cent of total assets and 72.8 per cent in 1945/46. Since more than 90 per cent of investments were held as medium and long-dated British Government stock, there was an inevitable squeeze on profits. Throughout the war years the dividend was maintained, but changes in income tax (from 13.75 to 47.5 per cent) meant that the return to individual Proprietors dropped steeply.

Regulations governing capital transfers, foreign exchange and building control remained in place. This placed a heavy burden on routine banking, particularly at Head Office, at London Chief Office, George Square, Glasgow, and Reform Street, Dundee, all of which had extensive overseas business. There is very little doubt that the Directors and the Treasurer, J.B. Crawford, found the whole situation immensely frustrating and a serious constraint on forward development. Monetary management had been used by the Government since 1931 but the Bank of England (1946) Act, bringing the Bank of England under Treasury direction, gave much tighter control over the whole banking system than had hitherto been considered necessary, or even, in Scottish banking theory, desirable. In an uncharacteristically unguarded moment, Crawford compared the situation to that of John Law's Bank of France, which burst like a bubble in 1720 leaving a spectacular financial catastrophe in its wake. Most bankers were more cautious in their remarks, since the Labour Party's programme included proposals for nationalising the insurance industry and many believed that the banks would not be far behind. In practice, however, from 1946 bankers were expected to respond to a variety of controls imposed or relaxed according to a Treasury definition of 'national interest'. In the immediate aftermath of the war the priorities were to provide 'cheap' money for investment in industries vital for the export drive, to refuse all 'non-essential' loans and to control inflation by retaining a tight control over the money supply.

One major problem was that the nationalisation of coal, steel, gas, electricity, railways and road haulage between 1946 and 1949 created particular problems for Bank of Scotland. Nationalisation broke many pre-existing banking relationships and bore particularly severely on the Scottish scene because the economy, and therefore Scottish banking, was committed to these industries. Their head offices tended to become concentrated in London, and in the process all the Scottish banks found themselves on the periphery of the decision-making process, with consequently reduced lending opportunities. The Scottish banks tried to divide up the remaining business among themselves according to the share of pre-nationalisation business which each had enjoyed. The detailed negotiations were lengthy, involving correspondence and meetings between the eight Scottish banks. Above all, this was time-consuming work which had to be dealt with by J.B. Crawford, the Treasurer, who in turn required the full-time assistance of James Letham, from 1948 designated Staff Manager.

Among the Ordinary Directors the interests of industry were argued for forcefully at Board meetings by S. Crawford Hogarth, the Glasgow ship-owner, and by Sir John Craig, chairman of Colvilles, the steel-founders, who became Deputy Governor in 1950. To many at the time, the logic of these nationalisations seemed impeccable: all the industries involved were in decline, and to compete internationally they required capital investment far beyond the lending resources of any single bank. In this race Bank of Scotland became acutely aware of the limitations imposed by its size in relation to English banks and the scale of new projects. Most ordinary bank managers felt themselves caught between the millstones of Government regulation and dissatisfied business customers. It also became clear that the system of taxation on company profits did not allow for internal capital generation. As a result most companies, even family companies, increasingly looked to the Bank to provide capital for investment rather than to cover cash flow, which had been its traditional role.

Against this restrictive background the process of readjustment for those returning from war service was painful as they tried to remember half-forgotten procedures and rebuild skills which had been irrelevant for six years. To those who had been used to taking decisions quickly and dealing with men in extreme situations, the pernickety slowness and rigidity of the Bank was irksome. The more senior men in most Bank branches were of an age group which was too young to have served in the 1914–18 war and too old for 1939–45. They had often worked in difficult and, in the case of London and Clydeside branches, dangerous circumstances, but their service lacked the glamour and comradeship of those who had seen active war service, and there were inevitable tensions. Temporary workers employed during the war, mostly female, began to disappear, although a significant number were transferred to the permanent staff. So far as new recruitment was concerned, from the early 1950s considerable numbers of unmarried women were taken on. The major difference was that women tended to leave the Bank's service on marriage, or shortly afterwards, and were not expected to possess the same

192   degree of ambition as their male colleagues. In September 1950 a
      conference on education and training in banking was held in St Andrews,
      at which these different expectations were discussed openly. It should be
      said that delegates from virtually every UK bank attended and the
      conclusions may therefore be said to represent the views of bankers as a
      whole. The core of the argument was that male recruits were expected to
      have a bank service 'life' of 40 years, whereas women, experience showed,
      had a bank service 'life' of ten years. Given this, the recommended
      recruitment pattern should be roughly two women to every male, a ratio
      followed almost exactly in the Bank during 1951–55.

      The key executive figures in the routine running of the Bank were the
      Superintendent of Branches and the five inspectors who shared
      responsibility for control of the Bank's 256 branches. Their teams, who
      were based in a large room above the banking hall at Head Office,
      descended unannounced on branches either for a 'book' inspection or,
      every other year, for a full inspection of a branch's business; and from the
      moment they crossed the branch threshold nothing could be done
      without their approval. Serving a period of time in the Inspection
      Department was the only route to the upper levels of the Bank because it
      effectively supervised lending, staffing and audit functions and was
      therefore the place in which an overview of the Bank's business was
      learned. The inspectors' tales provide one of the richest veins of anecdote
      in the Bank. Up to the 1960s their very appearance was distinctive. It was
      de rigueur for an inspector to wear a bowler hat and usually a riding
      mackintosh. In the 1940s and '50s to arrive unannounced in the Western
      or Northern Isles was not possible. A message from the ship's wireless
      operator to Lochmaddy or Stornoway that there were three gentlemen
      from Edinburgh on board gave sufficient time for all the banks and
      insurance agents to be prepared by the time the boat docked. The only
      alternative was that the bowler hats were tax inspectors, a species over
      which the Outer Isles took even more care. For the local staff there was
      always a conflict between pretending to be surprised and displaying their
      normal hospitable instincts of providing tea and scones for all mainland
      visitors. It was usually the youngest member of staff who gave the game
      away. In parts of Glasgow and the West of Scotland the bowler hat
      conveyed (and still conveys) an even less welcome message. Young
      inspectors had to be very careful about the public houses they used when
      'in uniform'. Much of the Bank's correspondence with Head Office
      passed across the inspectors' desks. It became the practice to record
      certain letters which were funny, consciously or unconsciously. The *bon*

mot book contains many examples of the misuse of the English language. Just three will have to suffice.

From Blairgowrie office
This account holder's family is increasing somewhat rapidly. He has three young daughters and is considering adding a further two rooms in case of further eventualities. This will depend on the raspberry season.

From Abbeyhill branch about a doubtful debt
The birth of the child is imminent, and therefore I have refrained from exerting pressure on the borrower meantime.

From Inverness branch on a property matter
'We recommend shoring up the earth embankment with the Bank's architect.' The district manager endorsed the letter with '. . . splendid solution. Couldn't happen to a nicer fellow.' And the Superintendent wrote, 'Who shall say there is no balm in Gilead?'. (An apt quotation from a man whose nickname was 'Moses', and who had direct access to the highest reaches of the firmament.)

The last example encapsulates what was for many local managers their main frustration with Head Office. The fact of the matter was that by 1946 most of the Bank's buildings were in need of refurbishment beyond the running repairs which had been normal for the previous 15 years. The situation had the added frustration that roughly half the branch managers lived 'above the shop' in the bank house and also had their family situation to consider. A survey was made in 1948 which showed the seriousness of the problem. Although a start was made, initially it proceeded slowly. The major constraint, as Lord Elphinstone reported to the Proprietors in 1950, was that 'The restrictions on building and renovations limit the attention we are able to give to our properties. But adequate maintenance has continued and provision has again been made for extensions and improvements as these can be undertaken.'

The Governor's remarks to the Proprietors, which always prefaced the presentation of the Annual Report, none of which were published before 1956, provide an interesting series of comments on the state of the Bank, the Scottish economy and the wider world. Each year a summary of the state of fishing and agriculture was given, reflecting the fact that, in 1950, some 21 per cent of Bank of Scotland's lending book was committed to this sector. One of the unintended consequences of the Government's policies had been to skew the shape of the Bank's lending. In 1938 agricultural advances, although important, had represented only an estimated 9 per cent of lending. The state of farming accounts was often at the mercy of events beyond human control. The hurricane which devastated Orkney, Shetland

194 and parts of the North of Scotland in 1952 provides just one example. However, the Bank had a very clear view that Scotland's future lay in diversifying out of heavy industry and improving the country's infrastructure. This also represented the Bank's main hope for its own future. The southward move of control of major industries was not compensated for by the arrival of new light-engineering companies. Those companies moving into Scotland tended to have their headquarters in England or, if American, in the United States. It followed therefore that they normally arrived with pre-existing banking arrangements which left only the personal banking arrangements of their employees for the Scottish banks.

J.B. Crawford and the Bank's management saw clearly that their own future lay with small and medium-sized indigenous firms. But the process of encouragement was severely hampered, first by Government restriction and secondly by the overdraft, which was the only instrument of lending used. Much ink has been spilled on this subject because the overdraft (or cash credit account as its variant was known in much of Scotland) was essentially a short-term method of lending which theoretically could be recalled on demand. Enough has been said in previous chapters to indicate that it developed as a response to a particular financing need, when most large businesses in Scotland were either privately owned or had a small number of shareholders and were capable of internally generating capital for investment. In practice, most firms had lending limits which remained unchanged for many years and which would be increased as business expanded. What conventional banking practice forbade was the acquisition by the Bank of a direct shareholding in a customer's company. This would have involved the Bank in becoming a commercial trading company or investment trust.

The Scottish Industries Exhibition, held in the Kelvin Hall, Glasgow, in September 1949, showed the possibilities of industrial development, and when in 1953 the Scottish Council (Development and Industry) published its survey of Scottish industry, progress had been made and much was possible if only Government restrictions on lending could be lifted and Government expenditure itself reined in. In fairness, the onset of the

Bronze bust of Sir John Craig,
Governor 1955-57, by Jacob Epstein

Korean War and the need for rearmament had given a boost to defence-related industries, in particular to shipbuilding on the Clyde, where the Bank had begun to acquire customers. In turn this increased the demand for quality steel products, which the denationalised steel industry was eager to meet. The major developments in north Lanarkshire were well known to the Bank because the Deputy Governor, Sir John Craig, was chairman of Colvilles, the dominant force in Scottish steelmaking. The needs of industry in the West of Scotland were fully understood in Edinburgh because every Treasurer of the Bank, since the appointment of George J. Scott in 1920 from the Union Bank of Scotland, had followed the same route to the top. A.W. Morton Beveridge, J.W. Macfarlane and J.B. Crawford had all spent time in the Inspection Department, then gone to Glasgow Office in George Square as Manager before returning to Head Office to serve as Bank Secretary or Assistant Treasurer.

The impact of Government policy, itself the result of Britain's external trading situation, cannot be over-emphasised. After June 1954 the current balance of payments began to deteriorate and reserves dropped. In February 1955 the bank rate, which had stood at 2.5 per cent a decade earlier, was raised to 4.5 per cent, hire-purchase restrictions were reimposed and the banks collectively agreed to reduce their advances by 10 per cent. In February 1956 the bank rate was raised again to 5.5 per cent, capital expenditure by the nationalised industries cut back and investment allowances withdrawn. The Suez crisis of autumn 1956 and the consequent drain on reserves led to a bank rate of 7 per cent in 1957, and banks were told to freeze their advances at the 1956 level. In 1957 the Government, dissatisfied with the banks' view that they ought to lend to all creditworthy customers, proposed statutory controls on bank lending.

In truth the problem lay elsewhere. An examination of Bank of Scotland's accounts for the period 1950–58 shows that many worthwhile lending situations had to be rejected and even good, long-standing customers were rationed. The gap left by the credit squeeze was filled by finance houses and other credit operators not directly answerable to the Bank of England. In 1945, advances to customers stood at 4.4 per cent of deposits and other credit balances; and although these rose to 5.46 per cent in 1951, they were reduced to 3.59 per cent in 1953–54 and remained at that level until 1958. Even allowing for special deposits required by the Treasury and the requirements for supporting the note issue, it was, above all, investments in gilts which rose as a percentage of total assets. These were invariably long-term securities which were kept until maturation date.

The major strategic error which the Bank made in the post-war years

196   was to continue with purchases of British Government securities (gilts) on the assumption that the price would remain stable whatever monetary policies the Government might have in place. Adjustments to the overall shape of the portfolio were more in the nature of fine-tuning than a radical reappraisal of policy. A steady slide in the value of gilts during 1948–49 had encouraged most of the Scottish life assurance companies to reduce the proportion of their investments held in gilts in favour of industrial capital. Similarly, there was no shortage of discussion of these matters in the financial and banking press during 1949 and 1950. The catalyst for the collapse of gilt prices was the election on 25 October 1951 of a Conservative Government committed to raising the bank rate and relaxing taxes on distributed dividends. By Christmas 1951 the difference between the purchase price of gilts and their market value was a deficit of £5.2 million. This collapse occurred over a period of eight weeks, a situation which did not improve during the spring of 1952 and was only partially addressed in the Bank's audited Annual Accounts for 1951, presented to the Proprietors in April 1952. In effect the Bank's inner reserves had been eliminated and would have to be rebuilt before major expansion could be safely undertaken. As if to emphasise the precariousness of the Bank's position, an engineer's report confirmed that there was severe subsidence under the retaining walls at the Mound: 'Collapse is possible at any time and little warning is likely to be given.'

Almost every Scottish bank was in a similar financial predicament. The position in both the Union Bank of Scotland and The British Linen Bank was, if anything, more serious. In the latter case its parent, Barclays, effectively recreated the reserve and insisted that it become normal practice for all senior managers to spend time in London to gain experience of large-scale investment banking. In the former case it gave an urgency to merger discussions between the Union Bank and Bank of Scotland which had begun two years earlier.

During 1950 the need to enlarge the Bank led to preliminary discussions with the Union Bank and with the Clydesdale and North of Scotland banks about a three-way merger. The Clydesdale proposal disappeared quickly for two reasons: first, it was in the middle of trying to integrate the staffs and systems of its own merger with the North of Scotland Bank, which took place on 1 January 1950; and second, any combined merger would have introduced the Midland Bank into the shareholding of the new combination. Rightly or wrongly this was seen once again as a threat to two banks determined to maintain their Scottish

Left: *One of the last two major variations of the old-style Bank of Scotland £5 note*
Right: *The last Union Bank of Scotland design for the £100 note*

Coat-of-arms granted to the Union Bank of Scotland in 1947

base and their independence of London banks. The negotiations were masterminded by William Watson, with Sir John Craig, Alastair Blair and Col Norman Kennedy as support from Bank of Scotland, while from the Union Bank side Lord Bilsland, Col Hugh Spens, Sir Samuel Beale and Sir Hugh Rose were the main negotiators. Detailed proposals for the merger of the shareholdings were put to an Extraordinary General Meeting of the Proprietors on 7 October 1952. Bank of Scotland proposed to acquire the whole shareholding of the Union Bank, one million 'A' shares and 200,000 'B' shares, by issuing additional Bank of Scotland stock in exchange. It was the retired Treasurer, A.W. Morton Beveridge, who proposed the motion, saying, 'I think I represent the views of the great majority of the 5,000 Proprietors when I say that I hope and pray that our old institution will continue to forge ahead and under the new conditions be assured of a higher degree of prosperity than it has ever obtained'.

Many of the underlying reasons for merger which coloured Bank of Scotland's decision applied with even greater force to the Union Bank of Scotland. Some of the reasons for the Union's relative decline are discussed in the previous chapter, but it had the additional handicap that it failed to attract a sufficient volume of deposits to allow it to develop its business. In 1930 it was in sixth position among the Scottish banks, and conditions after 1945 did not permit any attempt at expansion beyond its existing boundaries. There was a further consideration which applied with equal force to both banks: by any conventional ratio of number of branches to population, Scotland was reckoned to be over-banked. This was the subject of a paper, published in *The Scottish Bankers Magazine* in 1952, by the Union Bank's Perth Manager, Charles Tennant. He showed that in 1951 in Scotland each Scottish bank branch served 3,000 of the population as against 4,500 in England and Wales by English banks and

198 that deposits per branch were £429,000 in Scotland as against £641,000 in England and Wales. Basically there were too many bank branches in the main towns, and one of the attractions of the Bank of Scotland–Union Bank of Scotland merger was summed up by *The Economist*:

> The businesses of the two banks are competitive rather than complementary, and . . . both embrace extensive networks of branches. Throughout Scotland the potentialities for the concentration of branch business should be a good deal wider than those presented by the Clydesdale-North merger.

A mid-1950s newspaper advertisement

At the April 1953 Annual General Meeting of the Bank Lord Elphinstone was able to announce that the shareholders of the Union Bank had accepted the offer and that as from 23 October 1952 the banks were united. In fact, the real work of merging the two operations had only just begun.

In 1952 J.B. Crawford reached his sixtieth birthday and the question arose as to who would succeed him as Treasurer. He was asked to stay on for two years but declined because he felt that the process of integration would take longer, and also that he was too closely identified with Bank of Scotland to be wholly acceptable to Union Bank staff. The most senior possibilities in Bank of Scotland, John Wilson, the Secretary, and James Taggart, the Superintendent of Branches, were also approaching retirement age. The illness (and death in 1954) of John A. Morrison, General Manager of the Union Bank, removed another possibility. The question arose of appointing a much younger man in the shape of James Letham who, then 42 years old, had been involved with Bank policy for a number of years. The Directors felt this to be too radical a departure from tradition, and the precedent of Norman Hird was not wholly favourable; he had to wait a further 12 years before his moment arrived. The Directors nominated William Watson who, although a Director himself, had been involved full-time with the merger negotiations for over 18 months. He was therefore appointed Treasurer of Bank of Scotland and General Manager of the Union Bank with the task of merging the two. This appointment represented a sharp departure from tradition and there is little doubt that there was resentment, both among staff and in wider banking circles. William Watson was, as stated earlier, not a banker. One public indication of disapproval was a change in the rules of the Scottish General Managers' Committee. The chairmanship had traditionally gone to the Treasurer of Bank of Scotland as of right, but after 1952 it rotated among the general managers according to seniority. It is, however, in retrospect crystal-clear why he was chosen by the Directors of both banks in preference to the younger internal candidate, James Letham. His prime task was to rebuild the Bank's reserves, because until this was done there could be little prospect of expansion or development. At this stage in his career Letham, a good lending banker, had little direct experience of investment. In the 1950s this was an unglamorous and unseen role which relied upon a 'minimalist' approach to internal change beyond the necessities of merging the two banks. In the circumstances it was inevitable that William Watson should appear an austere and remote figure to most Bank staff. Down to 1958 a necessary holding operation was conducted because external circumstances permitted only a modest shift in the Bank's investment portfolio.

The exact date for complete merger depended on Parliament and on the successful passage of the amendments to the Bank of Scotland (1920) Act. This received the royal assent in November 1954, and the projected fusion date of 1 March 1955 was achieved. The paid-up capital of the new Bank of Scotland stood at £4.5 million with a like sum in reserve. In 1954–55 the administrative structure of the Bank, as established, combined elements of both banks. Under the Main Board of Directors, which met in Edinburgh, there were to be East and West Boards to deal with comparatively routine matters. This geographical split was followed through and branches were allocated to one area or the other. This led to some shifts which might surprise English readers. Berwick-on-Tweed was reclaimed for the East of Scotland and Cumbria was regarded as legitimate prey for the West! Parallel structures of inspection, lending control and superintendence of branches were retained, based on Head Office at the Mound and on the former Union Bank head office in St Vincent Street, Glasgow, now designated Glasgow Chief Office. Two Assistant Treasurers and Branch Superintendents were appointed: first, John Wilson, then in 1956 James Letham and James Taggart for the East area, and William Haddow and Dugald McIsaac for the West. In addition, two Local Boards were established, one for London and one for Aberdeen. In many ways the solution was a conservative one, doing as little

Sir William Watson, Treasurer 1952-65, by James Gunn

200   violence as possible to existing lines of communication and preserving an historical structure. The Aberdeen Local Board could trace its origins back to the Aberdeen Banking Company, founded in 1767, which amalgamated into the Union Bank in 1849. Similarly, the East Area Board was the direct descendant of the Union Bank Edinburgh Board, which was in its turn the successor to the Sir William Forbes & Company board. Whatever the initial logic, the fact of the matter is that, as a system, it has passed the test of time and served the Bank well for forty years.

Exchanges of staff between branches and departments began in 1954 and each side tried to adapt to 'other ways of doing'. There was a clear decision in favour of Bank of Scotland's accounting system, which under James Letham and Kenneth Minty of the Union Bank had made major strides towards mechanisation. Experiments with National Cash Register's electro-mechanical accounting machines in the earlier 1950s had proved successful and their wider introduction was in hand. Uniform procedures and standards had to be imposed and in 1956 a branch manual was produced detailing these. It is a measure of Bank of Scotland's conservatism that the previous book of regulations had been issued in 1865, and although seriously out of date in 1914 it had continued to be regarded as sufficient. The end of the old Bank of Scotland was marked by the retiral in 1955 of Lord Elphinstone, who had served as Governor since 1924 and was first made a Director in 1917. His successor was Sir John Craig, and Lord Bilsland was appointed Deputy Governor.

For many years, and for many staff, affection for one or other of the banks remained strong, particularly among Union Bank men, who felt that something of importance to them had been lost. It was also known that rationalisation of the branch network was scheduled and there was apprehension about individual prospects in the combined bank.

In fact, the amalgamation and rationalisation of branches proceeded more slowly than *The Economist* had suggested. In 1954 the combined banks had had 453 branches between them in Scotland and by 1959 there were still 433. There were four major reasons for this. First, there was actually less duplication of branches than had been suggested. Second, where there was duplication, amalgamation depended upon concentrating business on one or other branch, or, if neither was suitable, on finding premises appropriate for the enlarged business either by purchase or by building. Third, the surveys carried out by the Premises Manager, W.W. Malcolm, revealed a great backlog of maintenance work to be done in former Union Bank branches, which required most of the expenditure allocated for premises; and finally, down to late 1957,

Government restrictions on building had not been lifted completely.   201

It is hardly surprising that the bank manager was seen, as in one cartoon, as the 'abominable no-man'. All these matters were examined during 1958 by the Radcliffe Committee, from which emerged three recommendations. The first was that most of the instruments of credit restriction be abandoned; second that banks ought to introduce an American-style 'term loan' for businesses; and third that they needed to pay much greater attention to the small and medium-sized business customer. On personal customers there was little comment. For Bank of Scotland, wartime conditions ended in 1958 and the acceleration of both activity and change was noticeable to every member of staff in the Bank.

Against the background described it was noteworthy that in 1956 and 1957 the Bank's declared profit declined and the immediate benefits of merger were not realised on the balance sheet. Lord Bilsland, the Governor from 1957, commented in that year on the fact that Bank of Scotland had 11,000 Proprietors, of whom 83 per cent had holdings of £500 or less and controlled 70 per cent of the whole Bank stock. It was a matter of pride that the Bank was independent and Scottish in character. The asset base of the Bank was strong and more than ready to move in new directions. For most members of staff, appreciation of change took longer.

As if to confirm the close of one chapter and the opening of a new one, in 1957 the Bank's agency in Kelso was reconstituted as an ordinary branch. It was particularly appropriate that the Stormonth Darlings, a well-known family who had run one of the Bank's first successful branches from the early nineteenth century, should survive until the final flourish of the old system in which local men of business had been the Bank's representatives in their own locality. The last lawyer agencies of all were those in Pitlochry and Kirriemuir, which lasted for a few years more.

Silver casket by Hamilton & Inches, 1945

Head Office, the Mound, evening
(Inset) *The entrance hall, Head Office, the Mound, c.1964*

—15—

CHANGE AND NEW HORIZONS, 1958–70

AFTER the merger, the Union Bank of Scotland's dowry of customers among the shipbuilders and steelmakers of the West of Scotland dominated Bank of Scotland's lending book in the late 1950s and '60s. It is not an exaggeration to state that the problems and needs of Scottish heavy industry required more thought and effort from the Bank's Board and senior management than any other aspect of their business, with the possible exception of the Bank's investment portfolio. The close identification of many of the Directors with the prosperity of this sector of industry was analysed in Scott and Hughes's *The Anatomy of Scottish Capital* (1980). At the Annual General Meeting in April 1960 the Governor, Lord Bilsland (he was also a director of Colvilles, the steelmakers, and of John Brown & Co. (Clydebank) Ltd, the shipbuilders, a former president of Glasgow Chamber of Commerce and president of the Scottish Council, Development and Industry), commented to Proprietors on the Radcliffe Committee's recommendations that bank lending should include more long-term loans than had been common among English banks up to that time. He was able to confirm from personal experience that this was nothing new for Bank of Scotland and that 'the practice has proved beneficial both to our customers and to the Bank'. There was also a clear recognition among the Directors that Scotland's prosperity rested on a narrow and shifting industrial base. One major problem was that in many instances the very prosperity of these industries depended not necessarily on the economic viability of a particular firm or industry but on political decisions taken in London. It is, above all, this feature of Scottish life that

204   has created attitudes, even among conservative Scots, which are significantly different from those of their southern counterparts; though perhaps those operating in the Midlands and North of England (for example, the board of Martins Bank) might have found some of these preoccupations familiar.

The problems of Scottish industry were mirrored within the Bank. There was a growing understanding that the Bank itself had to make changes in its systems, methods and attitudes if it was to survive and remain independent, which the Directors believed passionately to be an overriding priority. It is perhaps ironic that one other part of the Union Bank legacy which affected Bank of Scotland was an intensification of central control under the Superintendents of Branches and in the Inspection Department (in itself a vestige of the Hird era in the Union Bank) which tended to make the Bank inward-looking.

If some of the older inspectors and managers felt that talk of change was simply 'young Turks and hot air', a more usual reaction was to acknowledge the need for change but to express great unease about where it might lead. This is probably best illustrated in a series of talks given to Bank officials' circle meetings in 1964 by Alex Robertson, then Assistant Superintendent of Branches in Glasgow. His theme was that changes were coming, some of which his audience already knew about. The Bank's first computer was installed in 1959 under the aegis of James Letham, and the process of extending centralised electronic accounting procedures to the branch network was well under way. The actual structure of the network itself was changing as branches amalgamated where there was duplication of Bank of Scotland and former Union Bank operations and new branches opened. Between 1958 and 1964 there were 45 closures and 19 new branches opened. Alex Robertson's underlying message to his audience was that, despite change, there were some traits of bankers that would remain constant. These included probity, character, human understanding and clear thinking. He pointed out that many branches were only marginally profitable; and foreseeing the end of the *Agreements and Understandings* among the Scottish banks (effectively a cartel, dissolved in 1965), argued strongly that competition and the search for new business would come to dominate the bank manager's working life. Finally, he predicted a greater degree of specialisation within banking careers, with a need for continuous training and updating of skills. In all these comments Robertson reflected the thinking of the senior Bank management at the time. The translation of this into a programme for change is the Bank's internal story during the period 1966-70, but the degree of inertia in the

Bank's structure which had first to be overcome was very great.

Both the Bank's oral history programme and the recollections of Duncan Ferguson, first Senior then Chief Inspector in these years, demonstrate that a more traditional and colourful Bank continued to flourish well into the 1960s. If particular incidents and 'characters' are remembered in retrospect with affectionate amusement, it should not be forgotten that they also often caused considerable frustrations at the time. Ferguson recalled that during an inspection of the Dornoch branch there was a power cut, so the junior was sent to the local office of the Hydroelectric Board with a message to the effect that the Bank inspector had arrived and they had better restore power quickly or face the consequences. Dingwall provides that most apocryphal of Bank tales, to which all swear the truth but which is told with variations in all the Scottish banks. Dingwall was almost unique in the 1950s in having a branch of each of the surviving Scottish banks on its High Street. The inspection team arrived promptly at 3.20 p.m., just after the branch closed, and proceeded as usual to take over the cash and tellers' notepads. Great displeasure was expressed at the volume of National Commercial Bank notes in the tills until it dawned on the inspectors that they were in the wrong bank. Apologies and a rapid exit followed, but in the meantime the delay had permitted the Bank's own branch (forewarned by telephone) to prepare for being surprised.

The Banking Hall, Glasgow Chief Office, in the 1960s
(Inset) *Staff of the Bank's first Computer Department, 1962*

A major characteristic of branch managers in the late 1950s was that they tended to stay in post in the same town for many years. They saw their role as sustaining the Bank's existing business, not extending it, in a life which did not draw too many distinctions between social contacts made for business and for personal reasons. A customer who wished to change banks could be a source of grave misgiving to a manager who feared being accused of poaching by his banking colleagues. In a number of cases there were managers whose entire career was spent among those they had been brought up with. It was always difficult for the Branch Superintendent to balance the merits of long-standing local knowledge against a tendency in those involved to identify completely with their locality and to regard Head Office as the opposition making unreasonable demands, to be mollified if possible and invariably blamed for hard decisions. Duncan Ferguson recalled being in Turriff on inspection and overhearing the manager and accountant discussing the overdrawn accounts list from Head Office: 'Noo Jeames Bloggs – fit hae we tae seay tae them aboot this ene?'

Such situations were not the exclusive property of Bank of Scotland. One former Linen Bank junior recalled being sent to the branch at Roslin in Midlothian and being totally nonplussed by the first customer, who on completing the banking business continued with 'Oh, and two pounds of carrots, a cabbage and seven pounds of potatoes.' Like one or two others, the bank house had a large garden which the then manager ran as a market gardening sideline (officially unknown to the inspectors).

For managers of the period their bank salary was only half the story. The most successful could more than double their salaries by commission on their insurance business, which was personal and which, on retirement or transfer, was passed to their successor for a fee. By 1965 this was an anachronism surviving from the days when the Bank agent was a local man of business, and banking was only one element in his income. In retrospect the personal benefits arising from commission can be seen to have affected a manager's readiness to look for new lending business for the branch. Any manager being asked to move to a new branch looked carefully at these 'extras'. From the Bank's point of view this distorted the ostensible branch structure because there were instances where a branch was only marginally profitable but had a large insurance business. Conversely, there were prestigious city branches with a large lending business and good salaries which were unpopular because the insurance commissions were small. Changing this situation was a prerequisite of rationalising the branch structure and introducing Bank-wide methods of assessing the viability of individual branches.

There was a further problem with the system of long-serving managers which was never quantified but was a well-established part of the chief inspector's lore. The problem was that no matter how vigorous and careful a manager might be early in his tenure of a particular branch, towards retirement there was a tendency to allow past experience of a customer, or even 'feel' about a proposal, to be the deciding factor. This is the kind of banking that newspaper editors think they remember as 'the good old days', but it had its down side in bad debt provision. There was, and is, a simple principle of lending: security for a loan was usually offered by the borrower and taken by the Bank, but no lending depended solely upon its collateral; if it did, then it was almost certainly a poor business proposition. The problem was that 'feel' could easily tip over into laxity, and the retiree's successor had to get the branch's lending back on course. In so doing he often acquired the reputation of being 'hard', which could make him personally unpopular with customers and affect the Bank's local standing. The only solution was to move such a manager on as soon as the job was well in hand. There were within the Bank a small number who came to be regarded as the experts in 'clearing up', a role that those concerned viewed as a very double-edged compliment. Part of the solution, which was evolved during the 1970s and has on the whole worked fairly well, is for a manager's final move to be made roughly six years before retiral.

The most visible changes for customers of the period 1958-65 were the steady modernisation of branches, in most cases long overdue, and the gradual disappearance of middle-aged male tellers and clerks. They were steadily replaced by young men and women. It was during the 1960s that female employment within the Bank's branches and departments began to be acknowledged as a permanent feature of banking and therefore to be taken seriously. Despite misgivings, the Bank discovered to its surprise that the Scottish public actually welcomed changes which made branches less forbidding. At December 1958 the Bank had some 2,418 staff members, of whom 1,848 were men and 570 women. Ten years later there were 3,771 employees, and the proportion of women had moved from nearly 24 per cent to 46 per cent, the majority of these concentrated at the younger end of the age range. The major worry for the Staff Committee in 1968 was 'wastage', the turnover of young staff of both sexes, which made a nonsense of the careful staffing strategies promulgated in 1951. The reasons for this were varied. Potential recruits thought of banking as dull and old-fashioned; and there was a large demand for young recruits, trained in banking skills, from a wide range of financial institutions not

208   constrained by Government wages policy. In 1961 there was one important staffing innovation: the Bank's first three graduate trainees were appointed, a move which can only be described as an outstanding success. Twenty years later one of those three, D. Bruce Pattullo, was Treasurer and General Manager and in 1991 became Governor and Group Chief Executive of the Bank.

There was one major staff matter arising from the 1955 amalgamation whose implications were ducked, and which therefore remained an open sore between Union Bank and Bank of Scotland people for nearly twenty years. Little attempt was made to integrate and standardise the benefits of service of those who had served in the two banks before 1955. Matters relating to salary scales, retirement age, pensions, widows' and orphans' rights were different. Thus a sense of discrimination was retained by middle-ranking and senior staff long after it was desirable, and in conditions where it was vital that they operated without reservation as a single unit.

Between 1957 and 1964 there were significant changes in the personal customer base of the Bank. Some of these were forecast in the Radcliffe Report, which also urged the banks to devise fresh methods of handling payments to meet the needs of these new customers. Computerisation of accounting meant that it was increasingly possible to pay wages directly into a bank account, and this became the norm by the later 1960s. Automatic cheque and bank-note sorters were also installed to speed up routine transaction processing. In 1957 only one-third of the working population had bank accounts and those being paid weekly usually received wage packets containing cash. In many branches, particularly those in industrial areas, the making up of wage packets (for a fee), or preparing the cash for transfer to a firm's own wage office, represented a substantial part of the Bank's routine work, particularly on Wednesdays and Thursdays. By 1964 the direct transfer of wages into bank accounts was gathering pace as the system developed in sophistication, and the Bank began to acquire a whole new constituency of customers whose attitudes and financial needs were significantly different from those of its traditional personal customer base.

It was with these new customers in mind that, as in other banks, schemes for personal loans were devised. There were numerous teething troubles in assessing the credit-worthiness of particular applicants because few managers had experience of consumer credit, and the pent-up demand for consumer goods far outstripped both the banks' and the Government's expectations. The problems with repayment were common to all the Scottish banks and were the subject of articles in *The Scottish Bankers Magazine*. In one particularly trenchant piece of advice the writer (from Glasgow) recommended never lending to newly-weds. 'Girls have an unquenchable faith in their ability to reform their fiancés after marriage, but they rarely pull it off.' The fact of the matter is that it took a number of years for bank managers to begin to match the expertise of the finance houses.

The major underlying internal problem confronting the Governor, Board and Treasurer between 1958 and 1964 continued to be the decline in value of British Government securities. In 1958 the difference between price paid and market valuation was £12 million (at 1993 figures this would represent £135.12 million). During the course of 1958–59 nearly £7 million of this gilt stock was sold as the market moved temporarily in the Bank's favour and permitted some losses to be written off the books. After a pause in 1960–61, by 1963 the Bank had reduced the value of its holdings to £33.2 million (in 1957 this had stood at nearly £77.5 million). The losses on sales were to some extent offset by a 50 per cent tax allowance, but the overall result was to contain the deficit on gilts to roughly £3 million for the rest of the 1960s. By the Annual General Meeting in April 1966, when Sir William Watson retired as Treasurer, British Government securities had been reduced to only 4.78 per cent of the Bank's total assets. The haemorrhage which the gilt book had represented for a generation was staunched and its relative importance changed as other parts of the Bank's business began to grow.

The second major need was to adjust the Bank's nominal capital to provide resources for development. In August 1959 the Board agreed that an additional £1.8 million was required to increase the capital base to £6.3 million. This was achieved by capitalising £900,000 of the reserve fund and distributing it to existing stockholders on a one for five capitalisation issue; the remaining £900,000 was raised by a successful rights issue at £2.50 per £1 stock. The reserve fund was replenished by the premium achieved by the rights issue, a transfer of £900,000 from the contingency fund and £150,000 from the year's profits, restoring it to £6 million in total. This stood until 1965, when the Bank's capital was increased to £8.4 million by issuing new stock to existing Proprietors (11,500 of them, 80 per cent with holdings of £600 or less) in a 1:3 rights issue.

The importance of diversifying the Bank's investments and rebuilding its inner reserves cannot be overestimated, because they formed the vital platform upon which all else was based. This process, unseen and unappreciated by most members of the Bank staff, lasted for nearly

210   fourteen years. It went in fits and starts, reflecting in part the long-held prejudices of some older members of the Investment Committee, but more often than not reflecting circumstances external to the Bank which affected the price of gilts and therefore the timing of sales. If, for no other reason, Sir William Watson's treasurership deserves to be remembered as the period in which the structure and spread of the Bank's investments were restored to the strong position they had been in before the First World War.

There is one major development in the Bank's history with which William Watson will always be linked: the purchase in August 1958 of North West Securities Limited, a subsidiary of the Braid Motor Group, whose story up to 1979 was indelibly shaped by Sydney A. Jones, its managing director. NWS's head office was in Chester and it had developed its business since 1947 by providing loans for industrial and commercial building, motor cars and household goods. In this acquisition Bank of Scotland was following where Ian Macdonald, General Manager of the Commercial Bank, had led when he bought two hire-purchase subsidiaries of the SMT Group in 1954. Treasury and Bank of England opposition to this method of escape from the rigours of Government lending policy meant that little more could be done before restrictions were lifted in 1958. It was an area of business very appropriate for banking, and it is noteworthy that the moment they were free most banks appeared to have a bride waiting in the side aisle.

The two parties met at the Adelphi Hotel in Liverpool: William Watson and James Dowling, CA, a Director, for the Bank, and Sydney Jones and David Mitchell, the Braid Motor Group accountant, for NWS. It was established and agreed that the net worth of the company was £250,000. The figure which was of particular interest to the Bank was the previous year's trading profit of £71,993, out of which the company had paid £37,273 to its bankers, Lloyds, in service and interest charges. For NWS the attraction was access to greater capital resources to fund expansion, which seemed all set to beat the 25 per cent growth of 1956–57. After negotiations a price of £700,000 was agreed upon and the two NWS men were assured of seats on the new board of NWS. William Watson's public position was that the Bank paid too much for the purchase, although he was somewhat mollified by the growth of NWS. The Bank increased NWS's capital to £450,000, and between January 1959 and January 1961 total assets grew from £1.89 million to £4.37 million. Nearly forty years after the event it can be revealed that the Bank Board had authorised a maximum price of £900,000, and could congratulate the negotiating team on their success.

Given that Bank of Scotland had little finance-house experience and that the management of NWS reflected the strong individualistic style of Sydney Jones, it is perhaps inevitable that there was a culture clash. During 1961–62 the consumer boom of Harold Macmillan's 'you've never had it so good' years began to fray at the edges, and bad-debt problems increased. The Bank's reaction was to try to integrate NWS into its own centralised control systems. This was characterised by two moves: first, premises were converted in George Street, Edinburgh, on the assumption that the base of operations would move from Chester; and second, Dan Mackay of the Bank's inspectorate was appointed company secretary. NWS operated a different kind of business in a very different way. The managers of its 23 branches, unlike their Bank counterparts, were allowed very little discretion. The only basis for lending was a well-developed system of credit rating. Disagreements came to a head in 1963 when Sydney Jones threatened to resign and take his senior management team with him. He was in a strong position. That year's profit of £181,196 permitted a 25 per cent dividend to be paid on the share capital of NWS, which by then stood at £1 million. This was talent the Bank could not afford to lose. Chester was confirmed as the head office location of NWS, and the company was given functional autonomy subject to supervision at Board level, with Sir Hugh Rose as chairman and Alastair Blair, James Dowling, William Marr (all non-executive Directors of the Bank) and William Watson as board members. This kept the company close to the geographical heart of its core business in the north-west and the industrial Midlands of England.

One other new venture, which was a direct outcome of the NWS experience, was begun in 1960. NWS and Standard Life Assurance Company became involved in the Capital Finance Company, which produced a scheme called Capital Plan, primarily for building new factories and financing industrial plant. Bank of Scotland was the banker. The focus of operations was Central Scotland. It began well, but in the aftermath of the collapse in 1964 of John Bloom's Rolls Razor (a direct-selling domestic appliance company), its financial situation deteriorated. By 1968 it showed a bottom line deficit of £5.4 million and was effectively bankrupt. In 1969 NWS agreed to take over the company to keep it afloat, provided the others underwrote the losses.

In 1957, advances by the Bank to customers represented only 28.6 per cent of assets. By 1963 they had reached 50 per cent of the total. By 1963 ships, shipbuilding, engineering and related trades represented over 20 per cent of the Bank's total lending of £103 million. The table below illustrates the spread and nature of the Bank's lending in 1963. These

212   figures do not correspond with those published in the Annual Accounts for that year for the simple reason that they do not include the provision for bad and doubtful debts.

Classification of Advances, 1963
(figures in £s sterling)

Sector	Year ending mid-February 1963 £	%
Manufacturing		
Food, drinks and tobacco	5,130,482	5.0
Chemicals	7,473,150	7.3
Iron, steel and allied trades	611,463	0.6
Non-ferrous metals	484,753	0.5
Engineering, etc.	5,092,885	5.0
Shipping and shipbuilding	14,579,489	14.2
Cotton	87,209	0.1
Wool	1,212,518	1.2
Other textiles	1,845,797	1.8
Leather and rubber	609,630	0.6
Unclassified Industry and trade	4,809,812	4.7
Other production		
Agriculture	14,667,255	14.3
Fishing	273,305	0.3
Coal mining	3,132	0.0
Quarrying, etc.	86,727	0.1
Builders and contractors	5,135,392	5.0
Building materials	1,256,015	1.2
Financial		
Hire-purchase finance companies	2,879,025	2.8
Stockbrokers	126,780	0.1
Other financial	9,388,683	9.2
Services		
Transport and communications	588,611	0.6
Public utilities (other than transport)	2,889,582	2.8
Local government authorities	1,046,590	1.0
Retail trade	6,489,465	6.3
Churches, charities, hospitals, etc.	98,749	0.1
Entertainment	271,582	0.3
Personal and professional	15,521,484	15.1
Total	102,659,565	100.0

The problems of shipbuilding and steelmaking in Scotland after 1957 have to be seen against a backdrop of increasing world demand for ships, and there were good reasons for believing that, with investment and restructuring of costs, output from the Clyde would increase again and with it demand for steel. In 1957 Colvilles, Scotland's only major steel producer, newly denationalised once again, spoke to both Bank of Scotland and the National Bank about a development programme in North Lanarkshire. The estimated cost was £25 million, of which £4 million would be put up by Bank of Scotland and £8 million by the National Bank. This plan had widespread support among politicians, but was overtaken by a more ambitious scheme costing nearly £50 million to build a new integrated steel plant at Ravenscraig, matched by a similar unit at Llanwern in South Wales. Essentially this was a political decision taken by the Macmillan Government. Although when it opened it provided a large general boost to business in the West of Scotland, servicing this level of financial commitment proved to be an enormous burden for Colvilles. The Bank was also heavily committed to Stewarts & Lloyds, the steel firm which had moved from Coatbridge to Corby in Northamptonshire in the 1930s with loans of over £14 million on the Bank's books.

The viability of steelmaking, particularly steel plate, depended crucially on exports and on the Clyde's shipbuilding industry. In 1951 around 446,000 tons of shipping were launched (35 per cent of gross world tonnage), but this had declined to 401,000 tons (31 per cent) in 1956–57. Although yards and order books were full in 1958, as ships came off the slipways they were not replaced by new orders. In 1963 only 258,600 tons of shipping were built, and Clydeside was down to 17 yards, of which only 11 were technically equipped to build the new super tankers and bulk carriers. Part of the story lies in successive Governments' treatment of the British Merchant Marine. It is a fact that throughout the 1950s and '60s Government policy on bank lending ensured that foreign owners received more favourable treatment from the UK for shipbuilding finance than British owners. One major initiative occurred in 1959, when the Bank entered into a consortium with Lithgow's, Fairfield's and John Brown's to build a graving dock at Greenock capable of taking the largest tankers. The Bank advanced £700,000 against equity and provided normal overdraft facilities to fund work in progress. The graving dock opened in November 1964, the month in which the new Cunard liner QE2 was laid down and the Forth Road Bridge opened.

A second scheme, Kingston Financial Services (Clyde) Ltd, was devised by the Bank as a means of financing the building of ships by Lithgow's and Fairfield's 'on spec'. Its capital was £1 million, but most of its interest-earning balances were to be kept with the Bank. The secretary of the company was William Hay, then Assistant General Manager of the Bank, and in 1964 William Watson, the Bank Treasurer, replaced Sir John

214   Erskine as chairman. Between 1961 and 1974 Kingston underwrote the building of 14 ships, and as a Bank subsidiary had no bad debts. It was a lifeline to Clydeside and British shipowners, but could hardly compensate for the incentives that foreign shipbuilders and shipowners received from their own governments.

The Fairfield's and subsequent Upper Clyde Shipbuilders story requires more space than is available here. Briefly, Fairfield's was in difficulties from 1964, and was technically bankrupt when receivers were called in in October of that year. There were 5,000 employees, of whom 3,400 were employed at Govan, and over 800 creditors, most of whom were small engineering companies in the West of Scotland, many of them Bank customers. The Bank was directly owed £3,894,000, but the Bank Board extended overdraft limits to pay wages. The yard was saved temporarily by the formation of a new company, Upper Clyde Shipbuilders, with £1.5 million from Government sources and £0.5 million from the private sector. This was a combination of five shipbuilding interests – Connell's, Yarrow's, Stephen's, John Brown's and Fairfield's. It was reorganised as a model of social democratic planning in which the workforce signed detailed agreements for the modernisation of work practices. Initially, in 1967, the shipping market seemed to be buoyant, but by 1969 the shipping boom was over and the company was in deep financial trouble. Bluntly, the reorganisation provided only a palliative for the problem, not a solution. The new capital was sufficient to complete existing orders, but it did not provide the capital investment necessary for re-equipping. This favoured treatment of one group of yards by the Labour Government created problems for most of the others and did not solve the underlying one of excess old-fashioned shipbuilding capacity chasing too few orders. Bank of Scotland lost most of its investment, but it is noteworthy that the Governor's remarks to stockholders in 1966 were studiously neutral in tone.

> Shipbuilders, too, though with full order books, are finding profits harder, sometimes impossible, to make. There is keen competition for orders and it is becoming clear that the spending of huge sums on modernisation can be nullified by shortages of certain skills and inflexibility in the use of labour and by the high rate of inflation of costs during the period of building a ship. One outcome of this crisis has been the new Fairfield company, where a consortium of Government, private enterprise and trade unions is endeavouring to operate a shipyard on the basis of greater flexibility of labour. This experiment will be watched with close interest and much goodwill for its success. More recently the Geddes Report has blown a fresh breeze through the industry, with proposals for rationalisation and Government aid. Successful results will demand a high

degree of co-operation within managements and within trade unions and between the two.

The question is whether the Bank could have done more to secure the future of Scottish heavy industry. In truth there were times when it felt it was the sole support for Scottish shipbuilding and steelmaking. Voices there were aplenty, but the requirements far outstripped the available resources of the Bank on its own. There was a general perception furth of Scotland that what was required was an orderly run down of these industries, hopefully to be replaced by light engineering and electronics. The Bank had little influence, outwith its own circle in Scotland, on those taking what were essentially political decisions.

In other cities and industries there were also problems. The terminal decline of the jute industry in Dundee and difficulties among Border knitwear firms all gave cause for concern. It would, however, be wrong to give the impression that all was doom and gloom. Between 1961 and 1964 Rootes established a car assembly plant at Linwood and the British Motor Corporation settled at Bathgate in West Lothian. The Scottish Council (Development and Industry) was praised for the Toothill Report on the integration, finance and management of Scottish industry. Two successive Scottish Council chairmen, Lord Polwarth and Lord Clydesmuir, together with the Council's chief executive, William Robertson, played a pioneering role in encouraging North American firms to locate in Scotland. By 1965 these were arriving at the rate of forty a year, and many were in the electronics sector, which by 1966 had built up to an employment figure of some 20,000. This collaboration between Polwarth and Clydesmuir created a valuable understanding of Scotland's probable financial needs; since they were, respectively, Governor of Bank of Scotland and Deputy Governor and Chairman of British Linen, this was important when the two banks came to discuss a possible merger a few years later.

It is perhaps noteworthy that in 1968 the Bank announced publicly for the first time that it had made no donations to any political party. This did not reflect any change of policy. Each time the matter had been discussed during the previous twenty years the conclusion reached by the Governor and Directors had always been the same. This is an attitude (and policy) which has not been modified since.

Sir William Watson's retiral in 1966 brought in James Letham as the new Treasurer. At the same time Lord Bilsland retired as the seventeenth Governor of the Bank, to be succeeded by Lord Polwarth. This new combination, irreverently referred to as the Dynamic Duo, introduced

The formal ending of the 'Agreements and Understandings' between the Scottish banks, September 1965

216 innovations and new ideas at a pace which was quite exceptional and to which most members of the Bank responded eagerly. It was an exciting and invigorating time. It was as if James Letham's energy and ideas, pent-up since 1952, were suddenly permitted free rein, and that he was acutely aware that the time for accomplishing his goals was short. These may be divided into three categories – new internal developments, new customer services and new initiatives.

In 1968 for the first time the Bank began to consider its overall corporate image, and a design consultant was brought in to streamline stationery, to develop a modern logo and to produce a standardised lettering for use throughout the Bank. Two new specialist appointments laid the foundations for much of the Bank's approach to its internal organisation during the 1970s and '80s. The first of these was the appointment of Sydney Hudson, formerly of Shell, as the Bank's first professional staff controller. In a short time formal staff assessment, training and managerial revitalisation were all on the agenda. In addition to the Edinburgh Training Centre at Tipperlinn a new centre was opened in Glasgow, and two recently retired members of staff, Eddie Bowen and James Bruce, organised a series of residential seminars at Peebles Hydro, the forerunners of the later managers' conferences.

The impact of the Wilson Government years on the Bank's lending policies will be discussed later, but the Labour Government put the banks under the spotlight. In 1967 the National Board for Prices and Incomes commissioned a firm of consultants to carry out a detailed survey of banking practices and charges. So far as Bank of Scotland itself was

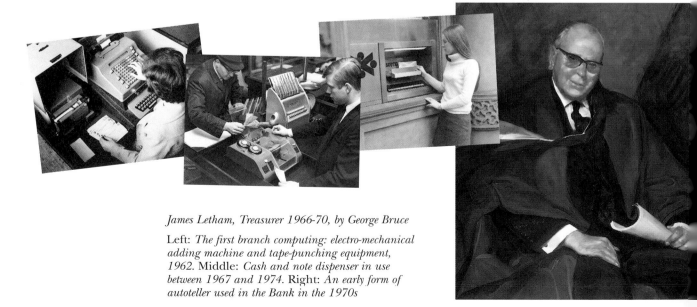

James Letham, Treasurer 1966-70, by George Bruce

Left: *The first branch computing: electro-mechanical adding machine and tape-punching equipment, 1962.* Middle: *Cash and note dispenser in use between 1967 and 1974.* Right: *An early form of autoteller used in the Bank in the 1970s*

concerned, the conclusions were that its charges were modest but that the Bank was over-staffed. The consultants Booz, Allen, when they had completed their Government work, were asked to undertake a full report for the Bank. This was the beginning of the Organisation and Methods department, and as a corollary in May 1969 a management accountant was hired, reporting to the chief accountant, John Wilson. The key figures in persuading the Board that this was worth while were Sir William Lithgow and the newly appointed Lord Balfour of Burleigh, who had had direct experience of forward profit planning as head of English Electric's operations in India. Alan Jessiman, a chartered accountant, came to the Bank from Fairfield's and was asked to design a budget and forecasting system which would be allied to profit planning and cost controls. The first full attempt at profit and cost budgeting took place in 1969/70. The idea was to compare projected costs by departments and branches against the actual out-turn and to compare this with the income generated. As the model was refined it became the basis in 1971 of a rolling projection of budgets over the succeeding five years. By 1971 the elements were in place for corporate planning which could quantify existing trends, identify areas likely to cause problems and forewarn management of the actions likely to be necessary to maintain real profits and push them higher. All this implied that the Bank should develop strategies and targets for all elements of its costs, including computing, marketing and staff. Although in retrospect these early projections were much less sophisticated than they later became, and as such were both resisted and resented in some quarters of the Bank, the fact of the matter is that they provided a consistent internal discipline which has been used ever since. This was almost certainly one of the key unseen elements in the Bank's success during the 1980s.

The literature on banking trends available to young Scots bankers was very sparse in the 1960s. Within the Bank itself it is possible to identify a group of energetic young managers who were beginning to map out future directions. Some of them began to meet regularly over tea in Crawford's restaurant in Edinburgh to discuss banking topics informally. The main vehicle for public discussion was *The Scottish Bankers Magazine*, in which appeared two prize-winning articles by Archie Gibson, at that time a young Bank Inspector. The second of these, 'All-Purpose Banking?' (August 1968), was noted in the Board minutes. The core of his argument was that traditional sources of deposits could be lost with greater competition and that banks should move into foreign and commercial lending, credit cards, hire-purchase finance and ever more computerisation to reduce internal costs. For the record, he also advocated longer opening hours to attract

218

working customers, and was nonplussed when the same year the Bank agreed to Saturday closing in negotiation with the National Union of Bank Employees. In December 1969 Archie Gibson was appointed Methods Planning Officer, with a list of issues to address and report on direct to the Treasurer and the Policy Development Committee comprising senior members of the Bank executive.

Meanwhile a number of young inspectors, including Bruce Pattullo and Robert Wickham, were sent on attachment for a period to stockbrokers and merchant banks in London. On his return, after a further period of secondment to Ivory & Sime in Edinburgh, Bruce Pattullo was appointed to head a brand-new investment services department in conjunction with Alasdair Macdonald.

The Bank realised in 1965 that in due course Britain would inevitably join the European Economic Community and that in any case Commonwealth links would become less important for British business. Bank of Scotland did not want to be dependent on the English clearers for handling its European business, so in February 1967, at a cost of £1.1 million, a 7.3 per cent stake was acquired in a French *banque d'affaires*, Banque Worms et Cie SA, which was Paris-based, and two years later a 15 per cent stake was taken in its Swiss subsidiary, Banque Worms et Associés (Genève) SA. The initial contact had been made by Lord Polwarth through his directorship of the Bank of London and South America.

As if to encapsulate the changes within the Bank and the new directions it was taking, on 1 January 1968 a completely new design of bank-note was issued in the £1 and £5 denominations. Plans to extend this to the £20 and £100 notes were overtaken by events. The 1968 issue was the first totally redesigned note to be issued by the Bank since 1885, although its printers, Waterston & Sons Ltd, had submitted trial designs on at least two previous occasions.

The background against which all this was achieved was a time of great difficulty for banks because of the intense credit restraints imposed by the Labour Government from the moment they came to power in 1964. In 1967 sterling had to be devalued and savage credit restrictions were imposed. Each bank had a fixed lending ceiling which made business very difficult. In November 1968 banks were instructed to reduce their lending to 98 per cent of the November 1967 figure, and the bank rate was raised to (a then unheard of) 8 per cent. The practical consequence of all this was to squeeze the number of loans to small and medium-sized firms, which were finding it difficult to trade profitably, let alone to expand.

One way in which the Bank tried to help its customers during the

Annual Report to the Proprietors
29th February 1968

Cover of the Annual Report to Proprietors, 1968

period of credit restriction was by forming in 1968 the Bank of Scotland Finance Company, which as a subsidiary had its own lending ceiling and was designed to deal with longer-term deposits and advances. From the beginning, under William Hay, one of the Bank's Assistant General Managers, it was much involved in shipbuilding finance. A further step in 1969 was the acquisition of a 50 per cent stake in Portland Group Factors (Scotland) Ltd.

Summing up the changes in the Bank between 1958 and 1970 is difficult, but some figures may indicate their scale. In 1958 the balance sheet totals were £227,476,636, with a net operating profit of £636,961. In the financial year ending February 1969 the comparable figures were £452,497,802 and £3,837,832 respectively. Most momentous of all, in May 1969 it was announced to the public and the Bank staff that Bank of Scotland was once again involved in a merger, this time with the smallest of the Scottish clearing banks, The British Linen Bank, which had been a wholly-owned subsidiary of Barclays Bank since 1919.

38 St Andrew Square, Edinburgh, Head Office of The British Linen Bank

Henry Hepburne-Scott, tenth Lord Polwarth, Governor, Bank of Scotland 1966-72, by George Bruce

Douglas Douglas-Hamilton, fourteenth Duke of Hamilton, Deputy Governor then Governer of The British Linen Bank 1963-70, by Alan Sutherland

*The Banking Hall of 38 St Andrew Square, Head Office of The British Linen Bank
(Inset) Ronald Bilsland Colville, second Baron Clydesmuir, Deputy Governor and Chairman of
The British Linen Bank 1963-70, and Governor of Bank
of Scotland 1972-81, by Alberto Morrocco*

—16—

AMALGAMATION AND OIL: THE 1970s

O N 23 July 1970 the Royal Assent was given to the Bank of Scotland Order Confirmation Act, which cleared the last hurdle for the amalgamation of Bank of Scotland with The British Linen Bank on the appointed day of 1 March 1971. Any discussion of this merger must retrace steps a little and consider the background against which the announcement was made on 9 May 1969. One hard lesson which the Scottish banks had learned during the 1960s was that their ability to influence political and therefore economic decision-making in London was virtually nil. When contrasted with the increasing financial and political power of the City of London, even (or perhaps especially) on Harold Wilson's Labour Government, the view from Edinburgh and Glasgow was that the standing and modest independence of the Scottish banking system was at risk. The Government's general strategy was to encourage amalgamations to create conglomerate firms, which were believed to be intrinsically more efficient. Small was perceived as anything but beautiful. The principles which allegedly applied to the car industry were believed to be equally valid for retail banking. In the wake of the creation of the National Westminster Bank in 1968 and the known discussions about a merger between Barclays, Lloyds and Martins, there was inevitable speculation in the City of London throughout 1968 about a bid for Bank of Scotland by one of the London clearers.

Within Scotland the creation of the National Commercial Banking Group Ltd, following the announcement in February 1968 of the amalgamation of the Royal Bank and the National Commercial, added

222 urgency to the situation. In fact Lord Polwarth, Governor of Bank of Scotland, and Lord Clydesmuir, Deputy Governor and Chairman of The British Linen Bank, had informally discussed a possible merger between the two banks during 1967 and the early months of 1968. The directors of both were convinced that a joint bank would be in a stronger position to develop than two separate banks. For The British Linen Bank's parent, Barclays, the merger solved the immediate problem of its Scottish subsidiary, which, as the smallest Scottish bank, appeared to have very limited prospects. It also reserved Barclays' position for the future. The terms involved a detailed audit of the resources of the two banks which revealed that Bank of Scotland possessed two-thirds and The British Linen Bank one-third of their combined assets. Consequently an additional £4.5 million stock was issued, which ensured that 35 per cent of Bank of Scotland stock was to be held in future by Barclays. The ground rules for the relationship between the two were spelled out in Lord Polwarth's statement to the Annual General Meeting on 21 April 1970:

> I would emphasise that a basic condition in our negotiations was that we would continue to maintain and uphold the independence of management that we have jealously guarded for so long as a Scottish bank, at the same time developing and benefiting in every way from the friendly relationship we would have with Barclays. They have also assured us that they will not seek to alter their holding without first consulting the Board of Bank of Scotland.

That assurance was implied in the Agreement document and spelled out in an exchange of letters between Lord Polwarth and Barclays' chairman, John Thompson. It has to be said that the scale of Barclays' concerns elsewhere meant that the proposed merger was from its point of view a straightforward 'deal', and that the decision to proceed or not had rested largely on the shoulders of one of its family directors, Theodore D. Barclay, and the general manager of British Linen, Thomas Walker. There were four strands to their thinking. First, Scotland was over-banked and the merger offered the possibility of rationalisation. Second, British Linen was attracting hostile publicity, particularly from the student population, over Barclays' South African connection and was therefore having difficulty recruiting young, skilled staff. Third, the accountant's examination of the two banks revealed that there was a good fit between their respective customer bases. Finally, looking twenty years ahead from 1968, although British Linen had some very good senior staff then, there did not appear to be talent in depth at lower levels in the bank to be brought on for the future. By contrast, Bank of Scotland's senior management appeared to be weaker (in part this was a function of the age structure of Bank of Scotland staff), but a raft of talented young managers were already beginning to make their mark.

The first step in the amalgamation was an exchange of directors between the banks. Lord Clydesmuir and James Gammell joined the Board of Bank of Scotland, while Lord Polwarth and Lord Balfour of Burleigh joined the board of British Linen. A steering committee of directors from both banks was established during the autumn of 1969 to examine the new bank's future direction. At the same time a number of working parties were created to deal with particular issues, such as the integration of accounting systems and computers. In some cases clear choices had to be made. Bank of Scotland's mainframe was a brand new IBM computer unit, installed in purpose-built premises at Robertson Avenue, Edinburgh. On the other hand British Linen Bank's accounting system was more streamlined and geared to the needs of a much larger clearer. One other major difference was that in the Barclays system, lending control was divorced from the inspection function, unlike Bank of Scotland's, where the two were combined. Approval of lending in Barclays – and therefore the system followed by British Linen – rested on the 'board note', which was very full, whereas Bank of Scotland used the simpler overdraft record sheet. If one were to characterise the differences of approach it would have to be said that Bank of Scotland's was a hierarchical system with centralised control, while the Barclays system relied on dispersed local head offices, which reflected their origins in a number of small partnership banks in different parts of England, in a number of cases strongly influenced by Quaker business principles.

The amalgamation document was in its way a triumph of Scots legal drafting. Sir Alastair Blair and his colleagues at Davidson & Syme, the Bank's constitutional lawyers, had managed to secure – with the agreement of the Privy Council – the legal continuance of The British Linen Bank as a separate Scottish company with a reduced nominal capital of £5,000; but all its other assets and liabilities, tangible and intangible, including the bank-note issue, were transferred to Bank of Scotland. Sentiment towards the British Linen name was strong and there was an underlying belief that it should be preserved for the future.

The amalgamation created a very powerful senior team, with wide and deep experience. James Letham would retire and be succeeded as Treasurer by Tom Walker, British Linen's General Manager. James Letham's second-in-command, Bill Renfrew, headed the Edinburgh team with William Hay, who amongst other duties was heavily involved in the

224   new Bank of Scotland Finance Company; and Duncan Ferguson, Chief Superintendent of Branches, and John F. Wilson, Chief Accountant, became Assistant General Managers. From the British Linen side came James Shearer, David Antonio, later Secretary of the Bank, and Robert Jamieson, while Robert Scott joined Ivan Robson of Bank of Scotland in the branch superintendence. Andrew Russell, the most senior of the British Linen men, went to Glasgow to work alongside Alex Robertson with a view to taking over the West of Scotland business on the latter's retiral. In London, matters were left unchanged, with Donald Kennedy at Threadneedle Street and the team at 30 Bishopsgate under Robert Runciman remaining, with Martin Cowan as senior manager and James Young and Andrew Davidson as assistants.

In 1970, before the arrangements were in place, the sudden illness and death of James Letham was a major setback. In Duncan Ferguson's words:

> A short while previously, the death of Mrs Letham had removed the only restraining influence her husband had ever heeded, and from that time forward he threw himself into the fray with almost frenzied vigour. It was as if a super top gear had been engaged causing the dynamo to spin out of control . . . suddenly the dynamo seized up. James Letham was ill and the Treasurer's room empty . . .

The first board meeting of the combined banks, March 1971

Just six months before the amalgamation date Thomas Walker, General Manager of The British Linen Bank, became Treasurer of Bank of Scotland. The merger was further complicated by the fact that UK decimalisation day was set for 15 February 1971. This involved a great deal of late-night working, particularly in the accountant's, cashier's and computer departments, simply to organise the logistics the changeover demanded. Angus Winton, the cashier, was able to report that all went well on the day. Yet another element in the equation was a completely new bank-note issue, the Sir Walter Scott series, the first of which, the £1 note, was issued to the public on 5 November 1970. The combined note issue almost doubled circulation, and in the event the contract for design, engraving and printing was won by Thomas De La Rue & Co. Ltd, who had been printing British Linen bank-notes since 1961.

To many Bank of Scotland people at the time it seemed to be almost a reverse takeover. There was, however, one publicly announced piece of reassurance to all staff of both banks – namely that, for five years after amalgamation, promotion would go alternately to a member of each bank and not necessarily on strict merit. With a combined staff of 7,223 this went a long way to alleviating the worst fears about branch rationalisation, which everyone knew was the natural corollary of the merger. In fact, the merger settled down very quickly, in no small measure thanks to the leadership and personal charisma of the Treasurer, Tom Walker. He rapidly earned the respect of all his colleagues.

The new Board of the Bank effectively combined the younger elements of the two bank boards, and the evidence suggests that in the early years of the merger their influence on the day-to-day running of the Bank grew. The full list as at the Annual General Meeting of 1971 is as follows:

Governor

The Right Hon. Lord Polwarth, TD, DL, LLD, DLITT, DUniv, CA

Deputy Governor

The Right Hon. Lord Clydesmuir, CB, MBE, TD, LLD

Ordinary Directors

Robert A. Allan, DSO, OBE, Publisher, London
The Right Hon. Lord Balfour of Burleigh, CEng, FIEE
Theodore D. Barclay, Banker, London
William Birkbeck, DL, Banker, London
Sir Alastair Blair, KCVO, TD, Writer to the Signet, Edinburgh
Thomas R. Craig, CBE, TD, LLD, Steelmaker, Glasgow
James T. Dowling, JP, Chartered Accountant, Glasgow
James G.S. Gammell, MBE, Chartered Accountant, Edinburgh
Sir William J. Lithgow, Baronet, Shipbuilder, Port Glasgow
James A. Lumsden, MBE, TD, DL, Writer, Glasgow

Thomas N. Risk, BL, Writer, Glasgow
William F. Robertson, LLD, Shipowner, Glasgow
Sir Hugh Rose, Baronet, TD, DL, Edinburgh
Charles F.J. Younger, DSO, TD, Brewer, Edinburgh

Extraordinary Director

His Grace the Duke of Hamilton, KT, GCVO, AFC, LLD

They represented both the board of Barclays and a wide range of Scottish business interests and, it is fair to say, saw change in a very positive light. As far as senior management was concerned, particular emphasis was to be given to the fields of staff administration, management services and computer applications, along with a further strong commitment to budgeting and cost control.

In the middle of negotiations for amalgamation in 1969 it was announced that oil had been discovered in commercially viable quantities in the North Sea. Aberdeen, as the nearest city and port to the northern sector, would have an important role to play, and Shetland was likely to be shaken out of its dependence on knitwear and fishing. Determined that Bank of Scotland should not miss out on any opportunities which this might present, the Bank subsequently approached Shell Petroleum and secured the services of David Fleming, an oil engineer with a lifetime of experience in the industry. Two years later this was followed by further

Computer Hall in the first Computer Centre, Robertson Avenue, Edinburgh

*Thomas W. Walker,
Treasurer 1970-74*

appointments, and the Bank in due course employed a petroleum reservoir engineer in Edinburgh and in North America. As American, particularly Texan, oil expertise flowed into the north-east of Scotland, it was the curious completion of a circle which had begun 150 years earlier. In the development of Texas, Scottish investment companies based in Dundee and Aberdeen had been so successful that in 1893 the legislature forbade them from acquiring further land or water rights. Many Texan oil families have names instantly recognisable in Banff and Buchan.

The major task after amalgamation was to deal with the duplication of branches. This was achieved in two distinct ways. Bill Park and John Kinniburgh, the premises managers of British Linen and Bank of Scotland respectively, with their staffs visited and reported on the physical condition of property, while joint inspectors' teams under Duncan Ferguson and Alex Robertson considered the business and staffing aspects of merger. In some instances there was no doubt at all about which office should be retained; in others the decision was difficult. In many places the office favoured was the purpose-built Victorian bank house, because it enabled back-office functions to be moved away from the telling areas and allowed for future expansion. The second approach was a direct outcome of the work of the management accountant. PA Management Consultants were commissioned to prepare *A Branch Location Study*, which was delivered in 1973. Its conclusions arrived after the bulk of the work had been done, and seeming only to be a final tidying up, it was on the whole not followed. On the other hand, it developed further the methods of assessing branch viability. In retrospect, and perhaps like most projections of future performance, it underestimated the impact of external circumstances on the Bank. Between 1971 and 1974, 130 branches were merged or closed as surplus to requirements and a further 50 identified for merger when premises or a suitable new site for building could be found. For all concerned this involved a great deal of work, but it was carried through with remarkably little fuss. There were two important matters which helped. First, in 1971 a joint management-staff liaison committee was formed at which local problems could be aired and if possible dealt with. This in turn was the key to good working relations with the National Union of Bank Employees. Second, the pre-retirement bulge in the age structure of branch management in Bank of Scotland and British Linen permitted a new generation of managers to begin with a clean slate.

It was in these complex situations that the personnel skills of Sydney Hudson began to prove their worth and to become accepted by some who had previously doubted their value. The benefits to the organisation of

The Sir Walter Scott bank-note design, first issued in 1971

228 recruiting individuals who possessed particular non-banking skills, for example lawyers and accountants, and the programme of sending young bankers on MBA and MSc degree courses was begun at this time. The groundwork laid provided the trained staff for the Bank's rapid expansion a decade later.

The process of amalgamation also permitted great strides to be made in the insurance commission problem discussed earlier. An insurance services department was set up under John Moore, trained by Royal Insurance and recruited from Alan J. Thompson, the Newcastle insurance brokers. After 1970 as managers retired, their insurance business was managed centrally, and concerted efforts were made to buy out those remaining. The process was largely completed by 1975, but there were a few individuals who resisted and carried their business on into the 1980s.

On 16 June 1970 Edward Heath and the Conservative Party were returned to power, determined to reverse wage-led inflation and to reduce public subsidies for 'lame duck' industries (for example, coal, steel, shipbuilding). As part of this, the bank rate was raised to 7 per cent and a month later all banks were asked once again to restrict their lending. The threatened demise of Rolls-Royce, the aero-engine company, in November of that year required Government support, and over the winter of 1970–71 lending controls were relaxed.

The Oil Bank

Six months after formal amalgamation in of the Bank and The British Linen in 1971 a new framework for all the clearing banks in the UK was put into place. The Government publication *Competition and Credit Control* was the acknowledgment by the Bank of England and the Treasury that tight quantitative controls on banks were unnecessary and that henceforth they would be permitted to compete for the business which up to then had become the preserve of secondary banks and finance houses. Specifically, existing liquidity and lending ceilings were to be replaced by reliance on interest rates, calls for special deposits with the Bank of England, and a new minimum assets ratio of 12.5 per cent of sterling deposit liabilities. The traditional liquidity ratio was to be stated in clearly defined reserve assets. This last caused immediate difficulty and the Treasurer went to the Bank of England on behalf of all the Scottish banks to argue that the cover held in the Bank of England for bank-note issue in Scotland should be included among reserve assets. This and other technical matters relating to short-term borrowing to cover the Scottish cheque-clearing system were of no interest in London. The report to the Scottish banks by Thomas Walker indicated that the Bank of England was primarily concerned with the uniformity of the system. Some informal concessions were made. One underlying purpose was to oblige the Scottish banks to hold more short-dated Government securities and it became necessary to split the Bank's investments into two: a 'liquidity or trading book' of gilt stocks maturing within two years, and an 'investment portfolio' of stocks maturing after two years or more.

The timing of the move to a more competitive marketplace was unfortunate because it speeded up to an unsustainable degree tendencies which were becoming apparent in the economy. Public sector borrowing rose and inflation began to gather momentum. The outcome of competition was that the Scottish and English clearers found their terms for business being challenged by new financial institutions which were not subject to the same degree of scrutiny or regulation. The Bank, like all banks, lost customers to a number of secondary banking institutions which offered a higher return rate on deposits and were prepared to lend on less rigorous examination of the proposals. One of the worst features of the situation was that customers borrowed cheaply on overdraft from their clearing bank and then redeposited the funds with a secondary institution at a profit. Much of this money found its way into speculative building and consumer spending: 1972 was a boom year, adding fuel to the fires that eventually led to the secondary banking crisis of 1974.

Within the Bank there were a number of difficulties. Throughout 1972 Bank of Scotland shares languished on the stock market. One reason for this was that the Actuary of the Bank Pension Fund discovered that it was underfunded and a special provision of 3 per cent had to be made from the Bank's pre-tax profits to cover the deficiency. Among other things this was the necessary precursor of further branch amalgamation. The same year Lord Polwarth was asked to join the Heath Government as a Minister of State at the Scottish Office with responsibility for oil and therefore had

Signing the first oil production loan on behalf of the Bank: Howard Duke, David Fleming, Thomas Walker

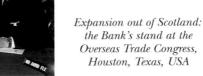

Semi-submersible exploration oil-rig in the North Sea

Expansion out of Scotland: the Bank's stand at the Overseas Trade Congress, Houston, Texas, USA

230   to resign all the directorships he then held, including the Governorship of Bank of Scotland. His successor was the Deputy Governor, Lord Clydesmuir, through whom the Bank's traditional connection with the Colville family was continued.

On 29 June 1972 the Bank gave the business community at large the clearest indication that it was moving in new directions. The Savoy Hotel in London saw the first UK conference on the funding and development of North Sea oil, sponsored by Bank of Scotland and organised by Bruce Pattullo under the guidance of Tom Walker. It was a vital step in raising the profile of the Bank, which shortly afterwards joined the consortium providing partial recourse funding for the development of the Forties Oil Field. The total requirement was for £360 million to provide production facilities and pipelines, one to Cruden Bay, Aberdeenshire, and the other to the BP refinery at Grangemouth. The Bank received a letter of congratulation from BP for being the first UK bank to commit itself to the Forties Field development. As a corollary to this the Bank began to look at organising oil development consortia with other, particularly Scandinavian, banks. William Hay, now General Manager, toured European banks, where he found much interest but little in the way of concrete proposals. Clearly, a Bank of Scotland initiative was needed if the Bank was to compete with American banks specialising in oil and gas financing. Discussions were opened with both Barclays and Banque Worms. From their own experience of consortia, Barclays insisted that the two lead banks should control 52 per cent of the equity. The major problem from Bank of Scotland's point of view was that Barclays wished to include nuclear power generation as part of the remit, whereas Bank of Scotland wanted to confine the consortium to oil and gas production. In the end, the International Energy Bank was set up in conjunction with the Canadian Imperial Bank and the Republic National Bank of Dallas, which insisted on a more democratic structure and clearly defined aims (Bank of Scotland 15 per cent, Barclays Bank International 15 per cent, Société Financière Européenne 20 per cent, Banque Worms 10 per cent, Canadian Imperial 20 per cent, Republic National 20 per cent).

On advice from its own experts Bank of Scotland concentrated its efforts on the development of oil and gas reservoirs and did not take a major part in the more speculative exploration end of the business. There were two exceptions to this. Participations were taken in Pict Petroleum, established by the young and dynamic Edinburgh merchant bank, Noble Grossart, and in Viking Oil, established by Ivory & Sime, the Scottish investment house. In most cases the Bank operated in the traditional way by providing term loans and overdrafts rather than taking equity stakes. The variety and scale of projects relating to oil was immense, and required a large commitment from

Classification of Advances 1973 and 1978
(figures in £s sterling)

Sector	Year ending mid-February 1973	%	Year ending mid-February 1978	%
Manufacturing				
Food, drinks and tobacco	16,791,000	3.8	36,483,000	4.3
Chemicals and allied industries	12,102,000	2.8	13,555,000	1.6
Metal manufacturing	4,810,000	1.1	5,495,000	0.6
Electrical engineering	4,755,000	1.1	5,944,000	0.7
Other engineering and metal goods	14,012,000	3.2	22,076,000	2.6
Shipbuilding	25,814,000	5.9	34,545,000	4.1
Vehicles	1,156,000	0.3	2,054,000	0.2
Textiles, leather and clothing	5,342,000	1.2	18,724,000	2.2
Other manufacturing	9,656,000	2.2	17,912,000	2.1
Other production				
Agriculture and forestry	40,122,000	9.1	79,471,000	9.4
Fishing	378,000	0.1	1,917,000	0.2
Mining and quarrying	210,000	0.0	25,500,000	3.0
Construction	15,363,000	3.5	26,987,000	3.2
Financial				
Hire-purchase finance companies	17,730,000	4.0	14,104,000	1.7
Property companies	11,977,000	2.7	18,429,000	2.2
Insurance enterprises (incl. pension funds)			14,206,000	1.7
Unit and quoted investment trusts			9,391,000	1.1
Stockbrokers and jobbers			154,000	0.0
Building societies			169,000	0.0
UK banks	2,063,000	0.5		
Other financial (incl. unquoted trusts from 1975)	54,424,000	12.4	9,966,000	1.2
Services				
Transport and communication	8,316,000	1.9	33,004,000	3.9
Public utilities/national govt	5,154,000	1.2	25,848,000	3.0
Local government services	18,313,000	4.2	3,704,000	0.4
Retail distribution	11,761,000	2.7	30,701,000	3.6
Other distribution	23,118,000	5.3	33,129,000	3.9
Professional, scientific, misc. services	51,340,000	11.7	71,973,000	8.5
Personal				
Bridging finance			7,089,000	0.8
House purchase	9,865,000	2.3	24,602,000	2.9
Other personal	64,764,000	14.8	86,372,000	10.2
Overseas residents (incl. banks overseas)	8,695,000	2.0	174,458,000	20.6
Total	438,031,000	100.0	847,962,000	99.9

the Bank's resources. This level of activity helped to keep the Bank out of the building and consumer boom of 1972–73, and therefore allowed it to escape the worst consequences of the secondary banking collapse when it came. A brief look at the table on page 231 demonstrates clearly how the quantum and structure of the Bank's lending had changed from that of a decade earlier (see page 212, Table 1). One important benefit for some of the Bank's customers was that the oil boom led to knock-on demand for its more traditional engineering and shipbuilding products. This in turn created a demand for additional borrowing from the Bank.

The main underlying problem of the boom of 1971–73 was that it was channelled into consumer spending, and imports were drawn into the country, producing a steadily deteriorating balance of trade. The hoped-for investment in British industrial capacity simply did not happen. A variety of new financial instruments were developed at this time which fuelled speculation. The first major casualty was the banking department of the Scottish Co-operative Wholesale Society, which had 'played the market' by issuing forward certificates of deposit on a very large scale. By June 1973 it faced a loss of £40 million and each rise in interest rates made the position worse. Collectively the three Scottish banks were clearing bankers for the Society, and the Bank of England initially took the view that this was a Scottish problem to be sorted out locally. However, the scale of the problem and the level of transactions with London-based banks were such that it required the creation of a 'lifeboat', with the losses shared out among the London clearers, the Scottish banks and the Bank of England. In one comment at the time, the Co-op's banking department was compared to a novice gin rummy player joining a professional poker game . . . with equally predictable results.

This provided a valuable training exercise for handling the much more widespread collapse of secondary banks during the winter of 1973–74, when the bank rate rose from 8 to 13 per cent. Among the clearers the National Westminster appeared to be the hardest hit, and its share price collapsed. In the wider world the impact of a great hike in oil prices by OPEC in the aftermath of the Yom Kippur War between Israel and the Arab States, and the three-day week, the result of the Government's struggle with the National Union of Mineworkers, induced a feeling close to panic. Bank of Scotland's portion of losses in the Bank of England's lifeboat operation for the secondary banks was to be 2.6 per cent of realised losses, with an aggregate ceiling for all the banks of £1.2 billion. Predictably, the impact of this absorption of available credit, which was followed in the new year of 1974 by a call for special deposits, hit first at business investment and produced a crisis of confidence in many of the Bank's customers. The best measure of the Bank's skills in avoiding the worst effects of these years is that in 1975, with advances of over £614 million, it made a provision of 1.1 per cent for losses.

On the Bank's home front the financial year 1973, which was reported in April 1974, saw significant changes in the Bank's top management. In reporting these matters to the Proprietors Lord Clydesmuir had this to say:

> The sudden death of Mr William Hay, Joint General Manager (Special Duties) . . . came as a great personal blow to all of us. He was right at the centre of our plans for the future and his untimely passing from the scene could have caused us serious dislocation.

The imminent retiral at the end of April 1974 of Thomas Walker, the Treasurer, created a potentially difficult situation. The Bank was very fortunate that it had in Andrew Russell, the Joint General Manager in Glasgow, someone willing and able to take on the Treasurership. His role in Glasgow was taken by Duncan Ferguson, who recalls the handover period with affection as one in which great care was taken to see that he was fully briefed and introduced to the Bank's major customers. The tasks facing the new Treasurer were formidable. Many of the initiatives to complete the Bank of Scotland–British Linen merger were not yet realised, requiring tact and restraint to bring them to a successful conclusion. Britain's external situation deteriorated rapidly from the autumn of 1973; inflation soared, reaching 22 per cent during the summer of 1975 and requiring an application to the International Monetary Fund in 1976. It would be difficult to dissent from the view that the situation required from a Treasurer all the traditional banking skills plus a very cool head.

There were also important changes in London. The businesses of Bank of Scotland and the former British Linen in the City were merged at the time of the retiral of Donald Kennedy from Threadneedle Street and Robert Runciman from Bishopsgate. Martin Cowan became Joint General Manager, London, with Andrew Davidson as manager of London Chief Office. One other significant development at that time was the relocation of the Bank of Scotland Finance Company Limited to its own premises at 4 Melville Street, Edinburgh.

The year 1975 saw two very important internal changes in organisation. The inspection and audit function was separated from lending control, and a branch administration was created which matched the geographical areas of the local boards of directors. Among other purposes it was

234

designed to speed up decision-making and allow the enlarged Bank to identify more closely with the local community. This was very much the work of Bill Renfrew, who had stayed on beyond retirement age to see it into place. The second important innovation was the creation of a fully fledged international division under James Young to deal with all aspects of energy financing, international trade and foreign exchange dealing. These were both important elements of the first Group Corporate Plan, which attempted to chart the way forward for the succeeding five years.

The most notable event of 1976 from a staff viewpoint was the successful merger of the three pension funds and two widows funds into the Bank of Scotland (1976) Pension Scheme. In some ways this was the most sensitive and difficult part of the task of merger. David Antonio, the Bank Secretary, aided by Alan Thomson among others, burned the midnight oil for many months over the details so that it would be right. The Governor and Treasurer had a difficult job persuading the Directors that this was the correct course of action. In 1977 Thomas Craig retired as Deputy Governor of the Bank, while Theodore Barclay of Barclays' board was succeeded by Sir Richard Pease. Two Deputy Governors were elected: Thomas Risk, who was also chairman of the Bank of Scotland Finance Company; and Lord Balfour of Burleigh, who chaired a number of the crucial Board committees which had supervised the changes of the previous ten years.

During the 1970s the Bank of Scotland Finance Company had been developing its corporate finance business and had begun to take on many of the characteristics of a merchant bank. The Bank's corporate plan of 1975 argued that the logic should be followed through and that it should have an independent and distinctive identity. To the delight of most former members of British Linen, a solution was available. The British Linen Bank was revived by increasing its capital from £5,000 to £8 million. Negotiations with both the Bank of England and the Department of Trade and Industry were very delicate. In the end, British Linen was permitted to resume trading, provided that it now registered as a limited company under Part VIII of the Companies Act 1948. On 30 November 1977, through the use of the Private Legislation (Scotland) Act, the functions (and staff) of the Finance Company were transferred to The British Linen Bank Limited, with Thomas Risk, former chairman of both the Bank of Scotland Finance Company and Standard Life Assurance Company, as its first chairman.

There was one matter which rumbled on in the background through these years. It had a number of different facets, but in the end it boiled down to the Bank's relationship with Barclays, and possible conflicts of

Cover of the Annual Report to Proprietors

interest. In January 1975 National Westminster Bank announced that it was to open its first branch in Scotland, and the next day Barclays, without further consulting Bank of Scotland, followed suit. It was a logical enough development out of *Competition and Credit Control*, but it did run contrary to both the 1875 'gentlemen's agreement' between Scottish and English banks about not encroaching on each other's territory and Bank of Scotland's understanding of the 1971 Agreement with Barclays. At first the direct expansion of English banks into Scotland appeared to be a great threat. It was particularly galling because the Bank of Scotland Board had recently rejected a proposal from West Area that a branch be opened in Carlisle on the grounds that it ran contrary to Barclays' interests. To be fair to the English clearers, during the 1970s some 33 non-indigenous banks opened offices in Scotland, hoping to take advantage of oil-related business, and Barclays felt that it could not afford to forego such opportunities. In reality, for Bank of Scotland it was a great liberation which permitted the Bank to look at expanding into the much larger English market. However, the margins for profit in Scottish retail banking in 1975 were then being squeezed by so many new arrivals that the vulnerability of the three Scots clearers to competition was increased. Informal conversations among the three banks (Bank of Scotland, the Royal and the Clydesdale) affirmed that survival would depend upon increasing the efficiency of their branch networks and preventing the English clearers from expanding their toehold. In contrast, as Bank of Scotland began to advance into the English market in the 1980s it found to its surprise that profit margins on corporate business in the provinces were better than it could then achieve north of the border. Even in the 1970s the rapid expansion of North West Securities from Chester had already provided competition to Barclays in their home territory. This was epitomised by NWS agreeing a new joint venture with the Automobile Association, which had previously been an important customer of Mercantile Credit Ltd, a Barclays subsidiary.

Andrew Russell,
Treasurer 1974-79

It also transpired that there was a deliberate effort to bring Bank of Scotland into Barclays' world-wide policy. This again was contrary to the spirit if not the letter of the 1971 Agreement. Rightly or wrongly, the confidence in Barclays, carefully developed by Theodore Barclay, evaporated and the 'Men on the Mound' (as the *Scotsman* had begun to call the Bank) determined to control their own destiny.

236 It was about this time, in 1976–77, that the Bank began to receive proposals about taking participations in large foreign loans. Some were led by Barclays, and a significant number were in South America. Bank of Scotland was very cautious for two reasons. In most of this consortia lending it was offered only minority participation and therefore would have little control over the conduct of any consortium. This was characterised in one Board paper (which turned down the application) as 'crumbs from others' tables'. More positively, the Directors, on the advice of the Treasurer, were cautious about lending to politically unstable countries and believed that the core of Bank of Scotland's lending should remain with its domestic customers and in businesses of which, from experience, it had developed detailed knowledge. In the event, some loans were made in Latin America, but not on a scale which skewed the Bank's lending book or posed a threat to its other activities.

In September 1978 Bruce Pattullo was made Deputy Treasurer of the Bank; it was subsequently announced that he would succeed Andrew Russell on 4 July 1979. Ian Brown was moved from International Division to be chief executive of The British Linen Bank. Sadly, Ronnie Craig, Divisional General Manager of the Computer Division, died. He, probably more than any other individual, was responsible for the Bank's pioneering use of computers. Much of his work was unseen and unsung, and it deserves a mention in the Bank's annals.

In 1978 a Bank Group-wide profit sharing scheme was introduced. Its provisions were such that the allocation could be taken by individual members of staff as either cash or stock. The Directors felt, despite some dilution of the shareholding, that this move acknowledged the great efforts that staff at all levels of the Bank had made in previous years. It was believed that staff would give even greater commitment if they had a direct stake in the Bank's success. This proved to be a very significant step.

Andrew Russell's strong belief that the key to success in retail banking lay in having the right people in the right places meant that great pains were taken over branch appointments. He also saw it as the proper duty of the Bank to take care of staff relationships and problems. This added considerably to the feeling of confidence and coherence of purpose within the Bank, which had been successfully steered through some turbulent years.

Bank of Scotland in the USSR, 1977

—17—

THE 1980s

I N May 1979, just two months before Bruce Pattullo became the twenty-fifth Treasurer of Bank of Scotland, a general election returned the Conservative Party to power at Westminster. The previous year had been one of widespread industrial action, culminating in the 'Winter of Discontent'; and the Scottish economy, which had begun to show signs of revival during 1978, was already slipping back into recession. One reason for this was the doubling of oil prices by OPEC earlier in the year. The seasonally adjusted unemployment total in Scotland (including school-leavers) stood at 8.6 per cent in February 1979 against a UK average of 5.7 per cent. Job losses continued to be particularly severe in heavy engineering and therefore in the West of Scotland. The Bank's reaction to the new Government's agenda, which was little less than the radical transformation of the old economic and social consensus, was cautious. On the one hand the earlier rejection of plans for a devolved Scottish Assembly was welcomed, because inherent flaws in the proposals made it a potent source of uncertainty. On the other hand, in its evidence to the Wilson Committee on Banking in 1976-77 the Bank had stated that it was very much alive to its responsibilities in the diversification and regeneration of Scottish industry. The problem, as Lord Clydesmuir, the Governor, made clear in his annual statement in May 1979, was that banks 'must operate within the bounds of commercial prudence' but that 'sometimes the co-operation of government agencies can tilt the scales in favour of a proposition which would not otherwise meet their criteria'. To the new Government, committed to the application of the market to

238   industry and commerce, such observations were almost heretical.

The Government's plans were made explicit in Geoffrey Howe's Budget of 1980, in which the medium-term financial strategy was outlined, with the stated aim of reducing monetary growth to achieve low wage-inflation and stable prices. The increase in interest rates to 14.6 per cent, coupled with the doubling of oil prices and the consequent upward adjustment of sterling's exchange rate as an 'oil' currency, produced a savage deflation. In the Annual Report to Proprietors in 1980 Lord Clydesmuir predicted that the measures would hurt Scottish business in the short term, but he hoped that they would result in a reinvigorated industrial and commercial sector in Scotland. Among the Bank's Directors and senior management there was ambivalence about the Government's approach to regional policy. On the positive side, the Bank's management was young and amongst the best-trained the Bank had ever possessed (a number had completed the Harvard Business School's Advanced Management Programme under Bank sponsorship). They were therefore well versed in the wider economic arguments, known to the public in Britain by the shorthand title of 'monetarism'. Their experience within the Bank during the 1970s had built a platform of confidence which made them eager to compete on equal terms with all comers. Moreover, North Sea oil prospered and needed new investment – an opportunity in which Bank of Scotland had a lively interest.

On the negative side, a great deal of senior management time in 1980–81 was spent on 'firefighting' to help the Bank's customers, many of them of very long standing, through an exceptionally difficult period of adjustment. The problem, certainly in Scotland (and in much of the English provinces), was that most companies had struggled to create sufficient profit to reinvest in new capital equipment during the 1970s. A tentative start during 1978-79 was brought to a halt by a rise in exchange rates which made British goods uncompetitive in international markets. Not all the Bank's efforts were successful, and Scotland lost some famous names. Within the Bank this strengthened the conviction that a policy which was effectively 'the deil tak' the hindmost' was not in keeping with either its own traditions or, more importantly, its future interests. A vibrant and growing Scottish economy was the only solid foundation upon which the Bank could base its plans for rapid expansion. One other consequence of the changes of these years was the rapid growth and centralisation of financial services. The increased dominance of City of London institutions over aspects of Scottish economic life, and their failure to understand the wider consequences of their actions, was a source of increasing disquiet.

There were two specific incidents in the early 1980s which more than any other shaped attitudes on the Mound. The full story will have to wait for a future historian, but there was sufficient comment in Scottish newspapers for the public to be well aware of the issues involved. On 7 August 1981 the Bank of England announced the sale of its recently completed Glasgow Office at 21 West George Street to the Royal Bank of Scotland. In the notes accompanying the press release the Bank of England said that it had:

> established an office in Glasgow in 1940 for the purpose of administering the Exchange Control Regulations, and later for maintaining contact with industry in Scotland. A decision to rebuild the agency was taken in 1970, and to extend its activities to include the issue and withdrawal of Bank of England notes in Scotland.

The note went on to say that the volume of work had proved less than anticipated and that the staff employed on note-issue work would be redeployed. Initially the Bank of England had felt that it was simply responding to the perceived needs of English and foreign banks which were attracted to Scotland during the 1970s and it saw no reason why these banks should be placed at a disadvantage by being forced to carry (and pay for) Scottish bank-notes. It was, however, a draft clause in the 1980 Currency Bill to have *all* Bank of England notes recognised as legal tender in Scotland – a status denied to Scottish bank-notes in Scotland, let alone in England and Wales – which set alarm bells ringing within the Committee of Scottish Clearing Bankers. The long-term future of the Scottish banks' note issue seemed to be in doubt. The announcement therefore acknowledged, amicably enough, that Scottish bank-note issue would continue as before and that the Bank of England would continue to operate through the three Scottish Clearers, with its Glasgow agency reverting to its former role of liaison with Scottish industry.

The second matter was the agreed takeover bid for the Royal Bank of Scotland by Standard Chartered Bank and the subsequent hostile bid by the Hong Kong and Shanghai Bank. These events were referred to the Monopolies and Mergers Commission, whose report in January 1982 eventually quashed both proposals. A team from the Bank had given evidence to the Monopolies Commission and had argued strongly for the retention of the Royal Bank as an independent Scottish bank with its head office in Edinburgh. It would be fair to say that many London commentators saw Scottish opposition to the proposals as merely parochial small-mindedness which ran directly contrary to the economic

240   logic of global banking and concentration in the City of London. This view showed a (characteristic) misreading of the forces at work and an underestimate of the issues involved. The failure of the bids left the Royal Bank to pursue the vigorous independent development which has led to its becoming an important and distinctive competitor in British banking. Within Bank of Scotland the principles raised brought into even sharper focus the strategy being shaped. Real competition in the UK market, it was seen, must come not from ever fewer (and larger) metropolitan banks, but from diversity. The fallacy of the merits-of-size argument in 1982 led to the risk of potential predators concluding that Bank of Scotland might want or need the protection of a 'big brother'. The conduct and successful outcome of this debate and the fierce resolve it engendered are seen by some of those involved as being important elements in the Bank's drive forward in the 1980s.

The regional element of the debate was (and is) a continuing one, and was most strongly worded by the Governor, Sir Thomas Risk, in his annual statement to the Bank's Proprietors in 1984:

> COMPETITION AND REGIONAL POLICY
>
> I make no apology for returning again this year to the theme of regional policy and, to the extent that it bears on the same subject, of competition policy. It cannot be stated too often that the prosperity of the United Kingdom depends upon proper use of all its assets. A policy which allows a centralising drift to operate without restraint, in response to the strong pull of London, will weaken the Regions without corresponding benefit to the centre. Short-term financial logic and stock market forces can always be used to make a case for concentration, but such influences are often destructive of local confidence and enterprise. The long-term good will be better served by a wide variety of companies, located throughout the regions and led by people who are identified, and identify themselves, with the communities in which their businesses operate. Scotland is distinctive with its vigorous financial services sector and burgeoning high technology industries. These are the elements of future success and prosperity and they must be used to the full.

The Bank's approach to its situation and business was brought together in 1984 in that year's marketing campaign, which launched the *Friend for Life* slogan, introduced staff outfits for the first time and planned to increase the number of regional offices in England. It was a high-profile strategy, increasing corporate identity and sense of purpose, the corollary of which was the need to deliver a quality service at all levels of the Bank's business. In 1986 the introduction of a corporate statement encapsulated the Bank's ambitions for itself and its customers and its place in Scottish life.

CORPORATE STATEMENT

The Bank of Scotland Group aims

to provide a range of distinctive financial services throughout the United Kingdom and internationally;

to maintain its reputation for stability and integrity and to show long-term growth in profits and dividends;

to be professional, friendly, prompt and imaginative in its dealings with customers;

to train, develop, inform, respect and encourage staff so that they can perform an effective and fulfilling role.

Through its branch network, the clearing bank aims to make a particular contribution to the cultural and economic prosperity of Scotland.

It was recognised that the strength of the Bank's stance depended on its success, which included dynamic changes in its own structure, a quite remarkable growth in business – and profitability. A strategy had been outlined by Bruce Pattullo and his senior team at the Managers' Conferences at Peebles in November 1979. Some of the elements were already in place. The key was to be expansion into the English market by building regional offices in the major provincial centres, primarily for business customers. The personal customer was served by a new Central Credit Services Department (in 1993 renamed Centrebank), initially to develop and market consumer credit products and mortgage business in England which could be run from Edinburgh. In June 1979 the Bank's House Purchase Loan Scheme had been launched throughout the Scottish branch system. Most banks produced similar loan schemes at about the same time; up to this point banks had not competed with the building society movement. Two major differences between Scotland and England were that in 1979 home-ownership in Scotland constituted just over 46 per cent of the market, compared with nearly 63 per cent in England, and that in Scotland the building society movement was much weaker. It was also clearly seen that the existence of a branch mortgage would provide opportunities for the Bank to offer other loans and insurance provision, an area of income in which the Bank was relatively weak compared with its rivals. Crucially, because of the expense and time it would take, it was decided that a high street branch network would not be built in England, but that the approach would be via computer technology and electronic banking services. The widespread introduction of autotellers required a very large increase in computing power, and the installation of IBM 3600s necessitated the building of a completely new Computer Centre at Sighthill, with the possibility of at least two phases of expansion. On the international front the Hong Kong Office was opened during the summer of 1979, and a further US Representative Office in Los Angeles.

242   When Lord Clydesmuir retired as Governor in 1981 he handed over to his successor, Thomas Risk, a bank which had made significant strides in the ten years since the Bank of Scotland–British Linen Bank merger and was already expanding rapidly. In 1971 Deposits stood at £578 million, Advances at £312 million, with Balance Sheet totals just short of £700 million. In 1981 the comparable figures were Deposits £3,113 million, Advances £2,085 million and Balance Sheet totals £3.5 billion, a remarkable achievement when set against the wider economic difficulties of the 1970s.

In 1981 the Bank's 150th autoteller was installed; the steady increase in computing capacity led to a number of experiments in self-service banking; and the first steps were taken in a computerised branch-located information system for customers. In these circumstances it was inevitable that the Bank

Sir Thomas Risk, Governor 1981-91, by David Donaldson

should see the rapid development of the electronics industry in the central belt of Scotland (known as Silicon Glen) as possibly an important direction for the future, and identify strongly with it. Another new direction was the acquisition of a 36 per cent shareholding (later increased to 100 per cent) in Kellock Factors Ltd, a company which, under Ben Allen, specialised in recourse factoring and, subsequently, invoice discounting, both growing areas of business for customers in many industries and services who needed to maximise the cash available against their debtors. Some customers went further and preferred to subcontract their entire 'sales ledger'. On the international front the Bank was granted a Banking Licence in New York and opened a full branch there under Brian Lambert. At home the science of reservoir engineering had proved very reliable, and great progress was shown in loans for oil and gas production. Effective use of sensitivity analysis demonstrated a new professionalism in bank lending.

It was not only the Clearing Bank which thrived. British Linen Bank was granted 'eligible status', which allowed it to rediscount bills of exchange at the Bank of England, thereby acknowledging it as Scotland's largest merchant bank. Similarly, North West Securities, with Lord Balfour as chairman, served a different customer group in a very different way, and rapidly expanded both its business and its profits.

The speed of expansion was made possible by the structural changes in organisation. Symbolic of the new sense of purpose was the early abolition of the central Business Development Unit, originally created to look for new business. Instead every branch manager (and every manager of a 'cost' centre) was to have responsibility for hunting out new business, and all were expected to be familiar with new developments in their 'patch'. But there were no geographical limits on branches. There was, for example, no objection to Edinburgh's Morningside branch developing significant business connections with Poole in Dorset, provided the customer was happy to use a long-distance connection and the branch could service the customer to their mutual satisfaction. The development of electronic banking and information systems during the 1980s meant that physical distance from one's customer became an increasingly less important issue.

The second change was possibly the most important of all, though it is doubtful if many people appreciated its full significance at the time. The Bank's Board of Directors, all of whom were non-executive, supported by committees consisting partly of Directors and partly of senior executives, carried responsibility for the Bank's policy decisions. By 1980 it had become apparent that the growth and diversity of the Bank's activities required

244   radical changes in the decision-making process if the Bank was to compete successfully. The solution was to retain a traditional Board of Directors, chaired by the Governor, but with Bruce Pattullo, the Treasurer, as the sole executive Director, and to create a new, wholly executive Management Board, chaired by the Treasurer and attended by the Governor, through which the principal line functions of the Clearing Bank would report. This was a revolutionary change in the way the Bank was managed, defining clearly the relative responsibilities of the Board of Directors and the Bank management. In 1981 the Management Board came into existence with just seven members: the Treasurer, Bruce Pattullo; Andrew Davidson, responsible for the Bank's business in England; James McMillan, Joint General Manager, West Area; Ivan Robson, his counterpart for East Area; Dr Joan Smith, the Bank Secretary; John F. Wilson, Joint General Manager, Head Office; and James Young, in charge of International Operations.

Over the next decade other General Managers were added to the Management Board, which became the 'engine of progress', as the Governor has described it, creating within the Bank short communication lines and speedy decision-making. In the words of one jaundiced wit, Bank of Scotland 'like to say *no* faster than any other bank'! The importance of the Management Board was recognised by including a list of its members in the Annual Report and Accounts. One other benefit of the change, which was not perhaps bankable but which permeated throughout, was a considerable *élan*, a feeling that banking was exciting and that Bank of Scotland was the best. This confidence was boosted by the fact that it was widely known that the Bank's prime strategy for growth within the UK was an organic one, relying on its own resources rather than on acquisition or merger. In the mid-1980s the Bank looked seriously at the possibility of acquiring a bank in Texas, where the Bank through its involvement with the oil industry had many friends, but where a number of local banks had encountered problems. The experience of other UK banks in the American market suggested care, but International Division examined all possibilities, including a Federal Deposit Insurance Corporation 'assisted transaction' where the acquirer was not obliged to take over troubled loans. Proposals were made to the FDIC in 1987 for First City National of Houston and in 1989 for the MCorp franchise in Dallas. Although unsuccessful – indeed the FDIC has never awarded a mandate to an overseas bank – it was believed that Bank of Scotland was only pipped at the post in Dallas by Banc One of Columbus, Ohio.

The speed of expansion required care to keep the Bank's capital ratios within the limits required by the Bank of England. In 1981 US$100 million

of subordinated floating rate stock was added to the Bank's Balance Sheet. 245
It was somewhat more than irritating to the Bank that in the same year the
Government imposed a special 4 per cent tax on retail banking deposits.
In line with its traditions, the Bank adopted an essentially prudent
approach to both liquidity and provisioning for bad debt.

During 1983 three new steps were taken. Firstly the Bank introduced its
Money Market Cheque Account, the first UK bank to offer near-market
rates on a chequing facility, to more substantial personal customers. It was
an instant success and was followed by all the other clearing banks in due
course. Secondly the Bank had begun to issue its own Visa credit card in
1982, and this led directly to a decision to build a credit card processing
centre of its own at Pitreavie, south of Dunfermline in Fife. Work began
during 1985 and the centre was fully operational by September 1987.
Thirdly a pilot experiment with the Nottingham Building Society on home
banking called Homelink, using a small keyboard and a telephone line,
hinted at the way ahead; at the same time systems work was begun within
the Management Services Division of the Bank to develop a full-scale
Home and Office Banking Service (HOBS) to be made available
nationwide. It was launched, the first electronic banking system in the UK,
in January 1985. The Bank's reputation for innovation had never been
higher. Archie Gibson played a significant role in product development,
and Robin Browning in pioneering electronic banking and foreseeing the
plastic card revolution.

The first Managers' Conferences at Peebles in 1979 were expanded
into major events in Glasgow in both 1984 and 1985. These provided a
progress report to all the Bank's managers about how they were doing
both in relation to each other and in comparison with the other banks.
The figures were very encouraging. One piece of analysis said it all.

UK Banking Groups (1984–85) Growth in Pre-Tax Profits

Percentage Growth Over:

	Last Year	Five Years Ago	Ten Years Ago
Barclays	17.6	23.7	314.3
Lloyds	11.7	69.2	524.8
Midland	(40.0)	(57.3)	40.5
NatWest	27.5	52.0	457.8
Royal Bank of Scotland	37.5	35.9	155.9
Bank of Scotland	35.6	98.0	474.3

246   The message was clear. With the exception of Midland Bank, which had run into particular problems of its own, the whole retail banking system in the UK was expanding rapidly, and Bank of Scotland was up with the best.

Hand in hand with this expansion, the Bank's branches underwent major alterations and updating to make them appropriate to the Bank's business. Branches continued to be closed or amalgamated according to the principles, suitably refined, of a decade earlier. The revamped branches were to be light, airy and customer-friendly. The most obvious visual change was the steady elimination of 'bandit screens' from all but the high-value cash areas, and the development of a distinctive house style. In London the former British Linen Bank office in Threadneedle Street was largely rebuilt as the Bank's London Chief Office, a decision simplified by the demand of the City authorities that the front of the Bishopsgate office be moved back 14 feet for road widening. From 1983 Head Office on the Mound was altered and refurbished to strip away some of the less happy accretions which time and business need had added to it since 1870. The old Inspectors' Department on the first floor was turned into a gallery, with five smaller rooms for the Mound-based senior executives. The Treasurer moved upstairs into the centre room overlooking Princes Street, and the Governor had a new office nearby within the west wing. Finally, in 1987 work began on Glasgow Chief Office to improve the one major twentieth-century building in the Bank's stewardship. In total the Bank's expenditure on its property far exceeded that in any similar period of its history.

Bank of Scotland's activities and expansion inevitably brought it into direct competition with its major shareholder, Barclays Bank plc. Strains in the relationship had begun to emerge during the late 1970s and from Barclays' point of view inclined in one of two directions: takeover, or sale of its shareholding. The Bank's response to the attempted takeover of the Royal Bank in 1982 made it very clear that any similar attempt would be fiercely resisted, particularly since under the terms of the 1971 agreement Barclays was obliged to inform Bank of Scotland of its intentions. There was little room for manoeuvre and therefore sale was the obvious option. It became a matter of when, how much, and to whom. For Bank of Scotland in 1982-84 this was a very sensitive issue. Barclays held 34.48 per cent of Bank stock, which enjoyed only 25 per cent of voting rights; the Kuwait Investment Office had 8.97 per cent and a reputation for maximising gain rather than viewing the Bank as a long-term investment. The key was to persuade Barclays to sell *en bloc* to a purchaser who had long-term aims similar to those of the Bank. Of the various alternatives, it was Standard Life Assurance Company which showed interest and fitted Bank of Scotland's requirements. The connection was one of very long standing (one hundred years plus) as a customer. The Directors were well known to each other (both Sir William Watson and Thomas Risk had been chairman of Standard Life). It is an Edinburgh-based company, the largest mutual assurance company in Europe, and it was interested in the long-term performance of its investments rather than in quick capital gains. Standard Life negotiated direct with Barclays Bank, and the completion of the sale on 30 January 1985, announced to an unsuspecting market, was the single most important event of the year for the Bank. After the announcement the Kuwait Investment Office began to reduce its holding. It is not an exaggeration to state that the Governor, Directors and Executives of the Bank felt this to be a liberation which freed them to pursue policies they felt best for the Bank without reference to the wishes of a commercial rival. It was also seen by Bank of Scotland and by Standard Life as an association which had potential commercial benefits for both.

The Bank's plans for continued investment in technology and expansion of services began to outpace its capital growth, so in both 1984 and 1985 rights issues were made to existing shareholders which after expenses produced £41.6 million and £81.3 million respectively. Both these matters were successfully handled by the recently appointed Bank Secretary, Hugh Young. In October 1985 the capital base was further strengthened by the issue of US$250 million undated floating rate capital notes. In 1988 the Bank's London brokers, Cazenove & Co., arranged an issue of £100 million of irredeemable preference stock, which was described by the 'Lex' column in the *Financial Times* as a 'trail blazing issue'. At the same time there was a further capitalisation issue, and the Bank stock was split into units of 25p. The issue of another £100 million of preference stock followed in 1990, and this in turn was followed in 1991 by both a capitalisation and a rights issue, which strengthened the Bank's Tier-one capital by £194 million. The net result of all this was that in 1992 the Bank's capital ratios stood at 6.4 per cent for Tier-one and 11.3 per cent for the total capital, all comfortably above the minimum levels established by the Basle Convergence Agreement – the key international measure of financial adequacy.

The financial year 1985/86 was a watershed in the Bank's development, since many of the initiatives begun in the first half of the '80s came to fruition. The strategy for the English market had been assessed correctly. There were now seven regional offices, dealing primarily with corporate

248 and business customers, which would be added to as site and opportunity presented. The personal sector was to be approached through centralised marketing and management of specific banking products such as Money Market Cheque Accounts, autoteller linkage, and HOBS, which had been greatly enhanced to make it more attractive to business customers. Some of these were handled from Central Banking Services, which was the fastest growing unit in the Bank. Another part of the strategy was to enter into joint ventures with other organisations. This was often done with or through NWS at Chester, the most successful of these being Automobile Association Financial Services Ltd, which was designed to provide consumer credit to AA members. Within Scotland, services were improved by the extension of opening hours to 4.45 p.m. on every weekday except Thursday, when there was a late session from 4.30 to 5.30 p.m.

Developments in technology later moved in two distinct directions. Within the Bank most effort went into CABINET, the acronym used for the customer and branch information network which aimed to create a customer database which could be accessed from any point on the Bank's network, providing information on customer accounts and a great deal of other information to assist marketing and control. One major spin-off from this project was that the new telephone network allowed HOBS customers to choose to use it rather than rely solely on BT's Prestel system. This made HOBS cheaper for customers to use. The Bank's increasing expertise in banking technology led to the creation of the Transcontinental Automated Payments System (TAPS), which won the Department of Health and Social Security's contract to handle the monthly payments of state pensions and other benefits to British citizens living abroad. Relying on satellite communication and using bilateral links to pass data between different countries' electronic clearing houses, the scheme initially encompassed 14 countries but this was gradually extended. Its great attractions were simplicity, speed, directness and the fact that the recipient of the payment had fewer commissions to pay en route, which had previously reduced significantly the value of the funds transferred.

During 1980 to 1985 the Bank developed a particular expertise in funding senior debt for management buy-outs. This was developed initially by Gavin Masterton, and subsequently carried out from both Edinburgh and London by teams under the three 'Cs' (Colin Leslie, Colin McGill and Colin Matthew). The units available for purchase were usually subsidiaries or functional units of larger companies, which were peripheral to its core business. These were sold to the incumbent management, supported by institutional investors. In most of the early successes it was noticeable that

*Sir Bruce Pattullo, Treasurer and General Manager 1979–88,
Deputy Governor and Group Chief Executive 1988–91, Governor since 1991*

Glasgow Chief Office Banking Hall

250

The 1995 bank-notes: front and reverse of the £5 note and reverse of the £10 note

the company's buy-out team usually possessed enthusiasm and production and sales skills, but initially often lacked those of finance and accounting. This reflected the fact that in large companies these were treated as central skills and were only exceptionally devolved to individual production units. This empirical observation gave good support to the case against takeovers and the necessity for strong, independent regional companies. The whole area experienced steady growth and by the time of the 1990-93 recession Bank of Scotland was handling more buy-out transactions than any other UK clearing bank.

Regional issues were not the only or the most important aspects of an event in 1986 which became notorious as 'the Guinness affair'. Distillers plc, an international company, producers of many brands of Scotch whisky with its head office in Edinburgh, became the target of competing takeover bids by Argyll Foods (owners of Safeway supermarkets, and a Scottish-based company) and Guinness (the UK and Irish brewers, but also a holding company). Both were therefore well-known public companies and were advised by major merchant banks. Distillers at first rejected both suitors but, recognising that their stance was likely to lack sufficient shareholder support, entered into discussions with Guinness about a merger. An agreed term of the resulting negotiation was that Sir Thomas Risk (knighted in 1984) should be chairman and that the new group should be headquartered in Edinburgh. Bank of Scotland had only a minor banking relationship with the Distillers Group, and none with the bidders, but had strong connections with the whisky industry in Scotland and believed it to be uniquely important for the Scottish economy as a whole. Despite initial reluctance to be seen as the token Scot, Sir Thomas Risk was persuaded to become non-executive chairman of the merged Distillers/Guinness Group. The Guinness bid did succeed, and in circumstances not then fully explained Mr Ernest Saunders was appointed chairman and the group did not move to Edinburgh. The most charitable view was that the whole episode was simply a tactic to neutralise Scottish opposition. But in the event there were many who were indignant at what they saw as a failure on the part of Guinness to fulfil their promise. Subsequently in 1987, with the appointment of Anthony Tennant as chief executive, good relations were restored, but the whole affair reinforced the Bank's attitudes and policies to Scottish industries and companies.

In 1986 two new subsidiaries were added to the Bank of Scotland Group. Bank of Wales, which was headquartered in Cardiff, offered the prospect of major participation in the regeneration and development of South Wales. The deregulation of financial services in New Zealand permitted the Bank to take a 40 per cent stake in Countrywide Building Society on its conversion to a full bank. Subsequently Bank of Scotland was able to move to 100 per cent shareholding when Countrywide bought United Bank, which had also earlier demutualised as a building society.

In 1988 there was a further change in the Bank's management structure. The increasing complexity of the Bank's business made it desirable to separate off responsibility for overall Group activities from day-to-day responsibility for the Clearing Bank. Bruce Pattullo became Deputy Governor and Group Chief Executive, while Peter Burt, previously head of International Division, became Treasurer and Chief General Manager, and therefore chairman of the Management Board.

The Bank's achievements in the 1980s were noted in two very different ways. *The Economist* magazine's survey of the financial sector in 1989 resulted in Bank of Scotland being voted 'the most admired bank' in the UK by its peer group because it appeared to use technology creatively in a banking environment and yet retain its traditional virtues of conservatism, consistency and solidity. There was one widely used aphorism within the Bank which summed up its attitude to expansion and acquisition: 'don't bet the Bank'. The second accolade was that in the same year the Bank was invited by the Institution of Electrical Engineers to deliver the prestigious Faraday Lectures, choosing as its title 'Electric Currency'. The team of Bank presenters took the message about the future directions of electronic banking to 20 cities in the UK and a total audience of 150,000. Many of the ideas that were promoted and implemented in the 1980s had come from lower down the organisation. The hierarchical structure had been reduced and the Management Board had positively encouraged the emergence of 'champions' which released an energy and enthusiasm which had previously been latent.

252   Viewed from the perspective of the Annual Report of 1991, the progress made by the Bank since 1981 was remarkable. Total assets had increased from £3.5 billion to £22.1 billion, while pre-tax profit had risen from £53 million to £134 million. If the longer perspective back to 1971 is considered, the appropriate figures are £700 million of assets and pre-tax profits of £9.7 million. In just twenty years the assets of Bank of Scotland had increased by a factor of 31.6 and profits by a factor of 14. There were other measures which testified to the Bank's growing efficiency in the 1980s. Although numbers of full and part-time members of staff rose from 9,318 to 16,100 within the Group, the operating profit per member of staff increased faster than numbers. By the end of the 1980s great emphasis was being placed on increased productivity, the usual measure of which was operating expenses as a percentage of net total income. In 1991 this stood at 54.6 per cent, ten percentage points below and clear of its nearest rival. The Treasurer set a target figure of 50 per cent for the future, which was achieved during the first half of 1994.

The 1990s contain too much that is unfinished or still in progress to provide any real historical perspective. Sir Thomas Risk retired as Governor at the 1991 AGM and his successor is Sir Bruce Pattullo, the first Governor in the Bank's history to have come up through the system. He is supported by two non-executive Deputy Governors, Professor Jack Shaw in Edinburgh and Tom Hutchison in London. The same AGM saw the retiral of Lord Balfour of Burleigh, a Director of the Bank since 1968 and Deputy Governor since 1977. He was chairman of the board of NWS and the East of Scotland Local Board. Perhaps his greatest contribution was that as chairman of the Joint Federation he steered the national joint Bank-Union negotiations with tact and skill during the period 1977 to 1986. The retirals of 1991 seemed to mark the end of an important phase in the Bank's story. The management team of the Bank was strengthened in a number of ways, notably by the appointment of Gavin Masterton as Deputy Treasurer. The steady growth in importance of the Treasury Division, housed from 1990 in the Broadgate Centre in London, resulted in March 1992 in the establishment of a new company, Bank of Scotland Treasury Services plc.

It is already clear that the actions taken by the management team in 1990-92, which included a 'no compulsory redundancies' policy for staff, have brought the Bank through the recession in better shape than most. Also, for the first time in over one hundred years the Scottish economy did not suffer in recession to anything like the same extent as that of the South-East of England. In no small measure this was due to the actions of the Scottish banks, which individually seem to have adopted attitudes similar to those of Bank of Scotland and were innovative during a difficult period in looking for ways to avoid, wherever possible, putting companies into receivership. At the time of writing, towards the end of the calendar year 1994, the Bank, having announced pre-tax profits of £213 million for the six months to the end of August 1994, is heading for the biggest profits and the largest return on Proprietors Funds in its three-hundred-year history.

The pace of change within the Bank is continuous and even quickening. To make predictions is inevitably to offer hostages to fortune. Similarly, it is difficult to know how to end the three-hundred-year history of an organisation that has every intention of continuing for the next three hundred, and clearly has the talent and tenacity to do so. It is a very singular institution, jealous of its independence, which still commands sufficient loyalty and affection from its employees for children to follow their parents in its service. Family connections within the bank are strong, the record being held by the Gourlay family, who can show at least six generations of continuous service. It remains too a very Scottish institution. Members of the Bank staff are involved in all aspects of Scottish life. They do seem to end up as treasurer of any organisation which they join! Scotland's traditional sport of golf has always had a wide support within the Bank, but few would willingly challenge Peter Burt, the Treasurer, who in 1993 set the new amateur course record of 69 at Muirfield, the Open Championship golf course in East Lothian. The Bank's future ambition for itself, its Proprietors and its customers is still expressed in its motto 'Tanto Uberior'. In the eighteenth century this was translated as 'The Mair tae Prosper', a toast rather than a boast, which cannot be bettered.

253

Peter Burt
Treasurer and Chief
General Manager
since 1988

256 *I will be equal to all persons, and give my best Advice for the Support of the Bank of Scotland; And in the said Office, Honestly Demean my self to the best of my Skill.* And this Oath, the first Governour shall take before the Lord Chancellor, or any other of the Officers of State, and then shall have power to Administrat the same to his Deputy and Directors. And the next Governour and Directors shall swear the same at their Entry as said is, before a General Meeting of the Company, certifying any who shall neglect to swear at his Entry, or within twenty days thereafter, his place shall be void, and an other shall be Elected to it: And the Governour, or Deputy-Governour, with the Directors or their *Quorum*, may choose a Thesaurer, Secretary, and other Officers for the Affairs of the said Company, who are to give their Oaths *de fideli* before the Governour, or his Deputy, or any two of the Directors; and may be removed from the said Offices, at the Pleasure of a General Meeting: *Providing alwise*, that neither the Governour, Deputy-Governour, or any of the Directors, may be chosen to any of the saids Inferior Offices. *And* it is further hereby *Statute and Ordained*, that it shall be lawful for the said Governour and Company, to Lend upon Real or Personal Security any Sum or Sums, and to receive Annualrent for the same at six *per Cent*, as shall be ordinary for the time: As also, that if the Person borrowing as said is, shall not make payment at the Term agreed upon with the Company; then it shall be lawful for the Governour and Company, to Sell and Dispose of the Security or Pledge, by a Publick Roup for the most that can be got, for payment to them of the Principal Annualrents and Reasonable Charges, and returning the Overplus to the Person who gave the said Security or Pledge. And it is further hereby *Enacted*, that the foresaid Company and Members thereof, or major part of them assembled at any General Meeting, may make and constitute such By-Laws and Ordinances, as to them shall seem necessary and convenient for the Good of the Company, and under such Penalties as shall be therein-contained; providing that the saids By-Laws and Ordinances, be not contrary to, (but consistent with the Laws of the Kingdom.) And for Ascertaining how the said Joynt Stock and Shares thereof, with all the Lands, Houses, or other Estate thereto belonging, may be Assigned or Transferred: It is hereby *Statute and Ordained*, that there be constantly keeped a Book or Register by the said Governour and Directors, where all the foresaid Assignments shal be Entered & Subscribed by both the Party Assigning, & the Party to whom the Assignment is made in Token of his Acceptance, and that such Assignments so Subscribed, shall make full, Compleat, and Absolute Rights, and no other shall be good, excepting that any Person having Interest in the said Company, may Dispose of the same by Latter Will or Testament, which shall be a Valid and Compleat Transmission in favours of the Person, to whom the Disposition is made, upon the Entering and Recording so much of the said Latter Will, as relates to the said Stock in the Books of the said Company, without necessity of Confirmation or further Formality whatsoever. And it is hereby further *Statute*, that no Dividend shall be made, save out of the Interest or Product arising out the Joynt Stock, and by the Consent of the Adventurers in a General Meeting: and for the better Encouragement of the said Company and Adventurers: It is hereby *Statute*, that the Joynt Stock of the said Bank continuing in Money, shall be free from all publick Burden to be imposed upon Money, for the space of twenty one years after the date hereof: And that during this space, it shall not be Leasom to any other persons to enter into, and set up an distinct Company of Bank within this Kingdom, besides these Persons allanarly, in whose Favours this Act is granted. And sicklike, it is hereby *Declared*, that summar Execution by Horning, shal proceed upon Bills or Tickets drawn upon, or granted by, or to, and in Favours of this Bank, and the Managers and Administrators thereof for the time, and Protests thereon in the same manner, as is appointed to pass upon Protests of Forraign Bills, by the 20. *Act, Parl. 1681. K. Ch.* 2. And sicklike, that no Suspension pass of any Charge, (for Sums lent by this Bank or to the same,) but upon Discharge or Consignation of the Sums Charged for allanarly. *And further*, for preventing the breaking of the said Joynt Stock and

Company, contrary to the Design thereof: It is hereby *Declared*, that the Sums of the foresaid Subscriptions and Shares, may only be Conveyed and Transmitted by the Owners to others, who shall become Partners of the Company in their place in manner above-mentioned, or by Adjudication, or other Legal Conveyance in Favours of one Person allanarly, who in like manner shall succeed to be a Partner in his Predecessors place, so that the foresaids Sums of Subscriptions, may neither be taken out of the Stock, nor parcelled amongst more persons by Legal Diligence in any sort, to the Diminishing or Disturbing the Stock of the said Company and good Order thereof. *And sicklike*, for the greater Security, and more convenient managing of the said Bank or Joynt Stock: It is hereby *Statute and Ordained*, that in case it shall happen any of the Members, Partners, or Subscribers, or other Proprietars of any part of the said Stock to be Registrat at the Horn, or to commit any Crime punishable by Confiscation, or Forefaulture of his said Share and Proportion of the said Joynt Stock and Profit thereof due at the time, then and in that case, it shall be lawful for the Governour, Deputy-Governour, and Directors, or their *Quorum* foresaid, to expose, by publick Roup, such Shares and Profit thereof to any other person, who shall bid the highest Price therefore, after such Legal Intimations to be made for that effect by the said Governour, Deputy-Governour, Directors, or their *Quorum*, as is prescribed by the Act of Parliament for the Sale of Bankrupts Lands, and the Price arising by the said Roup, to be made forthcoming by the said Company to the Creditors, Heirs, or other succeeding in the Right of the Party so Denunced or Forefeit: *Providing alwise*, as it is hereby expresly *Enacted, Provided, and Declared*, that it shall not be lawful nor allowable for the said Company, Governour, Deputy-Governour, Directors or Managers thereof, upon any Ground or Pretence whatsoever, Directly nor Indirectly, to Use, Exerce, or follow any other Commerce, Traffick, or Trade with the Joynt Stock to be imployed in the said Bank, or any part thereof, or Profits arising therefrae, excepting the Trade of Lending and Borrowing Money upon Interest, and Negotiating Bills of Exchange allanarly and no other. *Providing also*, Likeas it is hereby expresly *Provided, Enacted, and Declared*, that in case the Governour, Deputy-Governour, Directors, or other Managers of the said Company, shall at any time happen to Purchase for the Use and Behove of the said Company, any Lands, Rents, or other Heretage belonging to His Majesty, His Heirs, and Successors, or shall Advance or Lend to His Majesty, His Heirs, or Successors, any Sums of Money in Borrowing, or by way of Anticipation upon any part, Branch, or Fond of the Ordinary, Rent, or Casualities of the Crown, or of any Supply, Cess, Excise, Custom, Pole-Tax, or any other Supply or Taxation already granted, or which shall happen to be granted at any time hereafter to his Majesty and his foresaids, any manner of way whatsoever, excepting these Parts, Branches, or Fonds of the saids Rents, Casualities, or Impositions foresaids, upon which a Credit of Loan shall happen to be granted by Act of Parliament allanarly; Then and in that case, the said Governour, Deputy-Governour, Directors, or other Managers, one or more of the said Company who shal Consent, Agree to, or Approve of the said Purchase, Advance, or Lending to His Majesty and His foresaids, and ilk an of them so Agreeing and Approveing, and being found guilty thereof according to Law, shall be lyable for every such Fault, in the Triple of the Value of the Purchase so made, or the Sums so Lent, whereof a fifth part shall belong to the Informer, and the Remainder to be Disposed of towards such publick Uses, as shall be appointed by Parliament and not otherwise. *And* it is likewise hereby *Provided*, that all Forraigners, who shall joyn as Partners of this Bank shall thereby be and become Naturalized *Scots-men*, to all Intents and Purposes whatsover.

Extracted forth of the Records of Parliament, by
TARBAT, *Cl. Registri.*

BANK OF SCOTLAND   PRINCIPAL

Year ending (1):	Paid up capital	Reserves (2)	Note circulation (3)	Deposits (3)
1697	30000 [4]			
1707	10000			
1717	10000	2845		
1727	30000	4792		
1737	40000	5646		
1747	50000	5502		
1757	60000	13431		
1767	60000	23129		
1777	200000	15493		
1787	300000	48339		
1797	1000000	101814 [5]		
1807	1000000	108749	633000	
1817	1000000	158403	500000	
1827	1000000	157028		
1837	1000000	202574	449079	4373594
1847	1000000	193797	343318	4758926
1857	1000000	226144	510862	6366259
1867	1000000	304933	505391	7413022
1877	1250000	764581	639156	10409120
1887	1250000	797302	772077	13015471
1897	1250000	840905	1035781	14478328
1907	1250000	1056291	1099213	16204626
1917	1325000	774224	2492623	26912606
1927	1500000	1785966	3015709	31936520
1937	1500000	2605995	3239247	37635698
1947	2400000	2765948	10972730	87073848
1957	4500000	4753545	26061042	173894731
1967	8400000	8383101	28479946	248534169
1977	32250000	83629000	119071000	1399416000
1987	124200000	434400000	280200000	8104100000
1988	124600000	525700000	254000000	9623400000
1989	287600000	538400000	259800000	12440100000
1990	288600000	607200000	278100000	16376500000
1991	390600000	658400000	280000000	19899200000
1992	487100000	773900000	308800000	22064700000
1993	489300000	761500000	345000000	25946500000
1994	491100000	813000000	348700000	23437500000

NOTES
1. For years 1697-1833, financial year ended in March; for 1834-64 it ended December; thereafter it ended February
2. Prior to 1713 the dividend was paid directly from the year's profits. From 1713, a sum was paid into a separate account of undivided profits (known as the Adventurers' Account of Profit and Loss). There was no surplus (and hence no reserves) until 1716. An additional reserve account was set up in 1846. The reserves figure does not include hidden reserves (i.e. fund for losses).

BALANCE SHEET FIGURES, 1697-1994

Advances (3)	Net profit	Ordinary dividend	Extraordinary dividend	Dividend (%)	No of branches
	1520	600		6	
	1284	2000		20	
	4577	4500		15	
	2939	2000		5	
	3952	2500		5	
	5608	4000		6.67	
	4022	4000		6.67	
	19323	12000		6	6
	24671	24000		8	18
	76284	60000		6	27
	72143	70000		7	20
	88444	90000		9	15
	66833	60000		6	17
2590534	79379	60000		6	25
4208672	70049	70000		7	31
6038499	110176	80000		8	42
6657555	154429	120000		12	67
8444571	168353	157500		12.6	95
9348060	174266	168750		13.5	117
9908387	172342	150000		12	124
10006940	237007	193750		15.5	140
13424172	258369	161208		12.17	174
13332097	370119	192000		12.8	226
9799939	317713	205876		13.73	263
11816079	303214	158400		6.6	254
41998283	638984	362250		8.05	443 [6]
138332002	2060442	1428000		17	
961927000	12058000	3146000		9.76	
6928800000	71500000	20500000		16.51	
8240900000	82100000	23500000		18.86	482
10705800000	107800000	32800000		11.4	
14364200000	117100000	43500000		15.07	
17268900000	85400000	52400000		13.42	
18995700000	89400000	68900000		14.14	
22006300000	76700000	71800000		14.67	
25342500000	160900000	77700000		15.82	430

3. There was no source for notes in circulation, deposits or advances prior to 1794. The figures for the years 1794-1832 were obtained from BS 1/70/11 (Scrolls and states out of the common routine) and those for 1833-58 from the weekly states (BS 1/71, returns from each branch and head office) for the appropriate date.
4. Consists of £10000 paid up capital and £20000 loan from the Proprietors to the Bank which was repaid.
5. £12450 was transferred to the account of Capital Stock.
6. Includes Union Bank branches. Thereafter raw numbers do not reflect changes in branch structure.

SELECT BIBLIOGRAPHY

The following is a list of the works to which the author has most frequently referred. It is not exhaustive.

Manuscript Sources

The archive of Bank of Scotland and its constituent banks is very extensive; in particular, board minutes, ledgers, lending books and correspondence have all been used. The archive is reported in *National Register of Archives* (Scotland), Lists 945 and 1110.

Extensive use has also been made of the following:

Bank of Scotland, Oral History Programme, Tapes 1–50 and Summaries.

Duncan Ferguson. *A Memoir of Bank of Scotland* (unpublished typescript).

Further information about any of the above may be obtained from the Archivist, Bank of Scotland, PO Box 5, The Mound, Edinburgh.

Published Sources

Scottish Bankers Magazine – Journal of the Institute of Bankers in Scotland.

First and Second Reports from the Select Committee on Banks of Issue, Parliamentary Papers, 1841 (366).

Report from a Select Committee on Banks of Issue, Parliamentary Papers, 1875 (351).

Report of the Committee on Finance and Industry (Macmillan Committee), Cmnd 3897, 1931.

Report of the Committee of Inquiry into the Scottish Economy appointed by the Scottish Council (Development and Industry) (Toothill Report), HMSO (1961).

Committee [on] Consumer Credit Report, Cmnd 4596, 2 vols, HMSO, London, 1971.

Committee to Review the Functioning of Financial Institutions, Report and Appendices (The Wilson Committee), Cmnd 7937, HMSO, 1980.

Published Works

Boot, H. M., 'Salaries and Career Earnings in Bank of Scotland, 1730-1880', *Economic History Review*, vol. XLIV, 4 November 1991.

Boswell, James, *The Journal of a Tour to the Hebrides*, London, 1785.

Campbell, R. H., *The Rise and Fall of Scottish Industry*, John Donald, 1980.

Chalmers, Thomas (ed.), *Wallace and McNeil's Banking Law*, Greens, Edinburgh (many editions).

Checkland, S. G., *Scottish Banking, A History 1695-1973*, Collins, 1975.

Clapham, Sir John, *The Bank of England*, 2 vols, Cambridge University Press, 1944.

Cockburn, Henry (Lord), *Memorials of his Time*, 1856.

Collins, Michael, *Money and Banking in the UK: A History*, Routledge, 1988.

Craig, H. Charles, *The Scotch Whisky Industry Record*, Index Publishing Limited, 1994.

Douglas, James, *Scottish Banknotes*, Stanley Gibbons, 1975.

Twentieth Century Scottish Banknotes, Volume 1, Banking Memorabilia, Carlisle, 1984.

Durie, Alastair J., *The Scottish Linen Trade in the 18th Century*, John Donald, 1979.

Forbes, Sir William, *Memoirs of a Banking House* (published for private circulation), Edinburgh, 1859.

Gaskin, Maxwell, *The Scottish Banks, A Modern Survey*, Allen and Unwin, 1965.

Gibson, Archibald T., 'All-Purpose Banking?', *The Scottish Bankers Magazine* (vol. LX 1968-69), pp. 77-96.

'Glasaguensis', *Banking in Glasgow During Olden Times*, 2nd edition, Robertson, Glasgow, 1834.

Holmes, A. R., and Edwin Green, *Midland, 150 Years of Banking Business*, Batsford, 1985.

Kerr, Andrew William, *History of Banking in Scotland*, A. & C. Black, 1926.

Kynaston, David, *The City of London, 1815-1890*, vol. 1, Chatto & Windus, 1994.

Lenman, Bruce, *An Economic History of Modern Scotland*, B.T. Batsford, 1977.

Lewcock, Francis James, *The Organisation and Management of a Branch Bank*, Pitman, 1934.

McGill, Patrick, *Children of the Dead End*, Jenkins, 1914; Caliban, 1980.

Mackenzie, Peter, *Reminiscences of Glasgow and the West of Scotland*, 1865.

Malcolm, Charles A., *The Bank of Scotland 1695-1945*, Edinburgh, 1946.

The British Linen Bank, Edinburgh, 1950.

Moss, Michael, and Iain Russell, *Range and Vision, The First Hundred Years of Barr and Stroud*, Mainstream, 1988.

Munn, Charles, *The Scottish Provincial Banking Companies*, John Donald, 1981.

Clydesdale Bank, The First Hundred and Fifty Years, Collins, 1988.

Oakley, C. A. (ed.), *Scottish Industry*, Scottish Council (Development and Industry), 1953.

Payne, Peter L., *Colvilles and the Scottish Steel Industry*, Clarendon Press, Oxford, 1979.

Rait, Robert, *The History of the Union Bank of Scotland*, John Smith & Son, Glasgow, 1930.

Saville, Richard (ed.), *The Economic Development of Modern Scotland 1950-1980*, John Donald, 1985.

Scott, George J., *The Valley of Enchantment*, (printed for private circulation), 1934.

Scott, John, and Michael Hughes, *The Anatomy of Scottish Capital*, London, 1980.

Scott, Sir Walter, *Marmion: A Tale of Flodden Field*, 1808.

The Letters of Malachi Malagrowther, Edinburgh, 1826.

Slaven, A. (ed.), and Derek H. Aldcroft, *Business Banking and Urban History*, John Donald, 1982.

Smith, Adam, *Inquiry into the Nature and Causes of the Wealth of Nations*, 1776.

Smollett, Tobias, *The Expedition of Humphrey Clinker*, 1771.

Smout, T. C., *A Century of the Scottish People, 1830–1950*, Fontana, 1987.

Tamaki, Norio, *The Life Cycle of the Union Bank of Scotland, 1830-1954*, Aberdeen University Press, 1983.

INDEX

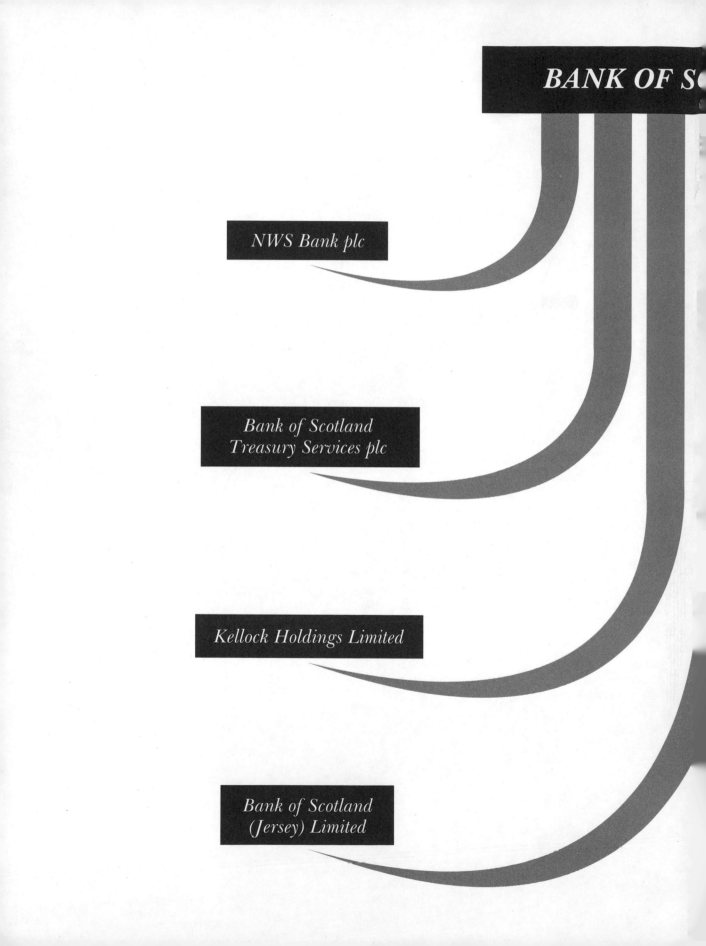

NWS Bank plc

Bank of Scotland
Treasury Services plc

Kellock Holdings Limited

Bank of Scotland
(Jersey) Limited